PASTORAL PSYCHOTHERAPY

COMMENTARY

Once again Dr. Carroll A. Wise has written a book which is destined to become a classic. *Pastoral Psychotherapy* is not a "how to" book. Rather it is the distillate of a lifetime of clinical practice. Written with a clarity rare in professional writing, Dr. Wise utilized his experience as a parish minister, teacher, supervisor and therapist to present a consistent theory and technique of pastoral psychology. It provides the pastoral therapist a uniform frame of reference from which to practice — be it in the pastor's study or a pastoral counseling center. It does away with psychotherapeutic nihilism rampant amongst many of the clergy. *Pastoral Psychotherapy* refutes eclecticism which often serves to disguise a lack of therapeutic technique, ignorance of psychological principles, inept supervision, and exploitation of clients.

Pastoral Psychotherapy integrates biblical wisdom with modern concepts of ego psychology, thus providing a biblical basis to pastoral psychotherapy. Employing religious language, Dr. Wise demonstrates how understanding religious symbolization can be utilized diagnostically. In the process he clarifies the manner in which people with problems use their religious beliefs in an attempt to cope with life's stresses. The function of an intake evaluation, the value of a working diagnosis and the importance of a dynamic formulation are clearly delineated as part of a procedure leading to knowledge of a person and the understanding of his behavior. Specific clinical entities are discussed so the pastor can recognize maladaptive coping mechanisms in the people he treats or refers.

Dr. Wise has made a unique contribution to psychotherapy. He demonstrates the import of a religious orientation and the special insights it can give. Values of Christian-Judeo theology are blended with the insights of ego psychology resulting in an amalgam which surpasses either. The book is must reading for seminarians, parish ministers and pastoral therapists. While there are some who will find it controversial, *Pastoral Psychotherapy* is an explicit statement of psychotherapy done by a minister. With its publication pastoral psychotherapy has come of age.

Carl W. Christensen, M.D.

PASTORAL PSYCHOTHERAPY

Theory and Practice

Carroll A. Wise

JASON ARONSON INC.
Northvale, New Jersey
London

New Printing 1987

ISBN: 0-87668-661-7

Library of Congress Catalog Number: 84-045025

Manufactured in the United States of America.

To my grandchildren
Richard, Larison, Alan, Laura, and Kathleen

Contents

Preface

This book is written primarily for pastors, theological students, and seminary and college teachers in the area of religion or psychology. It is written secondarily for professionals in the field of mental health and the helping professions. The expansion of the mental health field in the past fifty years has been such that no professional group can have a monopoly. Rather there is needed a great deal of interdisciplinary understanding. This book is intended as a contribution toward that end. It is therefore written not only for the clergy, but for professionals in the field. It is not a self-help book.

The book is a major departure in that it dispenses with the term *pastoral counseling* and uses the term *pastoral psychotherapy*. I have been using this term in my speaking and teaching for at least ten years, and have been encouraged by the acceptance it has received. Others have used it in print, notably in *Pilgrimage: The Journal of Pastoral Psychotherapy*.[1]

Some will find the term controversial. Some pastors will fear that the pastoral identity is being lost. Some psychiatrists and others will fear that we are moving in on their territory. But a solid pastoral identity is not lost in this way. Any movement which professes goals so closely related to religion as psychotherapy, and aims at the increase of the quality of human existence, cannot be avoided by the pastor. Indeed through the centuries pastors have been a major source of psychotherapy, usually called by other names, such as the cure of souls or pastoral care. Pastoral psychotherapy is by no means a new field for the pastor. What is new is the opportunity to combine pastoral concerns with a growing knowledge of personality.

Identity is a problem of being, not of techniques. The goal of the pastor, however, theologically expressed, has been the increase in the quality of life and in motivation for that life. This is clearly a concern in the New Testament, indeed, in the entire Bible. Specific meanings and methods have differed as they do today, but the goals have been there.

Pastoral identity does not mean narrowness and self-deprivation of knowledge. The pastor needs knowledge from many sources which he can hold in a comprehensive manner. He cannot know too much about people in a world where science is increasing that knowledge. Theology by itself tends to become ingrown and to feed on itself. Pastoral identity requires knowledge of persons for its fulfillment, and it requires that knowledge in usable form. It also requires skills beyond those conveyed by the image of the kindly but naive pastor.

Mental health professionals outside of the ministry evince one of two attitudes. Some are very friendly and helpful, and give real assistance to the pastor in the form of teaching, supervision, and general encouragement. Others are indifferent or antagonistic, seeking to limit the province of the clergy. Much of this is based on a misunderstanding of the function of the clergy. Some of it is grounded in outworn conceptions which need to be brought up to date.

The role of the pastor is not to be defined primarily in areas of beliefs or morals or social action as some do. Persons, their growth, enhancement, creativity, and fulfillment are the fundamental concern. Belief, morals, social action, and other concerns should contribute to this major goal. The ethical ideal of justice, for example, will become distorted if it is divorced in thought or action from the need of every human being for just treatment. Justice is not enough, however, as this can be cold and legalistic. The Christian faith insists that the cardinal need in human relationships is love; love that works no ill to its neighbor, love that is the fulfillment of the law, and love that provides the warmth and security in which those other two great religious virtues, faith and hope, are nurtured. Nothing human is outside the concern of the Christian faith.

Personality growth and fulfillment, being and becoming, are a central concern for the pastor. Whatever in religion robs persons of their autonomy promotes sickness. Pastoral psychotherapy, as interpreted here, will frighten many and encourage others because of its emphasis on autonomy or freedom. Such emphasis, however, is deeply Biblical. It is also strong in much modern psychological thought.

Our psychological analysis of religious experience will bother some and gratify others. The first group will fear the reduction of religion to psychological concepts. Careful reading of the entire book should show that this is far from the intent of the author. Psychological understanding is necessary in dealing with persons. But religious experience has its own validity regardless of the psychological processes involved. If these processes are immature or pathological, they may be used to help the person to a higher level of maturity and health, and to a fuller, more complete religious experience. For example, an immature person may be struggling through religion for a sense of integration or wholeness. By helping the person grow, the need for integration is not reduced or removed. It is fulfilled. The meteorological understanding of the forces that make rain does not invalidate the coming of rain to a parched land. The psychological understanding of religion, properly used, leads to an enrichment of life, not to reductionism, because there are validating aspects beyond psychological processes. Those who make a practice of discounting religious experience on psychological grounds are as mistaken as those who fear it.

The reader will quickly notice the orientation in ego psychology. No systematic attempt is made to discuss the merits of other points of view. This is largely due to my background and experience, and to my purpose in writing. I do know these other schools, and have tried some of them; for my purpose I have found them wanting. They tend to overmagnify some aspects of the person, such as feeling, cognition, or will, and ignore or discount other aspects. Some of these are popular with the pastor because they do not require extensive training, but by the same token their inadequacy is revealed. However, the major reason for using one orientation is that I have attempted to distill my own experience and this requires that I use the perspective from which I work.

The serious pastor often finds himself caught between the need for an understanding that does justice to the profound and complex aspects of human life and at the same time avoids esoteric language. It is characteristic of schools of psychological and theological thought that they develop their own peculiar terminology and formulations. Often the implication is that if the terminology and formulations are understood and passed on to others, therapy results. A very popular fantasy and fallacy is that therapy consists in explaining a person to himself, regardless of the particular vocabulary that is employed.

The essence of therapy is rather in helping a person discover the depths of his own being and express this in symbols that carry vital meaning. Technical language, theological or psychological, has little or no place in therapy. Living religious language does have a place, and by this is meant language which picks up and expresses vital experiences with which the person is struggling. Persons who have read books (students for example) often try to explain themselves in the language of a book that has impressed them, but this is defensive. They are keeping away from their real experiences. Modern ego psychology offers the pastor a sound basis for psychological thinking and one that has many points of relationship to theological thinking. But the essence of therapy—and of redemption—is in an intuitive and empathic relationship where a person is encouraged to discover the real self and to express this discovery and its meaning for his life in terms that are vital and viable. Occasionally one meets a pastor whose psychological training is very poor, and who does not prize theological language, but whose capacity for insight and for an empathic relationship is very deep, and his people call him blessed. This is a humbling experience. Most of us have to go through a rigorous process of training to develop such ability, and through a fairly deep therapy process in order to free ourselves from those inner, restrictive forces that block our empathy. To such empathy should be added sound knowledge.

My debt to many persons is obvious. I have learned much from the persons with whom I have been privileged to work, from students and pastors and colleagues in the seminary and ministry and from psychiatrists and other professional workers. I have learned from daily life itself. In my years of later maturity I have found evidences of new growth and new insights emerging in unexpected moments, and this has been exhilarating. To my younger colleagues I would say Yes, there are storms on the other side of the hill, but there are many beautiful vistas there too.

I have been blessed by the number of friends who wanted to read this manuscript, and who made helpful suggestions. Bernard Greene, M.D., Ronald Lee, Ph.D., and John Hinkle, Ph.D., read and commented on parts of it. Alfred Flarsheim, M.D., Carl Christensen, M.D., Bruce Hartung, Ph.D., Leila Foster, Ph.D., and David Moss, Ph.D., read and commented on it in its entirety. Drs. Ernest W. Saunders and Albert C. Sundberg, Jr., gave invaluable assistance on the Biblical material. To each I owe a real debt, not only for this but for many other acts of friendship over the years. To Robert Powell, M.D., Ph.D., I owe special thanks for some very helpful suggestions. To Miss Eleanor West and Mrs. Mary Lou Mumford go my thanks for secretarial assistance. To my wife, Addiene G. Wise, my gratitude for her constant encouragement and patience.

NOTE

1. *Pilgrimage: The Journal of Pastoral Psychotherapy.* David O. Bristow, D. Rel., editor, 427 Lakeshore Drive N.E., Atlanta, Ga. 30307.

Chapter 1

Pastoral Psychotherapy

PASTORAL COUNSELING AND PASTORAL PSYCHOTHERAPY

The work of the pastor with individuals has usually been called pastoral counseling. There are various reasons for this. However, in this book we shall discard the use of this term. Both in a broad and also in a more narrow sense, the pastor does a form of psychotherapy. By psychotherapy we mean a process, engaged in by two or more persons in which one is accepted as a healer or helper, who aims at assisting the other to change feelings, attitudes, and behavior, or, in other words, become in some ways a different person. Psychotherapy deals with intrapsychic processes, with interpersonal relationships, and with the person's response to his total environment, including his cultural milieu. There are many technical issues involved in psychotherapy in general, and pastoral psychotherapy in particular, some of which we shall deal with in this book.

In using the word *psychotherapy* rather than *counseling* we are returning to the roots of our religious tradition. The Greek word "psyche" in the New Testament refers, not to one part of the total person as distinguished from other parts, such as pneuma and soma. It rather refers to the living person as a total reality or unity. It cannot be taken to mean a spiritual aspect as distinguished from the mental or physical. It is man as a whole, an organic unity.

Sometimes "psyche" in the New Testament means "life" (Matt. 6:25; 10:39; Mark 10:45), but the individual life, not life in general. Sometimes it is translated "soul" (Matt. 11:29; 22:38). It is the seat of feelings such as joy or sorrow, love or hate (Matt. 12:18; Luke 12:19; Mark 14:34; Matt. 22:37). The "psyche" may be clutched nervously or it may find release and liberation by being offered up to God openly and without anxiety, and in this way find fulfillment (Matt. 6:25–34; Mark 9:34–37).

The word *therapy* is carried over from the Greek "therapia" or "therapeuo" in the New Testament, where it is used rather frequently. Here it means the "willingness to serve and the personal relation of him who serves to the one served by him."[1] It may express solicitude for someone in need. It also denotes the caring for the sick and the cure of illness. It is the word used in the commission of Jesus to "heal the sick" (Matt. 10:8; Luke 10:9), as well as in other passages in the New Testament. The fact that this word has been taken over today almost exclusively by the medical profession is an interesting chapter in the history of words. However, in terms of his tradition, the pastor has just as much right to the use of this word as does the physician, whose tradition grows more out of Greek thought. To avoid confusion, in this book we will use such terms as pastoral psychotherapy when referring to the work of the pastor. And since psychotherapy is indeed practiced by a number of professions today, we will either specify a particular profession by name, or speak of psychotherapy as a general practice.

Pastoral psychotherapy, taking its clues from the Biblical record, is concerned with the living person as a total reality, an organic unity which is broken and requires healing. Sometimes it is the "life" that needs healing or the "soul." Certainly the Biblical writers were aware of the presence of emotional conflict and responses. Feelings such as love and hate, faith or fear, hope or despair, sorrow or joy, anxiety, guilt and jealousy, and others, seem to have been as prominent in those days as today, and are frequently discussed in the Bible as either disruptive or healing factors in an individual's life. One of the difficult tasks in therapy is to help the person who is defensive and resistant with these attitudes which have been adopted to protect or save the self. A human being is not saved nor healed against his own will, but must be permitted the experience of self-discovery — coming to himself, as in the story of the Prodigal (Luke 15:17) — and the autonomous decision to change the direction of his life. Pastoral psychotherapy is not doing something to another person; it is assisting another person to do and be something.

Pastoral "counseling" has been defined by several methods. One is by building professional fences. In this method, one group says, "This is my province. You stay out." Such fences may be supported by certain cultural sanctions or practices. The point is that such a method aims at exclusion. Thus, we are told that the clergy should not deal with the mentally ill or emotionally disturbed, or that the pastor should not counsel with pathological persons, or he should work at prevention rather than cure, or that the psychiatrist should not deal with religion, but should leave that to the clergyman.

But who are the mentally ill, the emotionally disturbed, the pathological? The great majority of an average congregation today may be emotionally disturbed, depending on just what is meant by that phrase.[2] Persons in the severe throes of bereavement, or going through a family crisis, or suffering from certain physical illness, and in many other human situations, become emotionally disturbed. It is generally acknowledged that certain kinds of religious experiences usually involve emotional conflicts. The pastor must deal with emotionally disturbed persons, and at times with frankly mentally ill persons.

From Biblical days, the priest and the pastor have been concerned with and ministered to persons suffering from emotional conflict. But they have been called by other names, such as sinner, the penitent, the deviant, the depressed (dark night of the soul), the rebel, the overly scrupulous, the grandiose, the overcontrolled and the undercontrolled, the sensuous and the extreme puritan, the person with rigid conscience and the person who lacked conscience. Emotional disturbances and spiritual disturbances have had something of a common meaning. It has long been recognized that in the midst of profound emotional disturbance there may be a creative religious or spiritual process emerging. One thinks of men like George Fox, John Bunyan, and, more recently, Anton Boisen.[3]

When it comes to prevention the pastor is often described as the first line of defense against mental illness. A good case could be made for such a statement, and it would involve much more than being a handy referral agency. The question is, what is prevention? It may be thought of as keeping a pathological process from being started or developing. Certainly the pastor is in a strategic position here in terms of his ministry to the parents of very young children. More emphasis is needed at this point.

Real prevention in the field of personality is more than the product of some kind of manipulation of environmental forces in order to avoid a serious illness. Such approaches may only forestall a breakdown, but not deal therapeutically with the pathological process going on within the person.

Real prevention in the field of personality is achieved by helping a person deal constructively with the conflicts that might sooner or later lead to a full-blown breakdown. Such prevention is in a sense indirect. The real aim here is to help the person grow emotionally and find a greater degree of personal fulfillment.[4] For the pastor, and for certain others, the goal of helping persons realize the possibilities inherent within them is crucial. The goal of some kind of an adjustment to a status quo which will prevent a breakdown may be acceptable to some workers, but not to the pastor except as a last resort in some situations. Psychotherapy is one approach for the pastor in facilitating the growth of persons. It is not the only method for this. The understanding of persons gained in pastoral psychotherapy needs to be utilized in the other pastoral activities. For example, one hears sermons founded on such a faulty conception of the nature of personal life that they tend to contribute to illness rather than health, although this is not the intention of the preacher. Our real point here is that prevention in the field of personality requires positive measures that promote the growth of persons, often through the resolution of conflict.

There is another fallacy in this business of definition by setting up fences. It is that the nonpastoral psychotherapist, be he psychiatrist, psychologist or social worker, must not deal with the religion of a patient. This is a false assumption. Any therapist should deal with a patient's religion to the extent that religion is part of the patient's illness. A therapist should be able to deal with the healthy aspects of a patient's religion in terms of promoting the health of the whole person. Religion is fundamentally a resource for health, but in many persons it inevitably gets involved in the processes of illness. This means that the psychotherapist needs to know something about religion from a broad perspective. It means also that the psychotherapist should be able to make full allowance for his own personal biases in religion. He should be able to understand the healthy as well as the unhealthy aspects of a person's religion. He should be able to deal with religion with understanding, rather than with subtle or manifest hostility. Definition by setting up fences may be used as a justification for not doing these things.

Likewise the pastor cannot adequately understand a person's religious experience without dealing with the feeling components of that experience. Whatever else religion is, it usually involves the whole person. Beliefs, for example, while formulated conceptually, have deep emotional roots. There are profound nonrational elements in religious experience which are very necessary in the promotion of growth. To dismiss these as irrational is to show either bias or lack of understanding. The pastor can contribute to the production of mental illness by failing to understand the emotional roots of religious experiences. The psychiatrist can do likewise. Therefore, the fence conception of psychotherapy, which keeps the pastor away from deep, nonrational elements in persons, or the psychiatrist away from religious experience of persons, is totally inadequate in the light of our understanding.

Fences do give people security, and this is why we have them. Some fences may be quite helpful and necessary at times. At best they define only in terms of externals. They do not help in the definition of pastoral psychotherapy.

Another kind of definition is by the use of euphemisms to describe what a specific profession does. Thus, the psychiatrist does psychotherapy, the social worker does case work, the educator does guidance, and the pastor does pastoral counseling. Then some differences have to be described which make each term unique. Many pastors become anxious over the question as to what is unique in pastoral counseling. Sometimes psychologists describe their work as dealing with healthy persons, in contrast to psychiatrists, who deal with sick persons. The major point in this approach is to define differences in goals and methods, as well as similarities. Thus, Stewart[5] seems to identify the pastor with the social worker, placing the emphasis of his work in role relationships. Others see the pastor in a different light.

But "a rose is a rose is a rose," and psychotherapy done under any other name is still psychotherapy. The fact is that all helpers do the same things at various times, and attempts to make distinctions in terms of what is done is at its best superficial and unsatisfactory. It leaves the whole person out of account, and attempts to concentrate on some one aspect of the process.

The trend today, or perhaps it is more than a trend, is to give attention to the total process of helping persons, rather than to single out a particular aspect or technique. Thus, many nonmedical workers are openly thinking about their work as psychotherapy, and no longer need to make superficial distinctions. Perhaps we are all getting more honest.

The concept of pastoral therapy today is being formulated in terms of the process. The process of helping another involves an individual who is hurting and who wants to change; the ability of the therapist to create a relationship in which a change can take place; understanding various phases of the process from beginning to end; and, particularly, understanding the various qualities of relationship between the therapist and the sufferer that take place during the process.

The process of therapy may be understood from a number of different points of view. There are the psychoanalytic, the psychodynamic, the person-centered, the behavior modification, and the existential analytic, to mention a few. The therapist needs sufficient training so that he is at home with one conceptual approach and the methods it describes. There is a broad agreement today that change in psychotherapy is a function of the relationship, regardless of the theoretical formulations which are used to describe the process. However, conceptualizations do become a guide to the activity of the therapist in the relationship, and to some extent they define the relationship. A person working from a person-centered point of view would aim at quite a different kind of relationship than would one working from a behavior modification approach. The goals might be similar or different.

Our position is that what is called "pastoral counseling" is really pastoral psychotherapy and should be recognized as such. This position finds support from numerous authors from the medical point of view. Dr. Jerome Frank,[6] Professor of Psychiatry at the Johns Hopkins Medical School, writes:

We shall consider as psychotherapy only those types of influence characterized by the following features:

1. A trained, socially sanctioned healer, whose healing powers are accepted by the sufferer and by his social group or an important segment of it.

2. A sufferer who seeks relief from the healer.

3. A circumscribed, more or less structured, series of contacts between the healer and the sufferer, through which the healer, often with the aid of the group, tries to produce certain changes in the sufferer's emotional state, attitudes and behavior. All concerned believe these changes will help him. Although physical and chemical adjuncts may be used, the healing influence is primarily exercised by words, acts and rituals in which the sufferer, healer, and if there is one, group, participate jointly.

Later, Dr. Frank adds:

> The very same patient might be treated by a psychiatrist, a
> psychologist, a psychiatric social worker, or even a clergy-
> man, depending on where his feet carry him. As a result, the
> relationship among the different professions that conduct
> psychotherapy are in a state of flux. Clergymen and psychia-
> trists have formally recognized their field of common con-
> cern by forming the Academy of Religion and Mental
> Health. Jurisdictional problems are most acute in the larger
> cities where, in response to the increasing demand for
> psychotherapy, psychologists and psychiatric social workers
> have gone into independent private practice in direct compe-
> tition with psychiatrists, resulting in attempts by various
> groups involved to settle the issue by legislation.

Classical psychoanalysis is perhaps the most complex form of
psychotherapy in existence today. We are not identifying pastoral
therapy with classical psychoanalysis, though there are some
clergymen who are doing something very close to psychoanalysis.[7] But even for his classical discipline, Sigmund Freud[8]
wrote:

> For the patient, then, it is a matter of indifference whether
> the analyst is a doctor or not, providing only that the danger
> of his condition being misunderstood is excluded by the
> necessary medical report before the treatment begins and on
> some possible occasions during the course of it. For him it is
> incomparably more important that the analyst should pos-
> sess personal qualities that make him trustworthy, and that
> he should have acquired the knowledge and understanding
> as well as the experience which alone can make it possible for
> him to fulfill his task.
> A professional lay analyst will have no difficulty in win-
> ning as much respect as is due to a secular pastoral worker.
> Indeed, the words, "secular pastoral worker" might well serve

as a general formula for describing the function which the analyst, whether he is a doctor or a layman, has to perform in his relation to the public. Our friends among the protestant clergy, and more recently among the catholic clergy as well, are often able to relieve their parishioners of inhibitions of their daily life by confirming their faith — after having first offered them a little analytic information about the nature of their conflicts.

We shall present one more opinion from a physician. In his excellent book, *Psychiatry and Pastoral Care,*[9] Dr. Edgar Draper writes:

> Pastoral Counseling must be considered as a form of psychotherapy in which the therapist is a pastor. Although models, methods, training, accoutrements, skills, theories and goals may be different, our definition of psychotherapy includes him along with the psychoanalyst, psychiatrist, case worker, physician, psychologist, shaman and quack. How good or qualified or skilled or capable a psychotherapist is forms a different though *crucial* question.

Other statements might be added to the above.[10] Psychotherapy is recognized as a complex process which is susceptible to various forms of interpretation, and is practiced, whether acknowledged or not, by a variety of professional workers. It would seem very important for society, in our present state of change and disturbance, to have psychotherapists operating within it who have various professional identities. We have been making this emphasis here because in the remainder of this book we shall be speaking of pastoral psychotherapy rather than pastoral counseling. Pastoral counseling is a form of psychotherapy, and should be dealt with as such. The word *counseling* has long been an ambiguous word, subject to many definitions. At this point we are making no distinctions between long and short term therapy, so-called supportive therapy, or any of the other distinctions often applied to the word *counseling.*

Pastoral psychotherapy is that psychotherapy done by a person who has a professional identity and commitment within a religious faith group. This means that in addition to all of the problems of human values that are the concern of other kinds of therapist, the pastor openly recognizes the place of ultimate realities and values in all aspects of human life, and is, therefore, qualified to help persons to deal with their false ultimates, or in religious terms, their idolatries. As an illustration of what we mean, take love as a value. Love may be viewed solely as the best way to live, or as essential to health, or as necessary for satisfying interpersonal relationships. Much of what is said about a strictly human view of love is congenial to the pastor. But a religious orientation does not stop here. Indeed, it believes that to stop here is to invert the true order of life and to raise the human, or the penultimate, to the level of the ultimate. In the long run, this can destroy the strictly human aspects of love. Religious faith understands and accepts many of the human meanings of love, but it also sees love as a value which is rooted in the nature of the universe, or in God. The individual, the microcosm, is created and sustained by the Whole, by God, and partakes in the nature of God. Discussion of such dimensions in the therapeutic process would be determined by the context and content of the specific situation, and certainly would take place within an understanding of the dynamics of the person involved, including his religious orientation. But the context and orientation within which the pastor works in itself speaks of these ultimate meanings, and frequently verbalization is not necessary in the therapy process. Any therapist works not only as an individual but as a symbol of a larger unity, be that humanity, or the ideal of health, or of medicine as an art and a science, or, as in the case of the pastor, of religious faith and the structures through which that faith is expressed.

THE PASTORAL THERAPIST

What are the possibilities and limitations of the pastor as therapist? How, in the modern church, can he fulfill his traditional function in the cure of souls?

As in the case of any other profession, his possibilities and limitations are determined by (1) personal qualifications, (2) training and (3) the setting in which he works. There are, of course, other determinants of possibilities and limitations which are within persons.

Personal qualifications include such things as the ability to empathize with another sufferer; the qualities of patience, understanding, acceptance; the ability to establish a healing relationship with another person; and the ability to utilize personal feelings in terms of the needs of persons. Some pastors who are strong in the pulpit, or in administration, or in education are very poor therapists, though there are exceptions. Every parish needs to have a pastoral therapist available from time to time. The full work of the ministry cannot be accomplished if this aspect is missing.

On the personal side, another qualification is important. The pastoral therapist needs to have gone through his own therapy with some positive results. Having had therapy does not of itself make a therapist. But being in close touch with feelings, attitudes and motives is very important in any pastoral work, particularly when one is dealing with loneliness, suffering, frustration, and the like in others. This is considered of such importance that it is one of the requirements for membership in the American Association of Pastoral Counselors.[11]

Education and training is an important consideration for the pastoral therapist. It is available in some clinical centers and also in some theological seminaries. Solid grounding in theoretical understanding is important. Equally if not more important is the length and quality of the supervision of clinical work received during the training period. This period should be sufficiently long to enable a candidate to begin to learn how to use himself

effectively for the therapy process. This art is not gained quickly
or easily.[12]

The setting in which the pastor works offers both possibilities
and limitations. The therapeutically oriented pastor in the parish
has the opportunity to develop relationships of trust and confidence. Preaching, the conduct of worship, calling, educational
activities, for example, offer an unparalleled opportunity to
develop the quality of relationships which will bring people to
him.[13] Because of the pressure of other duties he may not have
time to take care of all who come. This means referral to other
sources of help. He also may have requests where long-term therapy is needed, and this has complications within the parish which
the trained pastor will understand.

On the other hand, pastors working within a pastoral therapy
center[14] are not troubled by some of these limitations, but they
lack the opportunity for the development of meaningful relationships within the parish. They have to depend on referrals from
pastors and others. They do have the opportunity to specialize.
They may develop rather long and rewarding relationships with
persons who come to them, and they may find themselves chan-
nels for a great deal of good.

It is not a matter of superiority of one form of ministry over
another, but of each pastor finding the setting which is congenial.
There are other settings, such as in hospitals or other institutions,
in colleges and universities, which attract some and offer excellent opportunities to trained pastors.

Whatever the setting, the pastor has the task of deciding just
how he will work in his situation. His own depth of understanding is important here. Will he take a history on persons who come
to him? How often will he see them? Do his other duties permit
regular appointments? Who determines the manner in which he
deals with a particular person, himself or the person? How
should hostilities, resistances, transferences, and countertransferences be handled? Some of these issues will be dealt with
later. However, it is the responsibility of the pastor to determine how he will work in the setting he has accepted or created

for himself. This is part of what it means to be a professional person.

Before getting away from the parish setting, we shall deal with a prevalent fallacy. It is the belief that one cannot preach to people and meet them in an actual therapeutic relationship. This may be true in regard to classical psychoanalysis. Those practicing this approach to healing are probably correct in refraining from other contacts with their patients.

The reasons given for the support of this fallacy often result from misconceptions of the work of the ministry, or they involve problems of transference[15] or countertransference that are not recognized as such. Some misconceptions are that the task of preaching is to reinforce the superego, or the unconscious, emotional sense of right and wrong, or to reinforce belief, or to promote the institutional program and loyalties, or to move people to some specific action. Transference and countertransference issues manifest themselves in various conceptions of the authority of the preacher, or his need to maintain dependencies, or his need to be overly dependent on his congregation. The pastor's conception of himself and his work, and of his congregation may be important factors here. The idea that a pastor cannot practice some level of therapy with members of his congregation may be true of some pastors, but it should not be accepted as a general truth.[16]

The general field of psychotherapy as it is emerging today must be seen as multidisciplinary. In our complex society there are many influences on the human mind and its development, so that no one discipline can have a monopoly of understanding or of cure. One of the values of the work of Erik Erikson[17] is that he has shown how biological and intrapsychic processes interact with cultural forces, including religion. Something deeper than a verbal knowledge of his work is essential for the modern pastor. In addition, many professions have an interest in persons and their development, and are, in one way or another, involved in changing feelings, attitudes and interpersonal relationships. The pastor should maintain relationships with other professionals

such as psychiatrists, psychologists, social workers, and educa-
tors. In some instances this would be for consultation and the
sharing of experience, and in some for supervision. With the disturbed schizophrenic, psychiatric consultation is certainly in
order. Sometimes the pastor is the first to see the personal and
social effects of a gradually developing organic brain disease, and
certainly here a referral is called for. Few pastors are trained to
give psychological tests, and here the services of a psychologist
should be sought. The pastor should make referrals to a lawyer in
cases where legal issues are involved, as in divorce. There is evidence today that some professionals are turning to qualified pastors for consultation in regard to emotional as well as religious
problems. In many instances adequately trained clergy are being
accepted on equal footing with other therapists. Indeed, interdisciplinary movements are occurring today in an encouraging
manner. The realities of human experience call for understandings and consultations on a multidisciplinary level, rather than
professional isolation.

RELIGIOUS SYMBOLS AND
ULTIMATE VALUES

The pastoral psychotherapist should understand the various
symbolic expressions of religion.[18] He should be able to distinguish clinically between the function of faith and the structures
of faith in a person. This means understanding the dynamics of
religious symbols and their uses. He should be able to distinguish
the healthy strivings in the religious life of a person, and also the
unhealthy defenses and patterns. Part of his task is to help others
discover this within themselves. He will soon learn that verbal
communication is essential, but it must take place in a process
and relationship of mutual discovery. The communication itself
must be understood. This is the therapy process.

The religious ideas of a person, if listened to carefully, become
a form of symbolic communication. They are more than ideas in
the abstract. They have a vital relationship to the inner life of

the person and to his interpersonal experiences. They are symbolic in form since they express intangibles like meaning, value, and relationships. When taken literally they may not make sense. But when seen as expressing processes, meanings, and relationships by which a person lives, they become very significant. Conceptually and socially validated theological ideas become a sort of a measuring stick or perspective which helps the pastoral therapist understand the relation of a person's religious ideas to his inner dynamics and human relationships. They serve somewhat the same function for the pastoral therapist as theoretical formulations serve the scientist or a knowledge of physiology and anatomy serve the surgeon. They are guidelines to help understand deviations and malfunctions, as well as adaptive functions.

The two-dimensional nature of religious symbols, the human or penultimate and the ultimate, are to be understood simultaneously and in their dynamic relationship. Theologians are correct in fearing the loss of emphasis on the transcendent meanings of religion, but pastors know that the internal dimensions of religious faith must also be dealt with. Overemphasis on structure or content to the neglect of inner dynamics, process and consequences lead to unhealthy results. The pastoral therapist must be equipped to deal with either or both dimensions according to what is required in a given situation, not forcing structures or contents on persons but dealing with the processes of faith and doubt. A genuine and secure pastoral and religious identity does not lead to forcing specific religious structures. Genuine faith cannot be passed on in the form of structures, but only through a relationship in which it is manifest.

What we have been saying about the concern of the pastor for ultimate values, and his interest in the internal dimensions of religious faith and language is also shared by some therapists who are not pastors, on the basis of their own religious experience and insights. The nature of religious faith is such that it cannot be contained within the formal structures of an ordained ministry. Neither is it created by those structures alone. This is the significance of the doctrine of the priesthood of the believer.

Perhaps we can formulate the goal of the pastor as that of enabling persons to attain a genuine religious quality of life in terms of the New Testament ideal. These include such attitudes as faith, hope, love, patience, understanding, courage, joy, and peace. The pastor is also aware of attitudes which are destructive of persons as portrayed in the Bible and elsewhere. One of the central concerns of the Bible is the power available to achieve a high quality of life, wholeness or salvation. This is the problem of motivation. Another Biblical concern is the primacy of relationships between persons and between persons and God which become a source of strength. In experiences such as prayer, meditation, and worship deep intuitive insights into the nature of life, its meaning, and values are found.

Whether in the general pastoral ministry or in the specialty such as pastoral therapy, these concepts of quality of life, power, or motivation, personal relationships and the intuitive source of insight (so denigrated and yet striven for in a scientific world) are central.

Dynamic psychology deals with many of these issues, but in the more descriptive manner and orientation of science. It offers the pastor, generalist or specialist, a source of knowledge and understanding which is indispensable in dealing with persons. In all of his work he needs to be sensitive to the issues involved in the emotional life of persons. For the pastor constant growth toward excellence is imperative. Especially does the concern for motivation in the New Testament need to be expanded by the more detailed modern knowledge of motivation, and the appropriation of this knowledge for both his own inner life and his work. He must learn to recognize and deal with those attitudes and feelings within himself and others which resist change. It is fundamental that change is necessary for either a religious quality of life or for health. Many want the blessings of religious faith or of emotional growth and health without fulfilling the conditions necessary for those benefits.

It is not our intention to draw simple parallels between Biblical ideas and those emerging today from psychotherapy. It is, however, our intention to point out broad relationships between ideas that have emerged from the two fields. Both are concerned with the individual's growth and fulfillment. Psychotherapy limits its perspective to the human dimension of personal existence. Religion with a broader perspective sees the individual in relation to ultimate meanings and values to God, however God is conceived. But religion also sees the individual in his wholeness and totality, and in his relationship to other human beings. It knows that individuals are hampered in fulfilling their ultimate destiny by experiences within the life process itself, as well as by conflicts within the individual (Gal. 6:7). The pastor has to be concerned with these, not just in general but also in the cause and effect relationships within the individual. The richness of the meanings of the words "psyche" and "therapeuo" in the New Testament, though at times confusing, gives the pastor guidelines which lead directly to the "cure of souls" as traditionally expressed, or to pastoral psychotherapy. In his total ministry the pastor is dealing with the inner life of the individual, with many who are anxiously holding on to self, rather than finding release and liberation by offering themselves to God and others in self-giving love (witness the present emphasis in psychotherapeutic literature on "narcissism"[19]). The pastor is called upon to give himself in service to others in a manner that makes it possible for them to use him for their own therapy, cure, or salvation. Pastoral therapy is not doing something to another person. It is offering a person a quality of relationship through which curative grace is mediated. In the chapters which follow we shall elaborate on the process of therapy.

NOTES

1. This quotation, and much of the material in this paragraph is taken from Kittel's *Theological Dictionary of the New Testament.* (English translation by G. W. Bromiley) Grand Rapids, Michigan: Wm. B. Eerdman's Publishing Co., Vol. III, pp. 128–129 and 194–215, 608–657. 1965.

For some other passages in the New Testament where these words are used, see Luke 7:21; Matt. 4:23–24; Matt. 8:7; John 5:1–9; Luke 5:15; 6:18; 19:2;

12:15; 17:18. This list is not exhaustive. For further study the reader is referred to Kittel.

For further discussion of the problems involved in an understanding of illness and the cure of illness see Aarne Siirala, *The Voice of Illness.* Philadelphia: Fortress Press, 1964, and Carroll A. Wise, *Religion in Illness and Health,* New York: Harper and Row, 1942.

2. The term *emotionally disturbed* requires careful scrutiny, especially in view of the question-begging statement that the task of the preacher is to comfort the afflicted and afflict the comfortable. The root sources of the emotional disturbance need careful assessment in terms of both internal and external factors, and the ways in which these play into each other in specific persons. In this book we use this term to connote those whose disturbance is grounded in intrapsychic factors and also those who are disturbed by bona fide objective conditions, either personal or social. Either condition is a context for growth and pastoral concern.

3. See Anton Boisen, *The Exploration of the Inner World,* New York: Harper and Row, 1936.

4. The literature which emphasizes personal fulfillment or self-realization rather than adjustment as the goal of psychotherapy is abundant. The student is referred to the writings of such persons as Erich Fromm, Carl Rogers, Edith Weigert, Rollo May, Erik Erikson, Karl Menninger, Andras Angyal. Christian theology also has formulated a similar goal in the concepts of the Imago Dei, the abundant life, and of salvation, where this term is conceived dynamically rather than statically.

5. Charles Stewart, *The Minister as a Marriage Counselor,* Nashville: Abingdon Press, 1961, pp. 142–143.

6. Jerome Frank, (1961) *Persuasion and Healing,* New York: Schocken Books, 1963, pp. 2, 3.

7. The best source of information in regard to classical psychoanalysis is, of course, Freud himself. A book such as *Systems of Psychotherapy,* by Donald H. Ford and Hugh B. Urban (New York: John Wiley, 1965), contains a good chapter on psychoanalysis. Or see Karl Menninger, *Theory of Psychoanalytic Technique,* New York: Basic Books, 1958.

8. Sigmund Freud (1926), *The Question of Lay Analysis,* in *The Standard Edition of the Complete Psychological Works of Sigmund Freud,* trans. James Strachey, London: Hogarth Press, 1959, pp. 244, 255–256.

9. Edgar Draper, *Psychiatry and Pastoral Care,* Englewood Cliffs, N.J.: Prentice-Hall, Inc., 1965, p. 79.

10. Mention should be made of the following works in this regard: Kurt Eissler, *Medical Orthodoxy and the Future of Psychoanalysis,* New York: International Universities Press, 1955; Harry Guntrip, *Healing the Sick Mind,* New York: Appleton-Century, 1964, pp. 119–128; Thomas Szasz, "Psychiatry,

Psychotherapy and Psychology," *Archives of General Psychiatry,* Vol. 1, 1959, No. 5, p. 455.

11. Those interested in a statement of standards for pastoral psychotherapists should contact the American Association of Pastoral Counselors, 3000 Connecticut Ave., N.W., Suite 300, Washington, D.C. 20008.

12. For further discussion of the training of pastoral therapists see the pertinent chapters in *Community Mental Health,* edited by Howard Clinebell, Jr., Nashville: Abingdon Press, 1970. Also Chris M. Meadows, Charles Kemp, et al, "A Symposium on Research for the Professional Doctorate," *The Journal of Pastoral Care,* Vol. XXVII, No. 4, pp. 267–282. (1973).

13. Carroll A. Wise, *The Meaning of Pastoral Care,* New York: Harper and Row, 1966.

14. Berkley C. Hathorne, *A Critical Analysis of Protestant Church Counseling Centers* (booklet), Washington, D.C.: Methodist Board of Social Concerns, 1964.

15. On the problems of transference and countertransference see Chapters 7 and 8.

16. Put in psychological terms, one of the issues here is whether the pastor should adopt a style which is authoritarian and thus seek to reinforce the super-ego, or whether the pastor should adopt a preaching style which appeals to the ego functions of the congregation, helping them to test their own lives in the light of religious truth, to arrive at a sense of values more congruous with their faith, and move them toward some desirable decision of their own making. For an excellent article on preaching, written from a therapeutic point of view, see Harry Levinson, "The Trouble with Sermons," in *The Journal of Pastoral Care,* Vol. XXII, No. 2, 1968, p. 65.

17. For a complete list of his books see Erik Erikson's *Life History and the Historical Moment,* New York: W. W. Norton, 1975.

18. Carroll A. Wise, *Religion in Illness and Health,* New York: Harper and Row, 1942.

19. Otto Kernberg, *Borderline Conditions and Pathological Narcissism,* New York: Jason Aronson, 1975; Heinz Kohut, *The Analysis of the Self,* New York: International Universities Press, 1971; Heinz Kohut, *The Restoration of the Self,* New York: International Universities Press, 1977; Marie Coleman Nelson, ed., *The Narcissistic Condition,* New York: Human Sciences Press, 1977.

Chapter 2

The Pastor as a Person
to Others

THE PASTOR'S DUAL ORIENTATION

One of the unique characteristics of the modern pastor is his dual orientation. His identity as a clergyman is given by the quality and meaning of his religious faith. Religious faith is more than personal. Through it he is bound to a group and that group helps to determine its meaning. Ordination is a ritual in which the individual accepts his pastoral identity as the group confers it, and in which the group confirms the identity of the pastor. It also is an act in time understood to have ultimate significance, for in this rite the church acts for the God of its faith. There may be some divergence between the various meanings of identity as conferred in ordination, and that which the pastor accepts for himself, either consciously or unconsciously.

Since he works with people, the pastor also needs a psychological orientation. This is crucial for the work of therapy. The pastoral therapist must not only know psychological theory, he must identify with it sufficiently so that he can use it. For example, he must not only know about anxiety and defenses, he must be able to recognize them and have a workable understanding of the nature of the experience behind them.

This dual orientation is not always comfortable. The abstractions of theology and psychology are not easily reconciled, nor should they be. They stem from completely different faith assumptions; they involve different dimensions of being; and they have their own ways of creating and resolving tensions. Furthermore, specific dynamic processes within the personality of the pastor, such as guilt feelings, come into conflict with theological and psychological ideas in a manner that cannot be resolved by reason alone. One side or the other then may be denied, or the pastor may vacillate from one to the other.

The resolution of this situation must come in the person of the pastor. This must involve his emotions and strivings, as well as his intellect. Such resolution usually requires emotional growth, moving to new levels of being. This may involve struggle, pain, personal therapy, long hours of reflection and meditation, and the ability to entertain and evaluate new insights. This requires a commitment to the process of being and becoming, to internal discovery rather than to the integration of diverse theories. How the pastor resolves this conflict becomes a determining factor in the kind of relationship he creates with others. It becomes part of his being a person to others. This chapter will be devoted to some of the considerations growing out of the religious orientation of the pastor and what it means for his being a person to others.

THE NATURE OF RELIGIOUS EXPERIENCE

Creative religious experiences involve deep intuitive processes. Many are difficult to adequately formulate either psychologically or theologically. Realities are experienced on the unconscious level that are difficult to formulate intellectually. The poet and the artist are aware of such experiences. They use an artistic medium to suggest realities they may only dimly apprehend. Such experiences may be expressed in religious symbols, but the more those symbols are organized rationally the more the deeper meaning may be lost. Symbols are, thus, cut off from their meaning, and become powerless to promote growth.

Freud[1] called this deeper level primary process thinking. He distinguished it from secondary process thinking, the logical thinking that deals with the realities of the external world and human relationships. It is an error to consider primary process thinking as always regressive and found only in sick persons, though it is found there sometimes in very distorted forms. All creative thinking contains a strong measure of primary process thinking, but here it is used in the service of the ego processes. It is even found in creative mathematical thinking.

Similar processes operate in any genuine religious experience and this is the reason theological or psychological theories of such experiences are never adequate. This is the reason that the psychology of religion, as a discipline, has been rather sterile. In a genuine religious experience, God meets man on the deepest levels of his being. From this experience new truth, integrations and actions break through to man's conscious levels. The health or the pathology has to be judged, not only in terms of processes, but also in terms of results in the person. It is on this basis that we can understand the insistence of some theologians that God breaks through to human consciousness in a way that creates discontinuities, especially those created by the experience of the ultimate within the contingent. One of the most powerful interpretative religious ideas is that of the Holy Spirit.

The discontinuities between the ultimate and the contingent have a very important practical significance for all pastoral work and therapy. In no way can finite Man control the ultimate. In no way can Man control the Holy Spirit, or God. Some people want to be controlled because it relieves them of the responsibility and the pain of dealing with their experiences. Others are too frightened to give up control. The pastor may feel that the uniqueness of the pastoral approach is that in some way he can bring God into the situation as a sort of a cotherapist. Whatever the pastor may or may not do, he has no way of guaranteeing or controlling the acts of God. The history of pastoral care is strewn with the wreckages of such attempts. We are called to do the will of God; God is not called on to conform to our wishes, nor does He!

What can the pastor do? On the level of relationships he is called upon not to do but to be. His manner of being with a person may in itself communicate the values central to the Christian

faith. The Christian faith is an incarnational religion.[2] The Word
became flesh and, to a lesser degree, still becomes flesh. Here
again we face the discontinuity between the ultimate and the
contingent, a profound mystery which none of our concepts adequately explain. Genuine love, hope and trust on the human side
of the equation may speak of these dimensions within God,
though not completely. Indeed, if these are not present in the
relationship, though not necessarily verbalized, speaking about
them may be futile. Wherever they are real they are communicated, unless the other person is unable to receive the communication. They may be rejected. The pastor cannot control the
responses of another person, nor should he try.

In spite of all that can be said about genuine, creative religious
experience, in the final analysis no other person can be involved
in it. The primary relationship is between the individual and the
Ultimate Power on which he feels dependent for his existence
though not dependent within his existence. The priesthood of the
believer, communication through relationships, the curative
power of the therapist are highly significant, but each has its limitations. The pastoral therapist is aware of the boundaries beyond
which he cannot trespass. If he were to try, he would be playing
God. In other words, there is no form of human intervention that
is certain to be effective on this deeper level. Here it is between
the individual and his God. It is often avoided because it is a
frightening, lonely experience. Part of the present disillusionment
with preaching is that the preacher too often has spoken for God
in ways on which God could not make good.

MODELS IN PSYCHOTHERAPY

What is the relation of the pastoral orientation to the model
adopted by the pastor? The word *model*[3] is part of current jargon
among therapists. Within the disciplines of medical psychotherapy, psychology, social work and theology, competing
models have been developed, each with their proponents and
their detractors. The history of psychotherapy and the history

of religion have much in common in terms of the development of sectarian or faith groups.

What is a model? A model is an approach and a pattern out of which a specific activity emerges. It is a way of working, based on a set of assumptions which become a guide. It also may be a standard of excellence. A model will present specific actions that are held to be necessary. In the medical model diagnosis always precedes treatment. Most medical psychotherapy, though not all, adheres to this pattern. In some pastoral and psychological models, diagnosis is not thought to be necessary. In some models a high degree of autonomy is granted the person; in others the person is closely directed. Interpretation is used extensively in some models; in others it is frowned upon. Some models emphasize feelings, others a more rational approach. Still others insist on getting behind feelings to underlying experiences and processes. Some make use of the past, present, and future dimensions of life; others concentrate on the present. Some models treat every person with the same techniques; other models vary technique with the person. Some models are incongruous with the pastoral orientation and identity. Sometimes pastors feel they must be eclectic, which leads them to present a confused picture to others.

The pastor with a strong religious identity will find much in the field of science which he can accept and use without sacrificing his religious orientation. On the other hand, there is a difference between using ideas and methods from science and replacing religious orientation with the faith of science. Secular therapists seem to understand this better than many pastors. They have been heard to question how a pastor could be interested in their point of view. Sometimes this questioning grows out of a misunderstanding of the theological orientation. Sometimes it is the result of awareness of deep incongruity in points of view and in conceptions of man. For example, in the preface of a volume on behavioral therapy, Dr. Joseph Wolpe[4] points out the value of the volume for those "attuned" to its message, and then says, "We can also hope that at least some of the individuals who wander confusedly in a phenomenological and mentalistic world devoid of determinable laws will likewise profit from this book, and will be guided by it into the path of science." While Dr. Wolpe does not mention pastoral therapists, we would certainly fall into the category of those he wants to convert to the faith of science, to the understanding of man on which behavioral therapy is grounded and the model of therapy which grows out of that understanding. The question for the pastoral therapist is, To what extent can the model of behavioral therapy be used by those who operate from a Christian understanding of the nature of man and of the healing experience? A second question is whether the faith and methods of science are able to give a completely adequate account of the nature of man, as Dr. Wolpe implies. However, he would be aware of the deep incongruities between his scientific understanding of man and that grounded in a religious orientation.

PASTORAL CARE AND
PASTORAL SENSITIVITY

Distinctions are often made between pastoral care and pastoral psychotherapy. Sometimes pastoral care is thought of as the activity of the pastor in calling on his people, especially if they are sick or in trouble. Or pastoral care suggests short contacts of varying frequencies rather than interviews carried on regularly for a period of time. Or pastoral care is thought of as contacts initiated by the pastor, while therapy suggests contacts initiated by the individual. Sometimes it is said that since pastoral care consists of a small number of short contacts, the task of the pastor is to bring the person to face his situation quickly, directly, and authoritatively. The pastor, it is held, does not have time for the kind of approaches which might be utilized in the longer therapy relationships. All of this suggests that the pastor is not with the person in pastoral care in the same manner in which he is with the person in therapy.

The resolution of this issue lies in a broader and more realistic concept of pastoral care. Pastoral care should not be thought of as an activity. It is a relationship in which the caring aspects of the Christian faith is communicated. Pastoral care is a quality of relationship which should infuse and inform all of the activities of the pastor. It is a way of being with persons. Preaching, calling, educational activities, the conduct of worship, and administration are all part of pastoral care, when such care is seen as basically a relationship in which the caring aspects of the faith are communicated.

The pastor will find his understanding of persons and his capacity to form healing relationships as useful and effective in a pastoral call, or in a casual contact, as in more formal therapeutic work. Wholeness requires that the pastor meet persons in the same spirit regardless of the activity, and that he always be sensitive to the internal dynamics of persons.

For example, if autonomy and personal responsibility are essential qualities in our understanding and healing of persons, then either pastoral calling or pastoral therapy would have to accept these as necessary in the relationship. This means that the pastor would be with the person in such a way as to grant autonomy and responsibility. It means a search for those areas in the life of the person where such virtues could be exercised. The potential for the exercise of autonomy and responsibility in a thirty-year-old woman who is dying of cancer is quite different than that of a woman of the same age who is physically healthy but facing a divorce. With the first person the task is clearly to help her with the experience of dying. In many aspects of life she has lost all possibility of autonomy and responsibility because she is being controlled by the cancer. But she still may be able to decide whether she will die in dignity or in fear. The possibilities are much greater with the second person, depending on her inner strength and circumstances. In each instance healing through a pastoral relationship may occur. In each the identity of the pastor will remain the same, though his techniques will differ somewhat. In each the needs and condition of the person will be a major consideration. One issue in all forms of pastoral care is whether we shall be a person to others in terms of their needs or our own. In each the understanding and sensitivity of the pastor to the motivational elements are indispensable. The pastor will be concerned with the quality of existence which each experiences.

THE CHRISTIAN UNDERSTANDING
OF CREATION

What does the Christian understanding of creation have to say about the pastor in his relationship to others?

A central element in the Christian understanding of man is that he was created in the image of God. This should be understood, as all theological concepts should be understood, in a dynamic rather than a static sense. This means, for one thing, that the pastor must be with a person as a fellow creature. The pastor is called upon to accept his basic humanity and to experience within himself the truth that ultimately he stands in the same need as others, and that he has the same potential for sin and illness as do all others. This must be more than an intellectual belief with the pastor. It must be grasped emotionally so that it becomes a functioning motive in his relationships. One obstacle to this is a quality which the pastor as a creature has in common with all men, his narcissism or love of self. The quality of human narcissism is one of the chief obstacles in finding healing or salvation. Two persons who seek to impose their self-centeredness on each other will hardly form a healing relationship. This is reaching down to the depths of human personality, but that is where the Christian faith reaches in its dynamic penetration. Being a person to others in a healing sense requires that the pastor be constantly open to the transformation of his self-centeredness.

THE PROBLEM OF NARCISSISM

The human need to place self in the center of the universe, to become a creator rather than a creature, is evident from the early pages of the Bible to the present. It is at the root of many human problems — the demand that the universe be revised according to my needs, regardless of the needs of others. Humans have great difficulty accepting themselves as "a little lower than the angels" (Psalm 9). The second temptation experience as recorded by Matthew gives us a particularly forceful view of this problem in the consciousness of Jesus (Matt. 4:5, 6).

Freud[5] met the same problem as he sought to explore the neurotic process in his patients. He used a symbol from Greek mythology to formulate it — the symbol of a young man, Narcissus, falling in love with his own reflection in a pool of water, and hence the term *narcissism*. Narcissism is essentially the attachment of energy on images of the self, the love of self through others, relating to others in terms of how they satisfy our needs. In early infancy the child is not aware of other objects or persons, but only of his own needs. Later he becomes aware of others, but they exist only to fulfill his needs. He is the center of his world and makes demands on others. Many persons retain this attitude to such a degree that they become pathological in one way or another. A final stage of growth comes as the individual learns to relate to others regardless of his state of need. In other words, persons do not exist solely for his satisfaction. Further, he can relate to others in terms of their needs or just as persons in themselves. This is a mature level of growth. The path to such maturity has many pitfalls, and a great deal depends on the quality of relationships responsible adults are able to give the child.[6]

On the other hand, some narcissism or love of self is necessary for self-protection and self-preservation. It can also serve as a basis for decisions which promote growth and well-being without harming others. Persons in whom narcissism is repressed to a pathological degree may make choices which are harmful or self-destructive, or may not be able to defend themselves against unreasonable demands of others.

The Great Commandments of Jesus (Matt. 22:34–40) deal directly and succinctly with the problem of love. The basic solution here is that the dominant force of love is to be directed toward God. God is more than the projection of the self-image. He is a Reality who lives through the pages of the Bible and in human history. The love for God is an overarching love, for it includes love for God's creation, including self and others. The mature relationship is from the whole to the part, not the part to the whole as in self-centered love. Genuine love for God means the acceptance of the self as a creature along with other persons, the love of others as oneself. This love makes no demands, but is able to respond to the needs of others, or to give others the freedom to be themselves.

There are many issues in the dynamic development of narcissism or self-love in its healthy and unhealthy dimensions. Here we are concerned with it as a factor in the way in which the pastor is with persons. His own narcissism can be an obstacle in his ministry. On the other hand, he cannot have a creative ministry so long as he allows others to determine how he shall be or how he shall meet their needs. He should project an image of constancy and consistency to his people. His love for God must be clear and unambiguous, a difficult assignment. He will need understanding of those who project their own infantile images on him, and expect him to conform. He should be able to recognize when a sacrificial attitude is necessary in himself or others, but not confuse this with neurotic self-punishment. His relationships with others should not be determined by how they meet his narcissistic needs. The task of being a Christian pastor requires a high level of personal maturity.

THE IMAGE OF GOD

The understanding symbolized by the "Image of God" has a deep significance for pastoral therapy. It carries the meaning that God has placed within man, as part of his created nature, resources which make for wholeness, health, growth, the resolution of conflict, the transformation of instinctive conflict and energy into creative living. Man as a creature has the power to take a hand in the creation of himself by utilizing and fulfilling the potentials which God has placed in him. There is a sense in which a person plays a decisive role in his own being and becoming through his decisions, commitments, and loyalties. The resources for healing are within the person; the pastor does not place them there. Again, this must be more than an intellectual belief; it must be made part of the emotional motivation of the pastor. He must be aware of models which encourage him to take on himself responsibility which only another can exercise for himself. The pastor has no blueprint of what another person should be. He must grant to each person what he wants for himself, freedom to work out his own destiny. Such freedom will produce anxiety in both pastor and person. It is essential to the quality of life envisioned in the Bible.

The symbol "Image of God" also brings the recognition of the relation of the ultimate within the contingent in the Christian understanding of man. Any living religious symbol points simultaneously to realities within the nature of man and to realities external and beyond him. Many so-called secular therapists today accept what we have been saying about internal human resources. But they either deny or are agnostic about any ultimate dimensions in these resources. They may be very effective therapists as far as problems on the strictly human level are concerned. The person himself, if a man of faith, might relate his therapeutic experience to his religious understanding. The pastor communicates this in the manner in which he is with a person, not necessarily verbally, but more deeply in his respect for and confirmation of the person and his faith.

Understanding man as a sinner created in the image of God brings the recognition of a depth in human conflict for which not condemnation but healing and salvation is needed. The deep realization of this constitutional conflict within all humans, the pastor as well as within the person, clarifies the goal of the pastoral relationship. It is not to change man's nature, but to help him find experiences through which love can overcome hate, faith can overcome fear, forgiveness accepted bring release of guilt, and healing is found for conflict. Such experiences will require change within the person. The psychodynamic schools have greatly elaborated the concept of ambivalence, but they did not discover human conflict. These conflicts find expression both on the human level and in the person-God relationship. Since this is a problem within the dynamic nature of persons, the answer must be found there, that is in experience rather than in some verbal formulation. The Cross has become an inescapable symbol for humans because it speaks to the depth of human ambivalence, whether in the person-to-person relationship or person to God. It says that the good may take the evil into itself in a way that leads to a redemptive quality of life. Such a change in the quality of life must be accompanied by a change in the motivation and organization of the person, a transformation.[7]

This is in contrast to another general approach to this problem which is that conflict or ambivalence is only the result of experience. Any deeper implications are denied. Because conflict is considered to be the result of human experience it is to be cured by the right approach and techniques. Some authors, such as Eric Fromm,[8] have developed a sociological and cultural emphasis in contrast to what is called Freud's "biological approach." Others account for human conflict in terms of learning and have devised techniques for unlearning and relearning. These approaches ignore the roots of conflict and concentrate on changing behavior, on the assumption that if behavior is changed the person is changed.[9] Still other approaches ignore the meaning of conflict altogether, and seek to bring about correct behavior through the use of drugs. Drug dependence, including dependence on tranquilizers, is one of the major substitutes for strong ego development and genuine religious faith.

The question here is not whether experience has anything to do with human conflict. Obviously it has much to do with it. The question is whether the experience theory is an adequate account of human conflict, and, therefore, whether a therapeutic approach which is based solely on an experiential theory is adequate for the pastor. Again, we point to the discontinuity between an understanding of man in the ultimate, religious dimension, and the cause and effect understanding of science. The Biblical view is that these two dimensions do not have to be viewed as in conflict or as if the acceptance of one means the rejection of the other. Each is required. A working relationship, however, is not a matter of rational theory. It is the result of a level of integration within the personality of the pastoral therapist which in turn expresses itself in his relationship with persons. It is the acceptance of a relationship with God as the Ground of Being who has given man freedom and power (within expandable or detractable limits) to deal with the cause and effect relationships in his daily existence. Such a relationship gives a man a home in the universe.

None of this should be taken to mean that we are not to help persons resolve conflicts within either dimension. A pastor may be able to help a man work out a more satisfying relationship to his wife without dealing with some deeper conflicts. Or a person may learn through group experience to behave in a manner which is more conforming to the expectations of others, but this may not mean that he is cured of his neurosis or has found a new relationship with God, or a new quality of life. He may have learned to manage his symptoms better, and one can only hope that new symptoms do not appear. One of the great temptations for pastors, in this day when there are so many quickie methods of therapy being offered, is that of creating false hopes in people. Another problem grows out of the nature of human conflict and its resolution. It is the fact that many persons who are hurting want easy, magical solutions, and they try to confer on the pastor or on to God's magical powers to take away their problems. Sometimes theology is used in a way to encourage this. This presents a real problem for the pastor. Should he accept the identity conferred on him by such persons, and seek to gratify their needs? If so, he will lead them further into illness. The other alternative is to create a relationship through which the pastor seeks to help such persons to a more realistic, responsible attitude. Such an approach has the possibilities of failure, but also of producing growth, increased strength and genuine wholeness. It is very difficult to overcome the resistance which many have to such a goal, and the pastor needs to be able to accept what seems to be failure rather than create more infantilism and disillusionment. The magical approach distorts the relationship between the ultimate and the contingent in human life. The individual seeks to control God so that God, with the aid of the pastor, will cure him of his neurosis. This does not happen.

Some pastors may find themselves in the grip of an orientation which is rather opposite of the magical. It is a very optimistic attitude which holds that if persons are helped on the human level they will rather automatically turn to God. This leads to avoiding the meaning of the ultimate dimension in the pastoral relationship. It may produce some good mental health results, but not help persons discover the meaning of a vital relationship with God. Pastoral therapy may not be the best means to such a discovery, and the pastor has other approaches such as worship, preaching and education at his disposal. While there is Biblical support for the idea that "he who does not love his brother whom he has seen cannot love God whom he has not seen" (I John 4:20), there is no evidence to support the idea that the love of man is bound to produce an awareness of love toward God.

THE ULTIMATE AND THE CONTINGENT

What can we say about the relationship of the ultimate and the contingent in pastoral therapy? We can first say that neither dimension should be used to try to manipulate the other dimension in the lives of people. A deep sense of the paradox in created human nature should be kept alive. That paradox is that we are created with a measure of freedom yet to be realized on the one hand, and on the other the seemingly contradictory understanding that we are creatures of cause and effect. This paradox, when alive, becomes the basis for understanding and insight into the nature and meaning of experience which may include both perspectives. When a person realizes these paradoxical dimensions simultaneously he is thrown into a tension that may result in creative resolution or a denial of freedom in regressive behavior.

There is no question but that experiences on the human level, especially in childhood, may distort the view of God a person holds in adult life. They will, at the same time, distort his view of himself and of others. This is an area for pastoral psychotherapy, although other pastoral activities may contribute to the resolution of such distortions. The pastor has no guarantee of success, as he is working with processes and realities quite beyond his control. This realization should be inherent in the way in which he is present with persons.

SALVATION, GRACE, LAW AND JUDGMENT

The Christian statement on salvation here is succinct — we are saved by grace through faith (Eph. 2:8). This statement points to qualities of relationship rather than procedures or steps in a process. Persons do not save themselves. They find inner peace, resolution of conflict and transformation through a relationship on the human level which mediates a grace which itself is rooted in the structure of life, in God. Grace operates in human life as part of the Creator-creature relationship. Love in human relationships may become a revelation of divine love, and trust in human relationships becomes a necessary foundation for trust in God, but not a guarantee. In salvation and healing we are dealing with qualities of being which involve every dimension of human life from the contingent to the ultimate.

The Christian understanding of grace and trust raises the issue of the opposite experience, that of law and judgment. Certainly these are also part of human experience and part of the therapeutic process. The issue here is whether the application of the law and judgment is part of the prerogative of the pastor, or whether it is part of the life processes, pronounced on the person through his life experience and to be understood and interpreted through grace on the part of the pastor. This raises real questions about the issues of confrontation, interpretation, acceptance, confirmation, and creation of guilt on the part of the therapist. For example, how does a given model of therapy and the relationship it offers relate to the person who feels no guilt for antisocial behavior? Is he condoned, is he condemned, or is he helped to read the meaning of his behavior in terms of its consequences to himself and others? Or is the issue ignored? How does the pastor handle the guilt once it is experienced and expressed? Is he aware of the difference between real and neurotic guilt, and does he understand that certain ways of handling guilt feelings may only drive them deeper? What about the person who is overburdened by guilt? Does he need the same kind of relationship and treatment? The understanding of various experiential problems of guilt will help to determine the manner in which the pastor is with a person.

The problem of law and judgment is tied into the problem of trust and grace. Grace has been interpreted as acceptance. Tillich[10] went a step beyond this and called attention to the need to accept onself as being accepted. It is difficult to accept forgiveness and make the changes in oneself that forgiveness would require. Acceptance is a central quality in much pastoral therapy. Many times it is expressed as a kind of sloppy relationship which eliminates all sense of judgment or evaluation and which really feeds the individual's narcissism. The person is not called to any sense of responsibility.

Whether conceived in psychological or theological terms, acceptance is the basis for any healing process, but it is not enough. Acceptance must be honest, and this means that not only the potential of the person must be accepted, but also his weaknesses, pride, and defensiveness. Many times the therapist must interpret the unhealthy or destructive responses of the person. This needs to be done in the spirit of gentleness and understanding. Only in this way is there healing and reconciliation rather than further alienation. Confrontation can be healing or it can be destructive.

There is another aspect of the experience of grace which has been overshadowed by our recent emphasis on acceptance. It is that of confirmation. In many churches confirmation is a ritual, but it must also be a reality to influence a human being. To be confirmed as a person by another is an important aspect of health or salvation. It is a quality of being with another so that doubts and uncertainties about himself as a person are removed. It is thus a liberating experience. It may happen suddenly, or it may be the result of a prolonged experience with another person as in the therapeutic process. It is essential to the development of a strong sense of ego worth and identity. While there are internal factors operating in the establishment of a sense of identity, the authenticity of this identity is confirmed by others, or there is self-doubt.

AUTHORITY

Closely related to the experience of grace and law is the experience of authority in human life and in the healing process. The way in which he engages in the therapy process reflects the nature of the pastor's practice of authority though it may not reflect his intellectualized concept of authority.

How the pastor views his source of authority is important. Who gives him the right to do what he does? Is it rooted in the profession? Is it conferred by God or by science? People sometimes ask what right does he have to say such things to me? How is he so sure of what I need or what I ought to do? Whatever his source, it will be communicated through the quality and process of his relationship.

Or is the pastor's source of authority vested in him by his parishioners? If so, what is the nature of the authority that others want him to exercise over them? Is it to assume responsibility for their lives, to give easy answers, or to help them develop autonomy as persons? Authority is power, whether the pastor takes it for himself or whether it is conferred on him by another. What is involved when the person wants a kind of authority which the pastor feels it is not his prerogative to exercise? Does this become a therapeutic impasse or is it used for therapeutic movement?

This is best dealt with by trying to help the person understand the emotional roots and meaning of the kind of authority for which he is asking.

The pastor must have a source of authority outside of himself, and presumably this would be in his relationship with his God. Part of his authority will be found in himself, in the kind of a person he is, the way in which he has dealt with his own hurts and anxieties, the values by which he lives, and what he can mediate to others from the depth of his own being. The real power of healing lies in the depth of one person speaking to the depth of another in a manner which calls out of the other more of his potential as a person. Whether he wills it or not, the values by which a pastor lives will be communicated to people, and the spirit which motivates him will be caught by the persons he seeks to help. Theoretical or factual learning is important. Far more important, however, is the development of the whole person and the quality of his being as a person with others. Out of what and who he is he will speak and also listen.

From the problem of authority we move to the paradoxical situation found in the experiences of autonomy and determinism. Anyone who accepts the Biblical view of man must accept this paradox within his own nature, and understand how it influences his being with others. Often clergy have overstressed freedom to the denial of determinism. The Bible is conversant with the deterministic aspects of life, even though the New Testament goal is that of freedom from legalism. The solution of this paradox is not by accepting one side to the exclusion of the other.[11]

Being with others from this perspective means helping others work out the patterns, feelings and behavior which have grown out of cause and effect processes, while also helping them to exercise whatever degree of autonomy of which they are capable at a given time. By understanding this paradox in his own experience and by constantly seeking to expand the margin of freedom in personal decision making, he places himself in a position to assist others in the same process.

One major point at which a person may exercise freedom is in learning to decide for himself what response he will make to experiences which come to him from the outside, and over which, as such, he may not be able to exercise much control. The self and its responses is the area for the exercise of autonomy. Therapy is to a large extent the process of helping persons work through the habitual harmful responses to previous experiences which handicap them. Autonomy is the self exercising one of its basic functions as a self, the function of determining its own responses rather than being determined from the outside. It is the self gaining freedom from both instinctive and environmental controls, and becoming more fully self-determining. It is the genuinely loving person finding release from internal compulsions and external legalisms. Theologically it is God giving freedom to accept or reject divine grace, with attending consequences in each case.

There are many times in the therapy process where the pastor must give a person the freedom to reject anything or everything that he says, or even to reject him. The person must be allowed to decide what his response to the pastor will be. The task of the pastor is to help the person deal creatively with whatever response he makes.

AWE AND REVERENCE

Finally, one of the modern cultural influences with which the pastor has to cope is the sense of superficiality and familiarity in today's mood. Some of this is evident in the manner in which many pastors conduct worship services—God is addressed as the man next door. There is no sense of awe and reverence before God. It finds further expression in the things which terrorize modern man. Fuel shortages, old age, illness, death, taxes, and, most of all, an atomic war are sources of terror. The popularity of horror novels and movies attests to man's need to be terrorized, if only in fantasy. Another source of terror is man's own unconscious processes though he is little aware of this. He thinks that his devils are outside. How frightening it is to be told that there is something in us, controlling us, of which we are not aware! This is heard in its destructive rather than in its constructive potential. The pastoral therapist has to deal with these destructive terrors. In recent years the emphasis on being human has led us to miss or deny a profoundly human response to that which is genuinely holy.

For the Christian faith, the object of awe and reverence and, therefore, of fright or terror is the living God, the mysterium tremendum.[12] This is a mood and orientation toward the creative, the healing, the salvatory. It involves the acknowledgment that there is a Reality in life we do not understand, that life is grounded in mystery. This Reality makes for wholeness, and brings fruits into human life such as love, joy, and peace. This Reality is high and lifted up, infinite in power, in wisdom, and in love. He is also immanent in the being of man. Man's proper stance is to stand in awe, in reverence, and in worship. God is not the man next door, and to reduce him to such familiarity is a symptom of our alienation. It is difficult to admit and accept our finiteness in the face of the Infinite. So we become terrorized by the destructive aspects of life rather than experiencing awe and reverence in the presence of a creative, loving, healing God. The pastor is called upon to help people understand that he does not cure them, nor do they cure themselves, but that healing comes through elements within themselves which they did not create, but before which they need to stand in reverence and obedience. The alternative is a vitiating self-worship. Healing happens to us, it is beyond our power to produce at will. Healing is evidence that in human beings there are forces which make for wholeness and which operate under some circumstances spontaneously, that is, apart from human causation but through human agency.

SUMMARY

There are many questions in regard to the theological interpretation of pastoral therapy. In our view, theology is a descriptive statement of the insights of faith. In this regard it is comparable to psychological theory, which states the psychologist's way of describing realities which he believes he understands. The tendency in human life is for verbal description to unwittingly replace the realities it seeks to formulate. The language used in the therapy process must be language of experience, direct, insightful and often figurative. It needs to be language in which the person can or has invested emotional meaning. Religious language, as distinguished from descriptive theological language, is often appropriate in a therapy relationship as it conveys insight. However, its use must be grounded in a relationship in which the person feels the concern of the pastor is to assist him in his struggles and pain, not to indoctrinate him in a creed. Thus we have come full circle. The presence of the pastor with another will inevitably reveal himself and his faith, as the person moves to reveal the sources of his terror. Since he is human the pastor will not always be with another in a therapeutic or salvatory manner. But it can be hoped that he is continually growing in grace and going on to realistic perfection. He must partake of that quality of life which he seeks to help others attain.

Pastoral therapy is the communication of the Gospel through personal relationships, as well as communication of elements of the pastor's own personality. The pastor as a person is called upon to be a person whom another may use in his own healing processes, or who may be rejected. In its deepest levels, in the New Testament sense, therapy is concerned with inner motivation, rather than "right behavior" (Matt. 5). The New Testament does not give rules or techniques for the cure of souls, nor for the restoration of the inner man to wholeness. It rather offers a Person who has tremendous healing power within himself and in his relationship to God, and it points to this as the root of all healing, whether recognized as such or not. Likewise the pastor is called upon in some measure to be a healing or therapeutic person to others. Pastoral therapy is a process in which the relationship of pastor and person is the essential element.

In the next chapter we shall discuss the use of religious lan-

guage in expressing emotional and volitional as well as intellectual meanings and processes in both health and sickness.

NOTES

1. S. Freud, *The Interpretation of Dreams.* (1900) N.Y.: Basic Books, 1953,
Ch. 7, Standard Edition. Vol. 4 & 5. London. Hogarth Press, 1953.

S. Freud, 1916 *A General Introduction to Psychoanalysis* (1916-1917). Standard Edition, London. Hogarth Press, 1961.

Silvano Arieti, *The Meaning of Pastoral Care.* N.Y.: Harper and Row, 1966.

2. C. A. Wise, *The Meaning of Pastoral Care.* New York: Harper and Row,
1966.

3. See Howard J. Clinebell, Jr., *Basic Types of Pastoral Counseling.* Nashville: Abingdon, 1966 for a description of a number of models.

4. Joseph Wolpe, In Preface to *Behavior Therapy: Appraisal and Status,* by
Cyril M. Franks, N.Y.: McGraw-Hill Co., 1970.

5. There are many references to narcissism in the writings of Freud. The following are helpful:

"On Narcissism." (1914). In *The Standard Edition.* Translated and edited by
James Strachey. London: Hogarth Press and the Institute of Psychoanalysis,
1953, Vol. 14.

S. Freud, *The Ego and the Id.* Translated by Joan Riviere. Revised and newly
edited by James Strachey, N.Y.: The Norton Co., 1960, Paper. Standard Edition. London. Hogarth Press, 1958.

S. Freud, *A General Introduction to Psychoanalysis.* (1916-1917) N.Y.:
Garden City Publishing Co., 1943 or Standard Edition. London, Hogarth
Press, 1958.

6. Narcissism has been an important topic among ego theorists and therapists
in recent years. The following are important sources:

Heinz Hartmann, *Essays in Ego Psychology.* N.Y.: International Universities
Press, 1964.

Otto F. Kernberg, *Borderline Conditions and Pathological Narcissism.* N.Y.:
Jason Aronson, Inc., 1975.

H. Kohut, *The Analysis of the Self.* N.Y.: International Universities Press,
1971.

Gertrude Blanck and Rubin Blanck, *Ego Psychology: Theory and Practice.*
N.Y.: Columbia U. Press, 1974.

7. Carroll A. Wise, "The Roots and Resolution of Conflict," *Journal of Pastoral Care,* Vol. XXIV, No. 1, 1970, p. 8.

8. Erich Fromm, *Man for Himself.* New York: Rinehart and Co., 1947.

9. Albert Bandura, *Principles of Behavior Modification.* Chicago: Holt,
Rinehart and Winston, Inc., 1969.

10. Paul Tillich, *The Courage to Be.* New Haven: Yale University Press, 1952.

11. B. F. Skinner, *Beyond Freedom and Dignity.* N.Y.: Knopf & Co., 1971 is a strong statement on the determinist point of view.

Silvano Arietti, *The Will To Be Human.* N.Y.: Quadrangle Books, 1972 gives an equally cogent view of autonomy.

Autonomy is accepted as a basic principle in therapy by a holistic therapist — Andras Angyal, in his *Neurosis and Human Treatment,* N.Y.: John Wiley and Sons, Inc., 1965. Autonomy is also a basic principle in the works of the ego psychologists. See references in Chapter 5.

12. Rudolph Otto, (1923) *The Idea of the Holy.* N.Y.: Oxford University Press, 1958.

Chapter 3

Religious Language and Personality Processes

COMMUNICATION AND
RELIGIOUS LANGUAGE

One suspects that the idea of communication is greatly over-worked today. Many comments are heard about communication which are strained, hollow and void of communication. In some quarters this is coming to be a magic word signifying that one is in the know. Talk about communication may be one way of not communicating.

Yet there is also a profound reality in the experience of communication or lack of communication. There is a sense in which all behavior is communication, a form of language to be read and understood by those who are capable of so doing. A simple experience like a headache, for example, is a form of language that may say that something is wrong in the head or elsewhere in the body. The physician has to be competent to understand the meaning of the language in each patient. The reader can think of many other instances where body language is very definitely a form of communication about feelings and attitudes, and also about interpersonal relationships.

Body language is not the only form of communication. There is also the language of art, of ritual, and of words. Actually these various forms of language should be seen as different ways in which the whole person can find expression. Thus, language of any kind may express conflict, suffering and illness, or it may express health and the drive toward wholeness. The processes of illness and of health may be expressed in the same language, and even in the same statement or act. The deep ambivalence between destructiveness and creativity finds full, but sometimes disguised, expression in all forms of language.

Communication takes place in two directions. One of these is between the inner world of the person and the conscious self. The other is between the self and his environment, especially other persons and culture.

COMMUNICATION BETWEEN SELF AND THE INNER AND OUTER WORLDS

Between the self and its inner world many messages are exchanged, some clear and some distorted and disguised. Impulses toward sexual behavior, or love or anger may be received into consciousness. The self may accept these and permit expression. Or it may reject them, and send back messages of control, anxiety and guilt. Thus, a sense of wholeness may be communicated, or a sense of alienation from the self. Psycho-analysis has elaborated on this conversation and conflict between the self and the deeper aspects of the person and has worked out the mechanisms involved in dealing with this experience of alienation.[1]

While this conversation is taking place, the self is engaged in communication to and from the external world. Sometimes this communication consists of messages as to what may or may not be done, what is approved or disapproved by the group. Or one may communicate to others some of his needs, his need for love, for example. These communications have within them the possibilities of frustration and conflict or of satisfaction. Thus, the self stands between two worlds, as it were, trying to resolve conflicts in either direction and trying to maintain a wholeness which involves both dimensions.

LANGUAGE TO REVEAL AND CONCEAL

Any kind of communicative language is something of a two-edged sword. Its purpose is to communicate, to reveal, and through this process to provide the basis for a sense of community and communion. On the other hand, language may be used as a means of concealment and evasion, a means of not communicating. The headache may conceal an intense hostility. A work of art, like dream symbols, may conceal a conflict between a wish and a fear. Ritualistic acts may disguise and express profound anxiety. Words are subject to all sorts of deceptive uses. Thus, the means for the expression of truth may actually communicate falsehood, and the means for communicating a sense of community may actually communicate a sense of alienation. The living truth within each of us are those processes and relationships by which qualities, abilities and possibilities inherent in the nature of the person are fulfilled. Truth is the expression of spirit or self.

FUNCTIONS OF RELIGIOUS LANGUAGE AND SYMBOLS

Religious language, verbal, ritual, or artistic, partakes of these functions, with some added dimensions. Through religious language the individual may be related to his tradition, so he knows from whence he came; to his present community, so he knows to whom he belongs; and to a future hope, so that he has some sense of what he and his community may become. The essence of religious tradition is spirit, not form. When religious experience is grounded in living truth it is in constant process of overcoming alienation, estrangement, and conflict. This task is never finally finished. In religious experience communication takes place not only between man and himself, man and others, but also between man and God. Religious truth and language is a process which continually moves toward union and reunion with the Source of life, the Sustainer of life, and the final Goal of life. The religious man sees all of this in God. When this process fails, idolatry and alienation result.

Religious language, or religious symbolism, is expressive, and therefore has the function of formulating insight or interpreting the meaning of inner experiences. It seeks to express truth as derived from deep intuitive processes. It is the language of faith. It is a window through which light may pass in both directions.

Religious language may be contrasted with language and symbols by which we handle our environment, or with language and symbols by which we express experiences on the level of the senses. Religious language deals with intangible aspects of experience. It seeks to probe into the unknown. It seeks to penetrate beneath external experiences to discover the laws and relationships that give meaning to life. Religious symbols are ways by which the deepest conscious or unconscious wishes, aspirations, conflicts, suffering, and hopes of man may be expressed.[2]

The deep struggle with which religion is concerned is the struggle between life and death. There are many lesser struggles which are derivatives of the struggle between life and death, and these take on different colorings depending on the cultural situation. One such conflict takes place in the area of sex, another in relationships between various groups within the culture. Another is the conflict between belonging and alienation. If religious symbols are used to gain insight into these struggles, and to find some answers that can be translated into actual relationships, there must be a living association between the symbol and the reality or relationship symbolized. When this association is broken, the reality is avoided or repressed, and the attention is focused on the symbol itself. The symbol then becomes reality, a condition described in the Bible as idolatry. Under these conditions religious symbols are subject to manipulation through all of the defense mechanisms the psychologists describe.

But who among us can maintain the strength to search for the living truth at all times? Who has the strength to face his inner world with all of its devious impulses, anxieties and guilts constantly? Who has the power to continually examine his relationships and discover when and what he is avoiding, against whom he is rebelling, and why he is not able to maintain an open, trusting relationship with all men at all times? To ask these questions is to point to the answer. We are dealing here with what the theologian might call original sin, or the experience of alienation. Freud called it the death instinct. By whatever name, the processes which make for illness are resident in all of us, and in our culture. They are in our culture because they are in individuals. It is much easier, in group relationships, to express the worst in us rather than the best. These processes are taking place in every person who consults a pastor. They are in the pastor himself. They find expression in religious language if we are able to read that language. They also find expression in many other human activities. To condemn an activity such as religion because of this fact is to misunderstand a basic quality of human nature. Any human activity has the potential of being contaminated by sin and illness, and the greater the promise of a mode of life like the religious life, the greater the possibility for its distortion.

THE PROCESSES OF DENIAL AND REPRESSION

To elaborate a theory of religious symbolism would require more space than is possible in this volume. We shall, therefore, deal with only two processes which become familiar to the pastoral therapist.

Many persons come to the pastor with the feeling that their religion has lost its meaning, and that the symbols of religion which once were powerful to them are now powerless. They have lost the living truth about themselves and their existence. Underneath they feel that their problem has a religious dimension, and they look to a pastor for help.

It is a common complaint today that religious language has lost its meaning. Some persons search for that meaning as they might look for the meaning of a word in the dictionary, but they do not find it. They do not realize that this loss of meaning grows out of the fact that they have split off some of their deeper wishes, aspirations and hopes from religious reality as expressed in their tradition, symbols, and rituals. They have lost the roots and motivation for their existence. The full flowering of this process is illustrated through the death of God movement. These theologians spoke for many people who had experienced this inner dissociation. As one depressed student said after hearing an advocate of the death of God, "God is not dead. I am dead, and I am just commencing to discover that." We must add the comment that this was the beginning of a new kind of life for that person.

The mechanism of denial, which was illustrated in this student's experience, is a common aspect of much religious life today. Denial is the process of refusing to recognize some unpleasant or painful aspect of external reality. It is used frequently by children as they reject the reality of their smallness and adult's largeness, and play that they are some powerful character. Through fantasy or action they pretend that they are something in a manner which denies what they actually are.[3] Both children and adults understand the game aspects of this behavior, since the adults also do it. But there comes a point where the child is required to give up his denial and accept reality. He is no longer the powerful Indian chief, but a little boy whose mother is about to put him to bed, perhaps against his will. As individuals mature, they also learn to deny unpleasant reality in the external world through fantasy or action.

DEPENDENCY

For many adults religion is a very acceptable part of their external reality as long as it satisfies certain narcissistic needs, such as dependency. But when religion enters with demands and requirements, it becomes unpleasant. The Gospel of Love sounds good until the Law is preached. The demands and requirements of religion challenge the sense of omnipotence in many persons. The high ethical and spiritual requirements of creative religion are more than they can accept. A much used defense against such reality is denial. Such persons will then act out a religiosity grounded in their narcissistic needs but denying the more mature aspects of their personalities. Their religion will give them little help in time of crisis, and it will keep them immature rather than promote their personal growth.

Such denial of external aspects of reality has its internal counterpart. When denial takes place, certain feelings are repressed. The denial of the demands and requirements of religious faith results in the repression of such feelings as trust, self-giving love, and a sense of responsibility. It may also lead to repression, or support the repression, of a healthy aggressiveness, and seriously inhibit the utilization of the creative aspects of the person.

Psychotherapists who are not pastors report that their patients do not talk about their religion, or do so under great difficulty. It is said that many patients talk about their sex life with much greater ease than they talk about their religion. This is part of the denial and repression of the religious dimension of experience, and its appropriate feelings. It may be encouraged by the attitude of the therapist toward religion, communicated consciously or unconsciously. The use of religious language by someone under stress either has to be in the form of a confession of faith, or it has to be defensive. Under some conditions an appropriate defensiveness may be in order.

GROWTH AND EXPANSION
OF RELIGIOUS SYMBOLS

Denial should not be confused with the growth of the person. Growth requires the constant expansion of the meaning of religious symbols, and at times the development of new symbols or formulations. Denial and repression block growth; like all defenses they get in the way of the living truth within oneself, even though they may also serve the process of integration at a given level. If the meaning of God at the age of six and of sixty remain the same there has been no growth, but there may be a certain rigid stability. Thus, an adult who uses religious symbols in a childish manner is revealing something of the childish level of his personal development. The expansion of the meaning of religious symbols is the opposite of denial.

We are living in a day when psychological symbols have profound meaning for many persons, and rightly so. But it can be questioned if psychological symbols serve the needs of the whole person as can religious symbols when used properly. There are levels of meaning and value in human experience that cannot be expressed within the scope of psychological symbols. Aspects of religion which involve pathological processes can be formulated in psychological symbols, as Freud amply illustrated. On the other hand, many today mistakenly make psychology into a religion. The humanistic psychologists, in their endeavor to break away from a strictly scientific view of man, seem to be developing a kind of quasi-religious interpretation, void of the very essential "beyond-the-human" dimension of religious faith. Humanistic psychology is, therefore, very easily assimilated by pastors as an understanding of man which seems to fit into the framework of their religious faith.

It is part of the function of the pastoral therapist to use the religious dimension, and the symbols by which the person formulates this, for the purpose of assisting the individual. For this reason the pastoral therapist must be well-trained in the dynamic processes underlying symbol formation and expression. The danger of the pastoral therapist is that he too becomes a victim of the person's defenses. Or of his own.

Before leaving the processes of repression and denial, we should deal with a closely related theme. It is the necessity of a certain kind of denial for the purpose of growth and health. In religious thought this is often called self-denial. Whether this is a valid term depends on the definition of the word *self*. To us, self is a very essential aspect of the person and is not to be denied. It is to be expanded and used creatively.

A more adequate religious word is "sacrifice." A sacrifice is the giving up of something for a higher goal. In personality growth it is necessary to give up childish feelings, ideas and behavior in order to develop more mature ways of living. "When I became a man I put away childish things," is a normative statement of growth. Freud[4] talked about this as renunciation. It is the principle of sacrifice in religion, the giving up of a lesser for a greater good. Renunciation or sacrifice is often preached with such negative connotations that people revolt. In pastoral therapy we discover that when persons find more mature satisfactions, they are quite ready to renounce childish pleasures. The search for restitution of what has been denied, given up or lost is part of the total process. The New Testament speaks of Jesus, "who for the joy that was set before him endured the cross" (Heb. 12:2). In the use of the word *denial* a distinction must be made between denial as a defensive process, and denial as renunciation of a lesser for the sake of a greater value, a childish identity for a more mature one (Matt. 16:24–28).

RELIGIOUS SYMBOLS AND INTELLECTUAL PROCESSES

We move now to a discussion of religious symbols in relation to intellectual processes. This will not be a thorough discussion of the problem of cognition. It will rather concentrate on the intellectual processes in the use of religious symbols and formulations for either health or illness.

The process of forming images and ideas, of formulating these ideas verbally so that they may be communicated and evaluated, is a unique ability of man. It distinguishes man from all other animals. The ability to think, to evaluate ideas in relation to each other, to put ideas into systematic or logical form, is part of what it means to be a person. Religious symbols and their related ideas become grist for the mill of the normal intellectual functions. The crowning product of this activity in religion is known as theology. It is interesting that theology was once known as the "queen of the sciences," a title which might be taken to indicate that it possesses a kind of authoritative, nurturing quality or function.

To put ideas referring to the external world in logical form is comparatively easy in comparison with ideas pertaining to man's inner world. There is a sense in which theology is a science, a way of knowing. But it is not a science in the sense of modern natural sciences or the behavioral sciences. It is a way of knowing about man's inner life, particularly as that life is related to God. But there is no relationship with God apart from self and others. There is an internal dimension in theological knowledge which fulfills its nurturing and redemptive purpose, even as it provides a structure and meaning for the universe in which the self lives.

The task of theology is to expand and test the meaning of religious symbols, and in so doing to expand the consciousness or awareness of the person in the religious dimension. But again we meet a paradox. It is necessary for growth and health to expand the meaning of symbols, but in so doing one is in danger of placing so much emphasis on the symbol and its formulations that the inner reality is lost. This means that the living, intrinsic relationship between meaning and symbol is broken. The symbol becomes unable to promote growth or the expansion of consciousness or wholeness. The symbol then becomes the reality, along with a driving need, derived from repressed feeling, to defend and maintain the symbolic system. This leads to dogmatism, to theological word games, and is one of the manifestations of the human propensity to sin and illness.

In psychological parlance, the process we have been describing is called intellectualization. In religious language intellectualization is a form of idolatry, of elevating verbal forms to the level of reality, of worshipping a false god. It means, psychologically, the act of placing such emphasis on verbal forms that the inner, affective meaning of the experience is lost. Thus, we may talk about being alienated from God without coming into contact with our feelings of alienation. Or we may talk about being a sinner without any consciousness of a sense of sin. The elaboration of religious systems may thus become a form of evasion, and foster processes of illness.

What is the meaning of this for pastoral therapy? For one thing, it may be a serious problem for the person especially if the person has been trained in theological disciplines, or if he has been an intensive student of religion. Through theological study, a person may so develop and refine his intellectualizing process as a defense that resistance is encountered in helping him to give up this defensive use and to understand the affective meaning of his symbolic formulations. The same may be true of persons learned in psychological formulations.

The process of therapy is that of the expansion of consciousness, the increase of awareness of inner and external reality, and the ways in which one deals with this reality. This means getting behind whatever words are used to the substance of a person's being and relationships. The task of the pastor is not to give the person religious words; it is that of helping him get behind his words to their truth. This truth deals not only with processes of illness, as do many of the symbols of pathology, but with the goals and processes of fulfilling one's nature.

Intellectualization may be a problem for the pastoral therapist himself.[5] One of the issues in the field today is the relation of theology and therapy. How do we understand the therapy process from a theological point of view? This requires the use of theological concepts in a manner which deals with living processes rather than static conditions. It also requires a disciplined ability on the part of the pastor to be more concerned with inner reality than with its formulation. There can be a profound understanding of the spiritual dimension of life without a highly developed theology. While the need for a theological understanding of the therapy process must be recognized, any final judgment of the process must be on the basis of its merits. True theological understanding must be distinguished from theological word games of a defensive variety.

The pastoral therapist may have to resist influences which would lead him to use the therapy relationship to promote a particular theological system. Unfortunately, the learning of a theological system or the manipulation of theological symbols does not change inner processes. Under some conditions such practices may increase anxiety, as, for example, when too much stress is placed on the idea of sin with a person who is already carrying a heavy burden of guilt. Whatever theological word is spoken should be a therapeutic word, that is, it should promote the healing process. Granted that a person may need some formal religious education, this should be done usually outside of the therapeutic relationship and probably by another teacher.

The pastoral therapist faces the experience of learning, unlearning, and relearning theology. In most courses in our seminaries, theology is taught as an objective mode of thought, in terms of doctrines and ideas. The teacher of theology is likely to complain that he finds the ideas of the teacher of pastoral psychology too subjective, as he insists on the objective aspect of theological thought. There may be many reasons for this situation. Our concern here is with its effect on the pastor.

When the student moves into the pastoral psychology or clinical pastoral education fields, he is faced with an entirely new set of questions. The question is not about the objectivity of religious thought. It is rather about what theology may have to say concerning the experience of a specific person, or how we understand the experiences of a person theologically. There will also be the question of the personal meaning of religious ideas. The student may find himself in a conflict so severe that more than educational experience is needed for resolution. When the student learns that the manipulation of himself or of others through theological concepts is neither salvatory nor therapeutic, he often reacts by discarding theology. Here practical values have a stronger appeal than theoretical values. This is the basis for the criticism that the pastoral care movement has lost its theological moorings. This is what we mean by unlearning.

The relearning of the pastor in theology may be a long and painful process. This is not primarily the intellectual learning of ideas and systems as presented in the classroom or in a book. It requires the growth of the pastor in his emotional and spiritual life, the accumulation of insight and understanding into life processes and relationships, and the formulation of these insights in theological concepts. This is a process which involves the whole man, not just intellect. Process of theological education must be developed so that this experience of learning, unlearning, and relearning does not have to occur in such a radical manner.

The fundamental problem is the nature of theological thought, and its relation to human experience. The day has long past when it is meaningful to talk about the objective and subjective aspects of experience as though they are fixed conditions. The relationship between the individual and his world, or the living organism and its environment is such that biologists tell us that one cannot tell where the organism leaves off and the environment begins. The relationships of the organism and its environment are so close that one can say that the organism and the environment are one. They are just two aspects of a total living process.

EXPRESSION OF THE SPIRITUAL LIFE

The genius of living religious language is that it does on the level of spirit, of meaning and value, what physical and chemical processes do on the biological level; that is, it is a process through which man's internal and external worlds become one. Living religious symbols are a means of expressing the intangibles of man's inner world through objects and events (symbols) taken from external world. The process through which this takes place is analogy. Processes and events in man's external world become means of formulating and understanding processes and experiences in man's inner world. Thus, the external and the internal are united in a living whole, or they exist in conflict.

The rational aspects of man seem to require the systematization and evaluation of living religious symbols. This is the task of theology, and it is a legitimate task. However, under the pressure in human beings for evasion and concealment of inner reality, theological thinking can be so dominated by the demands of logical thinking that the dynamic elements in the life of the person are completely repressed. This use of theology leads to a split in

the person, or it is the result of a split. The insistence on objectivity rather than subjectivity results in ignoring or neglecting the
inner dimension of the person. Also, much so-called objectivity is
really unrecognized subjectivity, that is, it is the projection of
subjective aspects. On the other side, the individual who seeks to
avoid all use of rational processes in dealing with religious symbols will regress into a kind of theology which is the mere expression of childish wishes. This is what the theologians rightfully
fear, as do pastoral therapists.

The pastoral therapist must bridge this chasm in a dynamic
manner. This is what is meant by relearning theology. The pastor
must learn to use the religious ideas of his clients as a means of
discovering those inner processes which also reveal the person's
relationship to himself and his world. He will come to understand
that in every person's religious ideas there is a logic of its own.
That logic[6] dictates the outcome of the wishes, feelings, and frustrations with which the person is coping. It may not have the
exactness of mathematical logic, but it is there. It is a logic which
is inherent in dynamic processes; it is not a logic which seeks to
control or deny those processes from the outside. It is a logic
through which either pathology and sin or the experiences of cure
and fulfillment may be expressed simultaneously. The pastoral
therapist learns to understand and utilize this kind of dynamic
theology.

The pastoral therapist, if he communicates his concern for his
person's religious ideas, will find many illustrations of this discussion. A young woman who was well trained theologically and
active in a church felt a division in her religious experience
that focused on the words God and Jesus. The word God evoked
strong anger whenever she heard it. She was sure that God did
not love her. But the word Jesus had a quite different meaning
for her. This word suggested kindness, tenderness, and concern.
When she heard the word Jesus in a worship service these experiences were evoked. Thus, a split between good and bad elements
in her feelings found continuous and painful expression in her
consciousness. She was aware of the incongruity and of the

difference between the meaning the word God had for her and the standard Christian meanings. She could be theologically correct (in a so-called objective sense) in conversation about God while at the same time she held back the anger the word evoked. She resisted talking about either word and their inner realities for some time, but gradually gained enough strength to do so. She had struggled for a number of years to resolve the incongruity through her rational processes, but this had been ineffective. For her to have been successful in this would have meant the rather complete repression of her anger about God and its transformation into a pathological symptom. The task of pastoral therapy was to help her discover the deep feelings involved in her conflict, and to work them out. This meant not only resolving a conflict arising out of early experiences with her parents, but also dealing with the fundamental ambivalence between love and hate of which the parental conflict was but one expression.

RELIGIOUS SYMBOLS AND
PERSONAL MEANING

The idea that religious symbols have a profound personal meaning, as well as meaning on the cultural and metaphysical levels, should surprise no one who knows the Bible. For here we read about a God who "dwells in the high and holy place, and also with him who is of a contrite and humble spirit" (Isa. 57:15). Indeed, there are evidences within the Bible that God may dwell in every heart, but sometimes this experience is one of intense conflict. Or as we read in the Book of Jeremiah, "This is the covenant which I will make with the house of Israel after those days, says the Lord: I will put my law within them, and I will write it upon their hearts; and I will be their God, and they shall be my people" (Jer. 31:33). When we turn to the New Testament we see the concern of Jesus for the inner, as well as for the ultimate dimension of life. He knew "what was in man" (John 2:25). "Out of the abundance of the heart the mouth speaks" (Matt. 12:34). In the parable of the Prodigal we see a young man working through some of the internal issues of his life, and coming to himself so that he could then return home (Luke 15:11–32). Clearly the implication here is that resolving internal conflicts about his own identity preceded the resolution of conflict in other dimensions. In the Sermon on the Mount, Jesus has some pointed words in regard to inner motivation in relation to the standard formulated meanings and behavior of religion.

The pastor is on very solid ground when he understands that religious symbols point to two dimensions of life. As he inquires about the inner meaning of religious symbols he will find great distortion and incongruity between those meanings and accepted theological meanings. If he seeks to understand persons, he will discover that there are reasons in human experience for this condition as well as reasons within the nature of man. If the theologian says that this incongruity is due to original sin, the pastor could well agree with him. The idea of original sin states that there are imperfections and ambivalences within the nature of man. But the pastor would want to go on to discover the peculiar ways in which these imperfections are worked out through life experiences, beginning in some persons in early infancy. Seeking to help persons understand the vital relationship between their feelings, intuitive processes and human relationships, as well as their relationship with God, is one of the tasks of the pastor. In actual process it may work in either direction, from symbol to experience or from experience to symbol.

A complete discussion of all of the inner processes which may be expressed in religious symbols would require a comprehensive review of personality development in both health and illness, combined with an understanding of the mutual interaction between individuals and their culture. To generalize, it can be said that religious meanings grow in part out of early family relationships. The experience of trust[7] which may develop later into religious faith begins in infancy as do other feelings, attitudes, and values. In later infancy the child may learn an experience of shame about his body, which becomes shame about himself as a person. From this may come many doubts which paralyze his capacity for decision or action. In adult life he may be called a "doubting Thomas" because he cannot accept formulated theology or creeds. But his inability to trust and to commit himself to a decision is really the pastoral problem. He needs an experience through which he can learn to exercise his autonomy, and this can be given through dealing with the meanings expressed in his religious symbols. Thus, the use and content of religious symbols is a pathway, sometimes very devious, which leads into the central themes of existence. This developmental approach could be followed into old age, for at every stage of life there are experiences of a potentially religious nature. Certainly the identity conflict of adolescence is one of these.

From a different perspective, experiences of grief and loss, of anxiety, guilt and hate, the characteristic and habitual ways of responding to human relationships, the sense of fulfillment or dissatisfaction in life, all find ample expression in religious ideas. Tendencies toward passivity, aggression, dependency, rebellion, and withdrawal, the need to hurt others, to be hurt by them, or to hurt oneself, the loss of love, the fear of love, guilt about loving or about not loving, the deep yearning in persons to be loved or to have love find full expression in religion. The experience of self-depreciation and guilt, the urge to place oneself in the center of the universe and to feel omnipotent, the fear of losing control or the need to be controlled, along with the need to control others, are other common examples. Nor should we lose sight of the ways in which sexual and religious experiences are related both openly and in disguised forms. There are profound analogical relationships between religious values and human sexuality. A religious understanding of the nature of man must include sexuality, in both its creative and destructive possibilities. In short, any of the processes and experiences which make up the person as a living, total organism within his culture may find expression through religious symbols, either in the direction of discovery, understanding, and appropriation for creative goals, or in terms of illness.

The salvatory or curative trends in persons, or the drive toward integration and wholeness, find their most complete form of expression in religion. This is because religion is that human activity that deals with man's ultimate destiny, of which his finite destiny is a part. In emphasizing the ambivalence in human nature, we mean to stress that there is always a positive, constructive side to every conflict, else there would be no conflict. Conflict always holds the possibility of growth, development, and more satisfying relationships, or of unhealthy regression, frustration, and unhappiness. Erik Erikson[7] has developed this principle through his concepts of nuclear conflict or crisis at the various stages of ego development. However conceptualized, the pastoral therapist should be alert to the positive, creative tendencies in the person, and should encourage these without exerting pressure. For example, if a person says to the pastor, "Look, I cannot trust you. I cannot trust anyone," he may be saying, "Really I want to trust you. Be to me the kind of person I can trust. Make it possible for me to trust." He wants to trust for this is part of what it means to be human. The pastor must learn how to communicate on the positive side of human conflict, as well as on the negative, in ways that are appropriate to the individual. These ways will differ from person to person, but the goal of all of his remarks should be that of fostering curative processes, understanding and growth.

RELIGIOUS SYMBOLS AND PSYCHODYNAMICS

Someone has said that if we want to know something about a person we should ask him.[8] This may sound very oversimplified, especially to a modern who has been trained in the latest research designs. Something can be learned through these research approaches, but fortunately we *can* learn much from persons just by asking them. But it is not quite as simple as it might sound. For asking means the intention and capacity to listen to the answers, to hear them accurately, and to bring to them an understanding that is a combination of empathy and knowledge about persons. What can be said through religious symbols has a depth of meaning which needs to be understood. Indeed, the person may not deeply understand the meaning of what he says. Genuine understanding is not the same as reading meaning into a person's remarks. The latter act is superficial and misses the person. Genuine understanding involves entering into the emotional and volitional aspects of the communication, as well as its rational content.

A RELIGIOUS QUESTION INTERVIEW AND ANALYSIS

The fruitful use of questions of a religious nature for both purposes of symptomatic diagnosis and for those of understanding personality structure and psychological dynamics is reported in an article by Edgar Draper, M.D.,[9] and a group of his associates from the University of Chicago and the University of Illinois. "A group of 50 randomly selected psychiatric patients . . . was seen in a 'religious interview' concurrent with, but completely independent of psychiatric evaluations done by non-team members." After the material had been gathered, and diagnoses and dynamic formulations had been written out, the two groups met to judge the accuracy of the evaluations done solely on the basis of the religious interviews. "With the exception of two patients, whose verbal communications were unusually constricted, no incorrect conclusions were drawn in differentiating neurotic from psychotic patients. In scoring the symptom and character diagnoses, the team members were correct in 92% of the cases." The interviews included such questions as the earliest religious memory, the favorite Bible story, Bible verse and Bible character, the most religious act which one can perform, questions about God, and life after death. A full list of the questions along with a number of the replies made by the patients will be found in this article. It is well worth the study of all persons concerned with pastoral therapy. It demonstrates clinically what we have been saying theoretically.

Stimulated by the Draper study, the Department of Pastoral Care of the Lutheran General Hospital in Park Ridge, Illinois, conducted a research using the same method, using both the Draper questions and a revised set of questions. This has been reported elsewhere.[10]

Following is the revised set of questions. It is suggested that the reader write down his own responses to these questions as he reads them.

1. What is your earliest memory of a religious nature?
2. What were your religious beliefs as a child?
3. What is God like to you now?
4. What is your favorite Bible or religious story? Why?
5. What is your favorite Bible verse or religious saying? Why?
6. Who is your favorite Bible or religious character? Why?
7. If you pray, what do you pray about?
8. What does religion or your faith mean to you?
9. How do you feel about the church, your clergyman?
10. How is (was) God meaningful to your father and mother?
11. What religious idea is most important to you now?
12. What is the most religious act one can perform?
13. What do you consider the greatest sin one could commit?
14. How do you see God involved in your illness?
15. What are your ideas about an afterlife?
16. If God granted you any three wishes, what would they be?

In my experience with applicants for pastoral therapy, I have found the following additional questions helpful: Does it seem that your life has any special purpose or meaning? and, What are your thoughts about death?

This approach was used with a forty-two-year-old woman with the following results. (Our interest here will be to interpret dynamics and relationship patterns in the light of the possibilities they offer for a pastoral therapy relationship. It is suggested that the reader write out his own understanding of this material before he goes on to read the comments by the author.)

1. What is your earliest religious memory? A. About the age of five. Being taken to Sunday School. It was an absolute must in our family. I was required to go. By my mother. Father insisted because Mother wanted him to. He wasn't interested in religion.

2. What were your religious beliefs as a child? A. I had no beliefs as a child. All I had were fears. We were taught to fear God. We would be punished by God. When I received low grades in school it was God doing this to me. I hated Sunday school, but I had to be quiet about it so God would not hear me. God would punish me if I thought evil.

3. What is your favorite Bible story? A. I do not have one. Everything was poured into us. I don't remember any of it.

4. What is your favorite Bible verse? A. The Lord is my shepherd. My mother was ill with cancer for seven and a half years. I kept saying that while she stayed alive. I felt that was why she stayed alive, because I said it so often.

5. How do you see God involved in your illness? A. I saw God involved in my mother's illness. I questioned why she had to be so sick. He could have changed things. Yet, I prayed to God to cure her.

6. If God could grant you any three wishes, what would they be? A. That my relations with my husband be good, that my children be happy, and that we all stay healthy.

The reader should not accept the following comments on the material as the absolute truth. He may see experiences and meanings which the author misses. The reader is somewhat at a disadvantage, since the kind of understanding involved here grows out of a mutual relationship between pastor and person, rather than answers printed on paper. But the effort will be worthwhile, even with this qualification.

This woman reveals in her answer to the first question that the life of her family was grounded in legalism. Her mother was the lawgiver, the authority, not the source of love. The role of the father was very weak, supporting the mother even though he did not agree with her. The child had no positive pattern of identification for coping with her mother. Religion was a matter of duty, not love or faith. We would expect this woman to have a very rigid conscience, with the possibility of a very restricted adult life or breakdown with rebellion. She would have a conflict between love and authority. On the more positive side, however, she was given a definite religious structure with which to form a relationship. Religion was not left a blank. While she remembers the method of introduction to this structure as authoritarian, yet there was a communication to her that religion was important.

In her answer to the second question we see a neurotic fear building up, with a strong component of guilt and punishment. God, like her mother, is a punishing deity. She related this to her school work, a place where success and failure became very important to her. There is a repressed reaction of hate toward the feared object, God, displaced from her mother. Her fear extended inwardly to her thoughts and feelings. Thus, she could not escape from God. She was in turmoil, created by her mother's attitudes, and reinforced in and through religious ideas God has taken on the character of the mother, much more law than of grace.

On the more positive side, there is some expression of autonomous ego functions in her answer. She had fears, she saw no choice but to conform in actions, but she had some inner freedom to accept or reject the cognitive content involved. Some strength is developing within her. She knows it is fragile, so she has to be defensive and protective of it. But it is there.

In her reply to the third question, there is an excellent expression of the process of forgetting motivated by hostility. What a commentary on one form of religious education! She cannot avoid Sunday School, but she can close her mind to everything she hears. She is in control of her own learning processes, over which she has a measure of autonomy.

In her reply to the fourth question, we see her ambivalence being expressed. With all of her fear, anger and guilt, she has a strong need for love, for mothering. In facing the death of her mother, legalism does not help. The mother's death means that she will be permanently deprived of her mother's love. She regresses to a childish level of trying to control the situation by the magical use of a Biblical verse. As she has been controlled, so she now will try to control God. She picks a verse which promises her the very things for which she yearns, loves and cares. She uses it in a magical manner, as a repetitive formula. She believed it worked because she said it so often, not because of vital faith. The experience of distrust was too strong to permit a vital faith which would have required and helped her to face the situation realistically. However, she has enough strength to reach out for help in her need. The alternative to this was some kind of disintegration. With some persons the mystery is not that they become sick. It is rather that they are able to maintain a degree of health in spite of intense conflicts. This is something of a confirmation of the theological insight that processes of illness and health, or of death and life, are working in all of us constantly.

She neatly avoids the question as to how she saw God involved in her illness, and again shifts to her mother. Here is the expression of both hostility to the question, and perhaps the questioner, as well as her need for her mother. Perhaps behind this answer there is a wish for her mother's death which would be completely unacceptable to her. She has to react against such a feeling by using any means to keep her mother alive. She had no one to help her resolve her ambivalence. Indeed, at this point many clergymen would have supported her magical use of religion, with the approval of some psychiatrists, on the ground that this expresses a healthy process within her, and is her way of holding herself together in face of inevitable loss. Her questioning of God reminds one of the protests and questioning of Job.

In her reply to the final question, her values of happiness and health emerge. These answers involve herself and her family. Thus, the narcissistic element is present. Such an element is always present in any regressive experience. In her situation, she has to be concerned for herself. When a person is sick there is usually neither energy nor interest for concerns beyond immediate needs. Concerns involving others are not part of infancy, but develop during later years, and then only if one has received enough genuine love so that he has grown to the place when he can have a genuine love and concern for others. Again, there is strength in healthy narcissistic wishes.[11] There are a few others in the world whose welfare is important to her, and for whom she might be helped to learn how to live and love more effectively. The pastoral therapist has a goal to work toward and a resource to work with. A trusting relationship with an understanding pastoral therapist could create a basis in experience for the reinterpretation of many of her religious symbols.

The interpretations given above should be accepted as tentative hypotheses by the pastoral therapist. They are not absolute truth. Good therapeutic work requires that the pastor have some idea as to what he is dealing with and where he is going. In the therapeutic process the feelings and processes related to these religious ideas would be explored. The pastor would be ready to modify or even discard any tentative interpretation in the light of new material. Our major emphasis here is that religious ideas and symbols are avenues into the inner processes of a person, and should be one of the major concerns of the pastoral therapist.

The pastor must bring to this method some understanding of theology, so that he can make distinctions between universal and group symbols, meanings, and rituals, and the private meanings and expressions of a person. Private meanings and uses might or might not be congruent with group meanings. Either way the pastoral task is to understand what is going on within the person in the light of a larger understanding. In the above record there are problems of conflict between love and authority, legalism and autonomy, with much fear, guilt and a strong need for punishment. These are also universal issues in religion. In the theological approach the issues are dealt with as such, largely intellectually. Here are some guidelines for the pastoral therapist. In the pastoral approach we deal with the issues as they are part of the emotional and spiritual processes of the person. It is a mistaken notion that applying the universal and group meanings in some manner will correct the emotional and spiritual problem. Life would be so much simpler if this were true. Problems of the inner life must be dealt with in that dimension. This is the pastoral task. Having a sound knowledge of theology is as essential to the pastoral therapist as a knowledge of anatomy is to the surgeon. In addition, the pastor must bring to this method some understanding of the inner processes of persons, regardless of the particular terminology in which this knowledge is formulated. In the words of Anton Boisen, pastors need to learn how to read the human document.

Another resource for the use of this method is an understanding of some of the principles of human communication. Every communication, especially about such vital matters as religion, not only has a cognitive content; it also implies a relationship. In the interview above the woman gave certain facts about her mother, her father, her home, and Sunday school. But with these facts she also communicated some very deep feelings about herself and her relationships. Another person might talk about the same subjects but with an entirely different communication about her inner processes and relationships. The pastoral therapist learns to understand both levels of communication, and to assist the person to an understanding of them.[12]

The approach outlined in this chapter has many positive values for other activities of the pastor, such as preaching, religious education, and worship. Discussion of these and other areas would take us too far afield. This approach requires the rethinking and revision of much that is done in these other areas, in terms of both methods and goals. This is a task for the entire theological curriculum.

The language used in pastoral therapy should be largely that of the person, especially words and phrases that have meaning to the person. The task of the pastor is to sense what the individual is expressing behind his words, and the manner in which he uses language. This means that conversation is a tool, not an end in itself. Even silence is a form of speech that needs interpretation. The real question is the level of empathy on the part of the pastor. It is an art to hear, in a deep sense, what another is saying. The manifest content of words often conceals the deeper meaning.

A person may say, "I do not feel angry," in a manner that expresses deep anger. Hence the pastor needs some understanding of the person with whom he is dealing, the nature of the person's life problems and methods of dealing with them, and the goals for which the individual is striving. At times he may bridge the gap between the language of the person and the language of the Bible by quoting a closely pertinent verse, and asking such questions as "Does that sound like something you are saying?" This becomes therapeutic only if the relationship is clear and it is not done in a "preachy" manner.

In the next two chapters we shall discuss evaluation or diagnosis as a tool in therapy, some related issues, and the pastor's use of himself in the process.

NOTES

1. See particularly Anna Freud, *The Ego and The Mechanisms of Defense,* New York: International Universities Press, 1946.

2. For more detailed discussion of symbols and symbolism see Carroll A. Wise, *Religion in Illness and Health.* New York: Harper and Row, 1942; Paul Tillich, *Theology of Culture,* New York: Oxford University Press, 1959; Erich Fromm, *The Forgotten Language,* New York: Rinehart, 1951; Martin Grotjahn, *The Voice of the Symbol,* New York: Dell, 1971; and Theodore Thass-Thienemann, *The Interpretation of Language,* 2 Vols., New York: Jason Aronson, 1973.

3. Anna Freud, Op. cit. Chs. 6, 7.

4. Sigmund Freud (1929), *Moses and Monotheism,* New York: Vintage Books, 1959, pp. 148–156; Gregory Rochlin, *Griefs and Discontents,* Boston: Little, Brown, 1965.

5. This is one of the problems in the training of pastoral therapists. Having mastered some theory, either theological or psychological, they set about to elucidate that theory to persons, rather than dealing with the experience and language of that person. The cure for this is not less theory, but more stress on the art of being with a person in terms of what he or she is experiencing.

6. On the logic of emotion see Franz Alexander, *The Scope of Psychoanalysis,* New York: Basic Books, 1961, p. 116.

7. The reference here is obviously to the work of Erik Erikson, and the reader is referred to his *Childhood and Society,* New York: W. W. Norton, rev. ed., 1963, and the fourth and fifth essays in his *Insight and Responsibility.* New York: W. W. Norton, 1964.

8. This statement has been attributed to Gordon Allport, whose work has been very helpful to pastors. His emphasis on the study of persons, rather than generalizations about persons, was strong. "Instead of growing impatient with a single case and hastening on to generalizations, why should we not grow impatient with our generalizations and hasten to the internal pattern" (Gordon Allport, *The Person in Psychology,* Boston: Beacon Press, 1968, p. 83).

9. Edgar Draper, et al., "On the Diagnostic Value of Religious Ideation," *Archives of General Psychiatry,* Vol. 13, Sept. 1965, pp. 202–207.

10. Lawrence E. Holst and Harold P. Kurtz, *Toward a Creative Chaplaincy,* Springfield, Ill.: Charles C Thomas, 1973.

11. See the chapter on "Narcissism: Benign and Malignant Forms" in Edith Weigert, *The Courage to Love,* New Haven: Yale University Press, 1970.

12. Paul Watzlawick, Janet H. Beavin, and Don C. Jackson, *Pragmatics of Human Communication,* New York: W. W. Norton, 1967.

Chapter 4

Evaluation in
Pastoral Psychotherapy

PASTORAL DIAGNOSIS

People come to the pastor because they are in emotional and spiritual pain. Inwardly, they are frightened, guilty, angry, frustrated, and hurting. These experiences are symptoms indicating that the inner quality of their life does not bring satisfaction and fulfillment. Instead of inner peace they experience conflict; instead of joy they know sadness; instead of love they feel anger; and instead of a clear vision of the road ahead they are baffled and perplexed. Many of them have tried the numerous panaceas offered in our culture today, panaceas that deal only with the symptoms and not with the underlying condition, and they have found these empty. The concern of the pastor is for the quality of life, the inner condition. But he must not jump to conclusions or generalize about this. His task is to help the person deal with his actual condition as he experiences it. This means that he must deal with the symptoms the person presents as indications of deeper issues. He must make an evaluation of the person and his experiences. He is not interested in labeling people. He is interested in understanding them, and whatever vocabulary he uses should convey that understanding.

The chief focus of pastoral therapy should be on the person. A major question is, What kind of a person is presenting himself for help? Additional questions are: What kind of help is he seeking, and does this come within the competence of the pastor? What does the pastor have to give, and how does this relate to what the person is seeking? And why is the individual seeking help at this particular time from this particular pastor? Is this the first time the individual has consulted a therapist? While the pastor must communicate a very accepting attitude toward the person, he will be misled if he accepts all of the person's statements as the whole truth. What the person is presenting is what he can present at this time, a picture of himself which is distorted by resistances and defenses and anxieties. The pastor, therefore, must not only listen carefully and attentively, but he must also do some thinking for himself as to the meaning of what the individual is telling him. How and when he seeks answers to the questions above depends on his style as a therapist and on what he feels is appropriate with a given person.

A traditional principle in both pastoral care and in medicine has been that the best approach to treatment depends upon a correct diagnosis. In recent years this word has become almost exclusively a medical term. Some have rejected it and what it stands for because it has been identified with a "medical model." This has been part of a somewhat general reaction against any scientific understanding of persons. However, any serious attempt to bring help to another must begin with a realistic appraisal of what is wrong and how it got that way. This means an accurate description and an understanding of the motivational factors behind the condition. The pastoral approach should be characterized by a profound respect, concern, and empathy for the other. A realistic attitude, combined with a genuine pastoral attitude, can prevent the pastor from having a kind of sentimentality, which at times borders on idolatry.

Anyone who thinks of pastoral diagnosis or evaluation as something new and, hence, dubious should read church history. A much used form of pastoral diagnosis has been in terms of the seven deadly sins.[1] These are pride, covetousness, lust, envy, gluttony, anger, and sloth. It should be noted that these are terms describing attitudes and feelings that result in sinful behavior and have their counterparts in modern psychopathology. The Ten Commandments are another favorite form of diagnosis stated more in terms of behavior. Modern psychological diagnosis seeks to refrain from the moral judgment usually associated with these terms, and adds the dimensions of the psychogenetic, dynamic, and developmental processes. It finds the beginning of these attitudes in experiences and relationships in infancy and early childhood. Gluttony, for example, is rather obviously a development out of the feeding experiences of infancy, and has to do not only with the taking of food and drink, but with love and intimacy. Pride is a defensive attitude growing out of early narcissistic overevaluation of the self which cannot permit the acknowledgment of faults. Pride finds expression in numerous defense mechanisms and illnesses, and in the inability of many to accept their need for redemption or therapy. Lust is the desire for physical pleasure in a relationship void of genuine love and respect for the other. Its overdevelopment can be traced psychogenetically and developmentally to relationships with parents or other adults in the formative years. Sloth is often identified with the inhibited withdrawn behavior of persons suffering from schizophrenia, or of those who in childhood were encouraged into a passive-dependent attitude which expects others to do everything for them. This attitude is sometimes falsely translated into religious concepts — God has to answer all of our needs, we can do nothing for ourselves. Historically, pastoral evaluation has much in common with modern psychological diagnosis. We believe that any concept of the pastor which denies him the use of modern psychological knowledge in his work with people is as sadly mistaken as were the divines of a past generation who fought against vaccination and anesthesia.

Another category of pastoral evaluation that has been used frequently in the past is that of good spirits and bad spirits, creative spirits or demonic spirits. I do not intend here to get involved in a long discussion of the Biblical concepts of Holy Spirit and human spirit,[2] but do wish to point out that modern psychology and psychotherapy has not been able to get along without a concept comparable to spirit. It is that of the self. "Self" is usually used in terms of the way in which the individual experiences himself. It describes the subjective experiences of a person, for example, his self-awareness or self-transcendence. We speak of a self-concept, or self-esteem, or self-blame, all of which indicate ways in which the individual understands and evaluates himself. The word *ego* is more of an objective concept, a description of certain functions observed by another, such as ego strength. A pastor might seek to understand the level of ego strength in a person by examining his insights into himself. These insights are possible because of the capacity for self-transcendence, the ability to stand back and look at oneself, and to be honest with what is seen. The individual is more likely to speak of this as his self-understanding. In actual practice, these two words are often used interchangeably. In pastoral evaluation it is highly desirable to inquire into the ways in which a person sees, understands, and evaluates himself. It is also highly desirable to evaluate his ego processes more objectively, and to note the degree of congruence with the self-report. Both concepts, insight and self-understanding, express something of the meanings found in the Biblical concept of human spirit.

Some of the meanings of the concept of the human spirit in the Biblical record[3] follow. First is man's self-awareness. Man knows his condition, its "grandeur and misery." Man has a responsibility to do something about his condition, but to do it in a context of faith and grace, or redemptive relationships. Second, man has the capacity to be open and responsive to all living things, including other men and God. With this there is the capacity to weigh, to judge and evaluate. He is to "test the spirits." Third, part of the concept of human spirit is human desires, wishes, or impulses, and the expression and control of these. Man's deepest desire is for union with others and with God. This is the ultimate meaning of love, in Tillich's phrase, the "reunion of the separated."[4] Fourth, man is a unity in which spiritual, psychological, and somatic processes function as a whole. This functioning unity can be destroyed or impaired. The task of therapy is to help persons reverse the destructive processes and gain whatever level of functioning unity is possible for them. This goal has often been thought of as salvation.

Religion, then, has had its methods of diagnosing or evaluating people as candidates for change or for a new quality of life. It is not sufficient to label a condition nor to condemn it. The pastor must seek to understand it from the psychogenetic, developmental, and internal dynamic or motivational perspectives. He must understand the quality of life for which the individual is striving, what blocks him, what drives him, and how this is related to the quality of life portrayed in the New Testament. He must give up the traditional conception that somehow a person can manipulate himself into a new quality of life. This may be a lengthy process, and we shall deal with it further as we go along.

Evaluation or diagnosis in the scientific sense involves an accurate description and history of the condition, an opinion as to possible causation, the differentiation from other similar conditions, a statement as to diagnosis, a recommendation for an approach to treatment, and a statement in regard to prognosis. One difference between the competent professional and the technician is that the professional has disciplined himself in the art of evaluation. He does not work blindly, but rather thinks through the problem of bringing whatever resources he might have to meet the situation. The technician is able to carry out certain techniques, and applies them indiscriminately without regard for the condition which he is treating. Much training in "counseling" is really training as a technician, not as a professional.

Two kinds of language are used in the evaluative process. One is the language of subjective experience in which the person describes and evaluates his own experience. The other is the technical jargon used professionally. Sometimes a person uses religious language, and the pastor must determine whether the person is communicating a genuine experience or whether it is used in a stereotyped, defensive manner. To avoid wallowing in the person's subjectivity, the therapist will have to translate the language of the person into his own technical language, but this is for his own use, not for communication to the person. For example, if the person says, "I am a loner," the therapist should seek to discover the kind of experiences to which the person refers. He should not respond in terms of "alienation," or "estrangement," or "neurotic distancing," or "schizophrenic reaction." The use of technical language is a pitfall for the beginning therapist, but even experienced therapists find themselves slipping, and not infrequently, into technical abstractions. We repeat that such language is an important tool in the thinking of the therapist and in his communication with other professionals, but not in communication with persons struggling with painful experiences. Unless the therapist can translate technical language into the language of experience and vice versa, he probably does not understand either. Furthermore, using technical language with a person tends to dehumanize him.

Objections to the evaluative procedures often center around the attitude of the therapist in obtaining information. A personal history or other data may be obtained in a cold, impersonal manner. Or it can be done in a manner which clearly indicates a preformed opinion of the person, a reading of prejudicial concepts into the person. These objections clearly concern the manner in which an evaluative process is carried out, and not with the process itself. We agree with the harmful effects of such attitudes. The pastor is not an inquisitor, nor is he a salesman looking for a motive that will get a signature on the dotted line. Neither should he be a person who flounders in a sea of ambiguous, disorganized, and undifferentiated data. Rather, the pastor should demonstrate his concern for the person by asking questions seeking to clarify the problems presented by the person. He needs to learn how to collect clinical data and then to think clearly and accurately about that data.

Evaluative interviews should be conducted within the framework of a therapeutic relationship.[5] The essence of a pastoral approach is the search for truth as an internal dynamic process within a relationship of trust, understanding, and respect. Questions may be asked in an open-ended manner. This allows the person freedom of response rather than a feeling that he is being cornered. In the process, feelings that are conscious should be recognized and accepted by the therapist. There should be no probing into deeper feelings at this stage. The person will sense that the therapist respects his privacy, but that he needs information as the basis for further work. Most people welcome a sound evaluative approach. It gives them the feeling that the pastor knows what he is doing. A person who comes to the first interview in a state of disturbance should be allowed whatever time the pastor feels desirable to deal with strong feelings, and, if necessary, the more formal evaluative process should not begin until the next session. However, such a first session usually reveals useful data for evaluation.

A woman came in for her first interview in a highly disturbed state. After about twenty minutes, because the pastor noted that her communications were becoming repetitive, he very gently began to take a history. The first question—"What is the earliest thing you remember from your childhood?"—brought forth a look of amazement and the response that it was as though she had no childhood. The process was continued with the usual questions about her relationship to her parents, her early childhood training, her school experiences, and the like. Gradually she remembered, and as she did her disturbance subsided. The final few minutes of the hour were spent discussing her present situation. She began the second session, a week later, with the words, "Last week you helped me regain a sense that I was a person who had a past. I had lost that. I have been living so much in the present that I completely blotted out my past. It gives me a new sense of strength."

In this situation, taking a history was of definite therapeutic value. It helped her regain a sense of her past, without which there is no identity. It laid the groundwork for future sessions in which she discovered how feelings and thoughts from her past, which she had "forgotten," were creating problems for her in the present. Her experience, like that of many others, illustrates the statement attributed to Santayana, that he who forgets his history is condemned to repeat its mistakes.

Another attitude that is essential for the pastor is that of holding all evaluative conclusions tentatively. Judgments arrived at in the evaluative process should be used as working hypotheses. They may be compared to the chart of a new territory to be explored. Not all of the topography is apparent. There is a sense in which therapy is a continuous diagnostic or evaluative process in which the person and therapist collaborate. As such, it contains an element of faith which is inherent in the pastoral approach, that of having some certainties which give courage to explore oneself. Such faith is not rigid dogmatism, nor does it demand unchanging formulations. It is more like a searchlight that illuminates some darkness ahead. If the pastor has a genuine therapeutic attitude, he will inevitably demonstrate it in the evaluative process. The sensitive pastor may believe it desirable to pause in the process and ask how the person is feeling about what is going on. In this way, he can learn something that will enable him to be of more value to the person.

Some therapists forego a systematic evaluation. They make a diagnosis from the data presented in the first interview. They may be experienced therapists who quickly recognize the signs and symptoms the person presents. From this they can generalize to the psychopathology and psychodynamics present in the person. If long-term psychotherapy is planned, knowledge of specific dynamic behavior patterns are not immediately necessary, as they will be clarified during the course of therapy. However, the pastoral therapist who is doing short-term therapy will want information revealing specific dynamic patterns since he will be treating only certain aspects of the person. This may be particularly true of the pastoral therapist working in therapy centers. Here a well-defined pastoral evaluation is essential if a continuity of treatment is to be maintained in view of a changing staff and shifting responsibility. This process should be participated in by the staff of the center, and decisions should be staff decisions. In this way a distinction is made between individual practice and group responsibility and consultation. This is also in the best interest of the person.

In a parish situation acute crises often occur that by their very nature do not require a formal diagnostic approach: for example, the experience of bereavement. Here the pastor is dealing with an immediate reality situation. If the grief work is successful in a reasonable amount of time, no extended evaluation process is necessary, though the pastor will be helped greatly by understanding the personality of the bereaved. However, if the grief process or any crisis involves reactions which are pathological, some evaluative procedure will be necessary. For example, a bereaved person may be reacting not only to the present situation, but to an unresolved bereavement some years before. Or the relationship between the bereaved and deceased may have contained a degree of projected anger or guilt which blocks the grief work. Thus, the pastor will have to distinguish between those situations requiring some evaluative process and those which do not. One criteria is the nature and depth of the problem. However, there are probably few marriage problems which do not require an evaluation.[6] For example, it is usually important in marriage therapy to know the history of the courtship, the factors leading to the marriage, as well as the nature of the parental and sibling relationships of each spouse as the probable basis for unhappy repetitive behavior.

THE LIFE HISTORY

The meaning of life history, including a statement of the presenting problem (which is itself history), is important. Life history is not a collection of cold facts. Neither is it merely recalling facts of the past to memory. It is essentially the understanding of those facts in terms of their dynamic and developmental significance to the person. If facts are the skeleton, the inner meaning of those facts is the life blood. The presenting problem is a culmination of the dynamic interrelation between facts and meaning as this has influenced the developmental process. The person's hope or lack of hope for the future is also part of the meaning of his history. "Meaning" in this context is more than an intellectual proposition. It is also the emotional responses of the individual to various experiences and relationships which determine whether growth or fixation will occur. These responses are made up of all of the potentials and processes involved in personality development. To take a history in the sense of understanding the background of a person one must have comprehended, both intellectually and emotionally, an understanding of the theory of personality development as it is available today, particularly ego development.[7] In addition, an empathic relationship with the person is necessary in order to sense the inner meaning of experiences. In taking the life history the emphasis of the pastor should be on the mutual exploration of the experience of the person in order to bring understanding.

In recent years there has been some emphasis on the idea of God working in human history. The idea is certainly Biblical. Usually it has been applied to the history of groups and of nations. For the pastoral therapist the idea of God working in the history of the individual and small groups, such as the family, is equally tenable as an article of faith. In a broad sense, certainly there are both destructive and creative forces at work in the lives of persons. There are forces and dynamics that make for illness and those that make for health. In these the pastor shares equally with all others, and he stands in the same need before God as the person before him. In searching out the history of persons, the pastor is dealing with a high order of God's creation, a creature like unto himself. Only attitudes of self-honesty, humility, and reverence do justice to the life experiences with which he deals.

The first thing which is needed in a systematic approach to evaluation is a clear statement from the person recorded in his own words as to why he is seeking help, why he is seeking it now, and why from you rather than another therapist. In short, what is bringing him to you now? It is desirable to note the manner of speech, whether it is slow or fast, halting or fluent, and other such details. The mood or feelings of the person, his attitude toward the pastor, and his general behavior in the office should be noted. Does he come in and take over, or is he shy and retiring? Does he pull his chair closer to you, or does he push it back? Does he show signs of nervousness, or is he composed? Is this genuine, or is he holding in strong feeling? If the individual is a woman does she sit in a seductive manner, either openly or by constantly trying to pull a miniskirt down below her knees? The pastor should be especially interested in the nature of the religious language a person uses. Is this a genuine expression of the experience of the individual, or is he trying to seduce the pastor for his own ends? Flattery, for example, may conceal hostility, and the experienced pastor wonders why the person has a need to use flattery, and how the hostility will be expressed later. Sometimes he asks about it.

The pastor should be alert to the communication problems and methods of the person. Hysterical persons, for example, are experts at talking a great deal, giving the impression that they are really communicating, but in the end they have said little of significance. Others will be compulsive talkers, going into great detail, elaborating inconsequential events, and otherwise talking in a manner that keeps away from themselves. Others will find it difficult to communicate, and will be silent or withdrawn. Still others may be hostile, especially the spouse who feels dragged into a marriage consultation. Communication problems need special attention in marriage counseling.

The pastor should also be alert to his own manner of communication. How does he sit and where? Behind a protective desk, in a face-to-face position, staring at the person, or at an angle to the person where each can avoid the gaze of the other, if it is desirable? Is the pastor concerned with papers or books on his desk or the telephone? Is he more concerned about taking notes than in maintaining emotional contact with the person? If he uses a tape recorder is it out in the open, and has he asked permission of the person to record? Does he hesitate and make false starts, giving the impression that he does not know what he is doing?

A fuller understanding of the person can be gained by involving him in a discussion of his present relationships within his family. This will reveal something of his interpersonal relationships within an intimate framework. The choice of an occupation can also reflect important facets of his personality growth. Likewise, the nature of his social and religious life and of other relationships which are important to him, such as recreational experiences, can add to the pastor's understanding. For instance, a young woman reported very angrily that her husband had gone on a fishing trip with his pals on the occasion of their wedding anniversary. Further inquiry brought out other such incidents. In many ways he seemed to avoid real involvement with his wife and to prefer male company. The pastor might have stopped here had he been sympathetic with the woman. Instead he inquired into her maneuvers. She told of incidents which revealed that unconsciously she gave him signals which indicated that she did not want involvement. She was busy in activities outside the home, had her own coterie of friends, and was often "tired" at night when he was interested in going out or in lovemaking. Her anger was in part a defense against her own fears of involvement, which took some time for her to face and work out. In evaluating a person, we should remember that what they tell us about their relationships with others usually reveals something about themselves of which they may not be aware. We use what they tell us about others, particularly their close relationships, to focus on what is going on within them and the kind of relationships they are creating.

The material that is gained about the present history should be organized and interpreted in a systematic manner. This is an attempt to make a tentative statement as to how the person is functioning in the present. Again, mere facts are not enough. The dynamic or motivational meaning of these facts is important. The meticulously dressed individual is communicating something about himself and the sloppily dressed person is communicating something else. Likewise, mannerisms, posture, gestures, and general behavior are important means of communication. For example, some men swing their arms as though they are shadow-boxing with someone. Perhaps they do want to demolish someone in their anger. The significance of an item like this must be considered in the light of what the person says about it, but also in the light of the total personality dynamics. An estimate of the general intelligence level is helpful, and this can be made from the history of the person's educational experiences, and the manner and content of the speech and thought in the interview. Lack of orientation for time, place, and person, or disorientation may be symptomatic of a psychotic condition. The individual's capacity to remember his use of imagination and fantasy, and his degree of awareness of what is going on around him should be considered. The feelings or moods which he manifests in the interview, his fears and angers and the objects of such feelings, his understanding of love and his ways of loving, and his defenses against strong or painful feelings, including love, should be understood. Any history of suicidal thoughts, or other forms of self-destruction, such as accidents, should be explored and understood. Symptoms of neurotic, psychotic, or character disorder reactions need to be explored from the point of onset. Some estimate of the individual's ego strength should be made. This includes an estimate of the conflicts between impulse and controls, the way of dealing with conflicts between wishes and conscience, or between wishes and cultural norms, the reality testing ability or weakness, object relationships, dependency on others and how this is handled, and how the person has put his life experiences together.

There are books[8] which offer outlines for the personal and family history. However, no outline should be used slavishly or mechanically, but rather with understanding. The general theory of personality development should be so mastered that the pastor can move naturally and spontaneously through material which is relevant for the person. Attention should be given to the cultural background, with special attention to those situations where the background is different from that of the pastor. It is the mark of a mature pastor that he can free himself from the prejudices and values of his own background sufficiently to understand a person from a different culture.

In taking the past history, stress should again be placed on the mutual exploration in order to understand the person. Any special factors surrounding the birth of the person may be significant. The first year of life is particularly important for personality growth. Experiences of closeness to or separation from the mother, feeding, weaning, and toilet training problems often have been communicated to the person and should be asked about. The early beginnings of trust or distrust need to be explored, or do the development of autonomy or shame and doubt about the self. This leads to an understanding of the difficulty or ease with which the person was able to differentiate himself from the mother and develop a distorted or healthy self-concept. The relationship of the parents to each other and to the child are important throughout this period. Especially in need of exploration is the three to six year level, when oedipal experiences should take place, to be resolved in healthy ways or unresolved in unhealthy patterns. Development of feelings of dependence, of passivity, of fear of normal aggressiveness, of fear of not being loved, of tendencies to work out anxieties in physiological reactions, and other such experiences need to be looked at. School experiences and the ways in which the child is able to form relationships with the outside world will reflect the strengths and weaknesses which have been developed in the earliest years. The child's play life, which later becomes a basis for his work life, may throw light on his developing personality. The whole gamut of sexual experiences and close attachments or rejections in the latent and adolescent periods reveals further dynamics. Success or failure in gaining emancipation from parents in adolescence, in developing a firm, functioning identity, and moving toward emotional independence is significant. Depending on the age of the person, the adult levels of ego development as expressed in love, in sexual experiences, and in vocational, social, and religious experiences should be explored. All of this may sound rather laborious, but it is necessary to prevent the pastor from falling into an ever-present danger, that of taking a superficial view of a person. Depending on the attitude of the pastor, the experience of exploring life experiences can have a definite therapeutic and professional value. On the professional side, it should give the pastor an understanding of whether he feels competent to embark on a therapeutic program, or whether he should only try to help the person with some immediate problems and then refer him for more intensive treatment.

While it is essential to be aware of and understand pathological processes, the pastoral therapist must also take into full account the healthy strivings of the person. He should keep in mind that there is a healthy aspect in the use of defense reactions. In the very act of defending himself against anxiety, the person is trying to maintain a certain level of integration. Without his defenses he would disintegrate. The strength of the defenses gives some estimate of the strength of the anxiety and also of ego strength. Sometimes the defenses are so rigid and the ego feels so weak that any exploration of underlying anxieties is impossible, and should not be attempted until ego growth has occurred. The ability to stand off and observe oneself and to report what he sees is an aspect of strength. The openness of the person to self-understanding, his idea about the kind of help he needs, his ability to entertain new ideas about himself, his willingness to meet conditions necessary for receiving help and for his own growth, the level of success he has had in various human relationships — these are indicators of strength. The drive toward integration and wholeness is one of the inherent elements of a person that is utilized in pastoral therapy. It is the motivation and goal of many religious experiences and is one of the God-given resources of a human being. It is, for example, utilized in pastoral therapy by setting up a relation in which the person becomes able to put his life together rather than the pastor trying to do it for him.

In the course of working with people, the pastor will be confronted with problems that have some relation to organic factors. The fact that a human being experiences himself within a body which is subject to various pathologies has been taken as a reason why only medically trained persons should do psychotherapy. Freud[9] disagreed with this view, as do many today. The pastor should know enough about the meaning of symptoms that he should recognize the possibility of organic conditions and make a referral for evaluation. Many medically trained psychotherapists do not attempt to make a diagnosis of organic conditions. They refer to a specialist in the condition. The pastoral therapist must be aware of two possible errors. First, there is the strong tendency on the part of some to attribute all symptoms to a psychological cause, forgetting that the body can malfunction. Second, the pastor may err in the other direction, of using physiological factors to help the person deny responsibility for his behavior. As part of the history-taking process, the pastor should inquire into the history of illnesses, and seek whatever consultation he needs for an assessment.[10]

As has been indicated previously, in the process of taking a life history and receiving other data, the pastor must be alert as to how the person relates to him. Does he hold back or does he offer more information than is required? Does he show suspicion of the therapist or does he show a degree of trust? Is he evasive or is he open? What does he tell easily, what does he omit? Whatever the behavior, it has transference[11] elements in it; that is, it reveals attitudes and ways of relating which grow out of his past experience. Some of these transference elements may be clear; others may not become clear until after a number of sessions. But as the pastor listens to an account of a person's relationships to significant persons in his past and present, he will discover the feelings by which the person will relate to him. This is important data in assessment and in the decision in regard to therapy. It also gives data as to problems and strengths which will be met in therapy.

The pastor should also examine his own feelings about the person. Is he frightened or made angry? strongly attached or repelled? anxious or indifferent? Some therapists make extensive use of their own feelings in assessing a person. This has value and dangers. Whence come the feelings of the pastor? Are they genuine person-to-person responses, or are they the products of his own past experiences and dynamics? What reactions is he provoking or stimulating in the person? Is he overzealous in collecting data? Overinterested in some aspects of the person's experience, underinterested in others? Whatever his feelings, he should examine them carefully and honestly. He should also know himself well enough to know what kind of persons he works with well, and the kind he does not work with well. No one works well with someone he does not like. In many ways there is no substitute for the self-knowledge of the pastor that comes through his own therapy. His self-knowledge should give him a sense of how he would feel were he in a situation similar to that of the other person, but it must be accurate self-knowledge.

THE WORKING RELATIONSHIP

In the process of seeking material for evaluation, a relationship has been developed between the pastor and the person. What is the nature of this relationship? Is it one that will promote the therapeutic process or will it retard or destroy the process? Can this particular pastor work therapeutically with this particular person?

We are speaking here of what has been called "the working alliance,"[12] or "the therapeutic alliance." A therapeutic alliance is a relationship in which the work of therapy can proceed. It is made up in part of the ability of the pastor to communicate concern, understanding, and competence to the person. On the person's part, it is the result of his willingness or ability to trust and cooperate in the therapeutic process, to say whatever comes to mind, to be willing and able to stand off and look at himself in the light of comments by the pastor which are aimed at understanding. This is not developed by any one procedure. By the time the first session is over, a beginning therapeutic alliance has been developed, or has not been, through all that has happened.

The relationship at the end of the first hour may not be conducive to therapy. This may be due to factors in either the pastor or the person. The failure of the pastor to understand the individual, or to communicate his understanding, his inability to listen to the underlying communication as well as to the words of the person, his inability to deal openly with resistances in the person — these are among the reasons for failure in developing a therapeutic alliance. On the individual's side, we would think first of resistances[13] to therapy (reasons why the person seeks to avoid a therapeutic relationship), such as fear of exploring himself, blaming his problems on others, a tendency to act out his problems rather than investigate them, a denial that his problems are internal — these and other such attitudes may be the reasons for avoiding a therapeutic relationship. They need to be brought up and dealt with by the pastor as resistances in the hope that the healthy aspects of the person will respond in a positive manner.[14]

As we have indicated in a previous chapter, the pastor has a special means of evaluating a person, namely his religious ideas and attitudes. The person will also evaluate the pastor's religious attitudes in the light of his own wishes. There should be no open disagreement, and there will not be if the pastor maintains an attitude of understanding the person's religion and religious attitudes, whatever they are. If the person is seeking a relationship of dependence through religion, the pastor has his choice of accepting this and destroying the therapy, or dealing with it as a resistance to understanding and growth toward autonomy and self-reliance. In the evaluation process, the pastor needs to arrive at some estimate of the person's use of his religion for either healthy or unhealthy goals. An anti-religious attitude is not necessarily an indication against pastoral therapy. It needs to be taken as a problem to be explored, and often it will be found to grow out of unfortunate experiences. It is a contribution to the health of the person if he finds a pastor who is more interested in understanding him and his religious attitudes than in changing his theology or practices. This communicates a fundamental aspect of religious faith, a respect for and an acceptance of the person and a concern to help him work out his fears of that acceptance.

At the proper time the pastor must inform the person as to his conclusions and recommendations. This must be done in the language of the person. If the pastor makes a clinical diagnosis, as he should for his own guidance, he should not communicate this. Some people who defend themselves by labels will want a diagnosis, but here the reasons for labeling rather than understanding oneself need to be explored.

It is important that the pastor try to impart some understanding as to why the person's attempts to solve his problems have failed, to reduce or remove any guilt about needing therapy, to deal with a false sense of independence—I should be able to solve my own problems—and to help the person understand what therapeutic help is, how it is given, and why it is needed. This should not be a long lecture, but done briefly and in nontechnical words. Sometimes there will be strong resistance to moving into therapy. Many times the person has come intent on getting assistance and the decision is made quickly.

At this point procedures need to be clarified. The time for appointment, the fees,[15] the policy of charging for missed appointments should be settled. The person should be told that the pastor will not ask informational questions as he has been doing in the evaluation, but will rather respond to whatever the person wishes to bring into the sessions. The person should be told that he should speak as freely as possible about whatever comes into his mind. In this way he cooperates in the therapeutic process.

Returning to the emphasis at the beginning of this chapter, we cannot emphasize too strongly that taking information about a person is not an end in itself. It is only as this information is used, along with an empathic working relationship, to understand the internal dynamics of the person, and for the therapeutic benefit of the person, that its purpose is fulfilled. Such understanding may be formulated in different ways, religiously or psychologically. An indispensable tool in this is a knowledge of modern psychodynamics. An indispensable attitude is the basic pastoral concern for persons and for the internal quality of life that is being experienced or desired. "A pastor should not only have a thorough knowledge of a human being as such, but as a true pastor or seelsorger, he must know how to diagnose and treat the peculiar spiritual conditions of an individual soul."[16]

If the pastor is to follow the concepts and spirit of the New Testament that were discussed in chapter 1, he must seek an understanding of the whole person and his life experiences, and particularly his responses to those experiences. Indeed, we could say that his response is part of the experience that is often neglected. Two persons may respond differently to very similar situations, and this indicates an important difference in them as persons. The pastor does not need to know everything there is to know about a person, but only enough to give him a sense of the individual's feelings and processes. He needs this knowledge in a relationship of "service" to the person, not one of probing or manipulation—indeed, in a relationship which in itself is curative or therapeutic. This can be a very important first step in helping a person understand himself. The pastor secures the cooperation of the person in helping the pastor understand. This requires a genuinely humble attitude on the part of the pastor. He allows the person to teach him.

In the next chapter we continue this theme, adding some concepts that should help in the interpretation of the history.

NOTES

1. William A. Clebsch and Charles R. Jaekle, *Pastoral Care in Historical Perspective,* New York: Prentice-Hall, 1964.

2. Arnold B. Come, *Human Spirit and Holy Spirit,* Philadelphia: Westminster Press, 1959.

3. Alan Richardson, *Theological Word Book of the Bible,* New York: Macmillan, 1951.

4. Paul Tillich, *Love, Power and Justice,* New York: Oxford University Press, 1954.

5. Edgar Draper, *Psychiatry and Pastoral Care,* New York: Prentice-Hall, 1965; Roger A. MacKinnon and Robert Michels, *The Psychiatric Interview in*

Clinical Practice, Philadelphia: W. B. Saunders, 1971; John C. Nemiah, *Foundations of Psychopathology,* New York: Jason Aronson, 1973.

6. An excellent approach to evaluation in marriage therapy is Bernard Greene's work, *A Clinical Approach to Marital Problems,* Springfield, Ill.: Charles C Thomas, 1970.

7. Theodore Lidz, *The Person,* New York: Basic Books, 1968.

8. Nathan W. Ackerman, *The Psychodynamics of Family Life,* New York: Basic Books, 1958; Harry Stack Sullivan, *The Psychiatric Interview,* New York: W. W. Norton, 1954; Group for the Advancement of Psychiatry, *Treatment of Families in Conflict,* New York: Jason Aronson, 1970.

9. Sigmund Freud (1926), *The Question of Lay Analysis,* in *The Standard Edition of the Complete Psychological Works of Sigmund Freud,* London: vol. 20, trans. James Strachey, Hogarth Press, 1953.

10. Leonard Small, *Neuropsychodiagnosis in Psychotherapy,* New York: Brunner-Mazel, 1973.

11. See chapter 7 on transference.

12. Richard Chessick, *How Psychotherapy Heals,* New York: Jason Aronson, 1969.

13. See chapter 6 on resistances.

14. Many pastors today are recording their interviews with the permission of the person. Listening to a recorded interview later can be a means of understanding the flow of the session, and the resistances and responses. This is what often occurs in supervision.

15. The subject of fees is not a clear issue for the pastor in the parish. Some have a policy of making a charge after the fourth or fifth interview. In a pastoral therapy center, fees are mandatory for adequate support. There is a difference of opinion as to whether they are necessary for good therapy to take place. Certainly the well-trained pastor is worthy of his hire.

16. John H. C. Fritz, *Pastoral Theology,* Saint Louis: Concordia Publishing House, 1932, p. 195.

Chapter 5

Evaluation in Pastoral Psychotherapy (Continued)

We have been stressing the need for information that yields understanding of the person who comes for help. This understanding is supplemental to that gained from the pastor's own sense of empathy. The description and history of the person is to be sought in a therapeutic or redemptive atmosphere rather than a critical, judgmental, or unconcerned atmosphere. There remains the task of evaluating the material received. In this chapter we shall suggest criteria for the purpose of evaluation, criteria that are concerned with ego processes. These processes have to do largely with the relation of the individual within himself and within his environment.

REALITY TESTING

Most discussions[1] of ego processes will make reality testing one of its primary functions. This usually refers to processes through which the person relates himself, for better or worse, to the outer world. The ego has the function of seeking to evaluate the external environment so that the person can find the satisfaction of inner needs in ways which are adaptive to the opportunities, demands and prohibitions of the environment. The external environment includes other persons, culture in all of its satisfying, frustrating and alleviating aspects, as well as the natural world.

People today tend to neglect interrelationships between themselves and their natural environment.

The pastor will be aware of another level of meaning to the word *reality*. His concern is also with the concept of ultimate reality, or God. For the religious person there is a reality above and beyond the immediate environment, a reality of love and of law which makes demands but also is the source of sustaining grace. Religious faith is a witness to the relationships between ultimate reality, the external environment and the inner world of the individual. These relationships may be both a source of pronounced tension and also a source of strength and peace. We are dealing here with knowledge or insight that is known only through faith, and is not subject to scientific verification. Those who insist that reality is only that which is subject to scientific verification will deny the validity of concern about an ultimate. This problem need not constitute a practical barrier to pastoral therapy. The first step in reality testing on either level is our perception of reality, and this perception is likely to be of the same quality for both levels. Perception is not controlled by the reality perceived. The personality of the perceiver,[2] his feelings, attitudes, patterns of response, defenses, and basic personality qualities (such as dependency on the environment or rebellion against it) have strong influence on the quality of perception. This is an expression of the ability of the organism to function as a whole and of the capacity of the self to seek to maintain the process of integration or wholeness. To the extent which this fails, the person is sick. This will be revealed in interpretations of reality which the pastoral therapist should recognize as distorted. The depressed person will have a gloomy view of reality (any reality); the paranoid person will see reality as threatening to him; the naive person will see reality as confusing and want to withdraw. It is this functioning as a whole that gives point to the use of questions about religion in the diagnostic process, for such questions can reveal a person's perceptions of himself, of immediate reality, and of ultimate reality. There is always a relationship between the condition of a person's inner world and his perception of his external world. The focus on the "world view" is controlled from within.

The relation of personality factors to the perception of reality can be a problem for the pastoral therapist. His perception of reality can be distorted by his past experiences, personal biases, and future goals. He may use either theology or psychology to reinforce his perceptions intellectually. His own perceptions can lead him to misinterpret or to be unable to grasp how another perceives reality. This is the problem of countertransference.[3] Some therapists today try to resolve this problem and act (or say they do) as though they deny their own perceptions and work entirely within the perceptions of the person. But this is self-deception as well as deception of the person, and can result in a kind of countertransference harmful to each. Problems of interpretation will be discussed later, but in a skillful manner the therapist often has to confront the person with what are obvious distortions of reality. Within the pastoral field this may extend to religious reality, and this is a special problem for the pastoral therapist. Any kind of pastoral therapy requires a substantial level of health in the therapist.

Reality testing may be considered in terms of everyday experiences. How does the person understand the gratifications offered him by his environment, does he accept them or is he afraid of them? How does he sense the prohibitions or restrictions of his environment, the opportunities for growth that it offers, or denial of growth experiences? A person may complain that he is not loved by his family. He has "tested" this aspect of his own reality, and this is what he believes it to be. But he may be afraid of love, of giving or receiving love. A common defense against fear of love is to perceive others as not being loving when actually they are. Or a person may feel that the restrictions of society are completely unjust and get himself into serious trouble when, as a matter of fact, he is not subject to any restrictions that others do not experience. Or a man may feel that reality is a big fat breast that will pamper him and allow him to get away with anything. A sound knowledge of psychopathology will acquaint the pastor with the kind of distorted perceptions that arise out of various feelings and defenses, and in turn help him to see these things when they are present. However, the basic principle is true also of persons without gross psychopathology.

A person's inner world is also part of his reality. How does he evaluate his feelings, thoughts, impulses, desires? Is it a case of what he wants he gets or of the opposite, what he wants he denies? Is he able to compromise? Does he overevaluate the open expression of anger, or is he afraid of his anger and its expression? Part of reality testing involves the meanings and values which he professes, and then those by which he lives. It includes the level of insight into himself, as well as awareness of his own self-processes, and what is going on between himself and his world. The use of language is also a clue to a person's perception and evaluation of his inner world, as well as his external world, whether his language is used to reveal or to conceal.

This means that for pastoral evaluation there are really three aspects of reality that need examination. One is the person's concept of ultimate reality and how this functions in his life. A second is reality as the external world. The third is the person's own inner world, his self or spirit. Religion has always been concerned with the cultivation of the inner life. Mystical elements in religion have tended to identify ultimate and inner reality — the finding of God and the finding of the self are simultaneous experiences and identical.[4] Sometimes the emphasis is placed on the intellectual aspects of religion to the neglect or denial of the feeling and striving aspects; sometimes the reverse is true. There are many in our secular and religious culture who place great emphasis on feeling and intimacy to the denial of both ultimate reality and the reality of the external world. One of our most difficult problems is that of maintaining a sense of wholeness in which all aspects of life receive their proper emphasis and are experienced in an integral relationship with each other. Since pastoral psychotherapy should deal with the whole person, evaluation for that experience must seek to understand something of the person in his totality. Furthermore, pastoral psychotherapy should aim at helping the person deal with the problems of the inner life, the problems of the human spirit. For this reason we have expanded the concept of reality testing. Pastoral therapy is concerned to help persons growth in faith, hope, and love, rather than a kind of adaptation to external reality which may be conformity gained at the price of inner integrity, growth, and creativity. Many secular therapists strive for the same goals, so the major differences may be one of formulation. Here we are trying to keep our formulations consistent with a long pastoral tradition, as well as to place emphasis on the importance of the inner life and motivation. The New Testament test for the reality of a life is "you will know them by their fruits" (Matt. 7:16–20).

The way in which a person uses his religion in his psychological economy is an important part of understanding his capacity for reality testing. A young man made a great point with a pastor that he "was living under grace." Becoming healthily suspicious, the pastor inquired about his behavior and discovered that the man very readily and without conscious guilt confessed many and various acts of sexual deviation. But he insisted that these things were unimportant, since he "was living under grace." His use of religion was obviously as distorted as his use of his sexuality. His capacity for evaluating his behavior was very poor, either in terms of everyday experience or of religion. His ego was at the mercy of id impulses.

Another person may use religion in just the opposite manner, as a means of rationalizing exaggerated guilt and self-punishment processes far in excess of the reality of the situation. Or a person may use religion to justify control of the family beyond anything which is reasonable or which is required by the situation. It is quite common for people to use religion to express omnipotent impulses or magical wishes which run directly counter to the real situation. A person may hold a very naive concept of God as support for an immature personality, which in turn prevents a real evaluation of his concepts of both God and self.

On the other hand, countless persons use religion as a means of testing their own attitudes and behavior, or of evaluating their relationships with others, or with some aspect of their environment honestly. People who are moving toward more mature attitudes will use religion to support this endeavor. Others will find stimulation for growth in religion. While the motivation for social reform obviously grows out of unhealthy defenses in some people, the true social and religious prophet is a person who uses both inner capacities and religion to sensitize himself to human needs, to understand conditions which require change, and to gain the courage to seek to bring about the change.

The pastoral therapist must look for evidences of the healthy and creative use of religion. He should keep in mind that there are persons who test and reject many of the values of their environment, not because they are sick but because they accept values which they feel are more ultimate and universal. The pastoral therapist may not see these persons; they may have little need of him, although they may be persons who earlier resolved many of their everyday reality problems through therapy. Genuine religious persons use their commitment to ultimate and universal values as a means of relating to their everyday reality in order to bring a redemptive presence into that reality, even though this may bring suffering and even death. This is difficult for many who have not experienced it to understand.

We have spoken of pride as one very important category in a traditional scheme of pastoral diagnosis. Pride is a failure in reality testing, the testing of the reality of oneself, of one's world and of ultimate values. It is an inversion of actuality. It is the expression of narcissism and omnipotence. In social and clinical experience it may show up in the person who exalts himself and understands any aspect of reality as something which he should have the right to control. The pastoral therapist will see many who suffer from the pride of depression, they degrade themselves to the exalted position of being the chief of sinners. There are many forms in which manifestations of pride appear, including the other deadly sins. These sins are deadly because pride causes the victim to feel that he does not need to change, and he therefore rejects help to gain either health or salvation. He cannot trust another sufficiently to put himself into a helping or saving relationship. Pride in the pastoral therapist may show up either in a highly overconfident feeling that he can and should help everyone, or the denial of help to some who present difficult problems, or in an attempt to be arbitrary and dictatorial.

The religious answer to the problem of pride is a kind of emptying of oneself.[5] This is genuine humility. It is the basis for a true appraisal of reality on all levels, and is accompanied by genuine self-giving. Only a deeply trusting and committed person can move toward this ideal. The therapist cannot demand this of persons, and he will see few who achieve this high level of fulfillment. Without a real measure of this, the therapist himself will be something of a mechanical robot, or his pride in what he does for others will be destructive. The genuine religious leader is the one who can help others discover their pain and their pride, revealing to them an image of the kind of person they want to be but hardly dare.

IMPULSES AND CONTROL

Another aspect of ego functioning that is important in pastoral appraisal or diagnosis is the manner in which the person handles his impulse and feeling of life. The Biblical concept of spirit has always included the element of power, of drive, of choice among ends or values. Wishes and desires are the motive power behind the seven deadly sins. They are a major factor in the production of emotional disorders of various kinds. They also provide the power for creative life, or for what St. Paul calls "the fruits of the Spirit" (Gal. 6:22).

One central issue here is that of control or direction. Those who are pictured in the New Testament as being possessed by demons are persons who have lost control. Here the source of the power is projected outside of the individual to an external force. Modern psychology brings this back into the person and sees the problem in terms of conflicting forces within him. This idea is not foreign to Biblical thought. The conflict between "the law and the Gospel" in the New Testament and in Christian theology is a

projection of the conflict within man's inner world. This should
not be taken, however, as a basis for denial of a transcendent
or ultimate dimension in that conflict. Man's projections are a
major way through which he comes to understand his world, inner
and outer. The real issue is the nature and purpose of the projection, whether it is really a search for understanding or a means of
evasion, concealment and of expressing pathological process. It
should be added that the central message of the New Testament is
a positive one, that there is a redeeming and curative power in life
and in man, and this is the glory of man's spirit. Modern psychotherapy is founded on a similar faith, that the healing forces with
which the therapist works are within the person.

Clinically, the pastor will meet the problem of control in the
two extremes of overcontrol and undercontrol, with much shad-
ing in between. Overscrupulosity in regard to moral and religious
behavior has long been an issue for the pastor. The intensely
inhibited person filled with guilt and anxiety about his desires
may appeal to the pastor for help in finding some measure of
release. Often people will come with marriage conflicts where
there is clearly overcontrol in expressing love on the part of one
or both of the partners. Sometimes the pastor will meet the person with a strong self-righteous pride which is a reaction to guilt
or anxiety. The overcontrolled person is likely to want to control
others, and sometimes works his way into a position in a family,
church or elsewhere where control of others seems to be a justifiable responsibility. This can be a motive for entering one of the
helping professions.

The undercontrolled person is frequently a problem in general
pastoral care or in the therapeutic situation. This person is
addicted to uncontrollable and irresponsible impulse expression.
It may be difficult to distinguish between a compulsive element in
such persons and a need to have desires satisfied immediately or
periodically. These persons are very self-centered, pleasure-
oriented, seductive, and are usually excellent rationalizers, able
to talk themselves and others into justification for their behavior.
Their behavior is acceptable to their ego. They must be helped to

realize that it is undesirable in order to proceed in therapy. Their impulse expression may be in such areas as sex, anger, overeating, excessive drinking, uncontrollable gambling, and stealing or otherwise unlawfully appropriating the money or possessions of others. They have little or no guilt about their behavior. They are adept at talking others out of a serious view of their actions, at getting "easy" forgiveness. The pastor has to be on his guard not to be taken in by them. Underneath the impulsive behavior there is a sense of deprivation or injury to their self-esteem going back to early childhood, often felt by them as depression. They have usually been overstimulated and then frustrated in some of their desires by a significant person in childhood.

Every culture has its methods of teaching its members to control the impulses of love, sex, and anger. It also arranges acceptable ways and means of expression, and has its ways of tolerating or disapproving compromise expressions. In Western culture the overcontrolled person is usually a cold, unloving individual, sometimes able to engage in sexual activities, but largely for his own pleasure rather than genuine concern for the mate. Likewise, the impulse-ridden person may feel that he can love, but it is a very egocentric kind of love which is really destructive of others. Over- or under-control of anger creates problems of adaptation in the individual and destructive behavior toward others. Anger, aggression, and hostility are among the crucial problems in many areas of our society. Various elements in our culture have ways of approving or disapproving either overcontrol or undercontrol. Sometimes the messages given by the Church on this theme are mixed and contradictory, as when people are taught to love in a "spiritual" sense but to avoid physical expressions of affection. Man loves as a whole being, or he does not love. It is fear and guilt which demand control; it is the demand for pleasure which requires impulsive satisfactions. Freedom of the human spirit within the Christian faith requires a spontaneity of warmth, tenderness, and intimacy within an appropriate context and within a commitment that recognizes the full personhood of the other.

In making an appraisal for pastoral therapy around the problem of control, some understanding of control or lack of it in relationship to the developmental process can be helpful. Erikson,[6] for example, places the major period for learning control in the second stage of ego development, and characterizes the basic conflict here as one between autonomy on the one hand and shame and doubt on the other. Success or failure at this stage depends on the level of trust or distrust experienced in the first stage, infancy. Autonomy cannot be developed on the foundation of anxiety or distrust. In the second stage, shame and doubt are experienced through those responsible for helping the child learn to control his bodily functions. In this stage also, autonomy — the ability of the child to learn to regulate his functions out of love for the mother and a desire to emulate the parents — is learned. In many cases, a measure of each is learned. Where doubt and shame seriously outweigh the freedom to be self-regulating within a context of security, psychological problems of control are likely to appear in adult life. This is a major factor in the later development of obsessive-compulsive pathology. The problem of control arises again in the next stage, where the basic conflict is described as one between initiative and guilt involving love and sexuality. This is the stage of increased sexual awareness, of clearer emotional delineation between male and female with hopefully appropriate identifications, of attraction to the parent of the opposite sex, and some degree of competitiveness with the parent of the same sex. Many of the feelings and attitudes which later lead either to fulfillment or to serious problems in marriage begin here, although some of them are brought into this stage from earlier stages. Persons who convert painful feelings into physical symptoms will be found to have had problems in this stage.

Understanding the problems of control of impulses in persons fitting into the various diagnostic categories can be helpful to the pastor. Obviously these problems cannot be thoroughly discussed here, and the thoughtful reader is referred elsewhere.[7] The obsessional-compulsive group has been mentioned, and a few comments should be added for illustrative purposes. These persons tend to inhibit severely the direct expression of needs or impulses, but find substitute outlets which are only partially satisfying. These people have a deep discontent but do not know why. They repress guilt feelings. Invariably they are possessed by a strong and rigid conscience. The ego has to deal with all of the prohibitions and controls of this conscience, but also find some level of satisfaction for the impulse. The ego has some strength, but cannot resolve the conflict between the desire for direct impulse expression and inhibition. In this situation the specific obsessive or compulsive symptom becomes the way of maintaining control, while at the same time allowing partial expression of the unacceptable impulse and a certain amount of self-punishment for the alleviation of guilt.

As an illustration, a certain young woman had an intense desire to kill the wife of her pastor. This was so strong that she studiously avoided the wife, even though this presented problems. She hotly denied any love or sexual feelings toward the pastor, but this denial was due to repression because of guilt. She was afraid of losing control of her impulses if she acknowledged them even to herself. She also had very angry feelings toward the wife which she could not acknowledge. Her strong, unreasonable desire to kill the woman was completely beyond her comprehension. Therapy gradually helped her to bring these feelings to the surface, and with them the discovery that she was reenacting childhood feelings toward her own mother and father. She was a meticulous, overly clean, overly conscientious person, and hence her obsession caused her no end of anxiety, which was the factor bringing her into treatment.

There is a somewhat different attempt to cope in the person who takes an hysterical reaction. In this individual the controls and repression are very strong, but the impulses against the controls are also strong. As with any neurotic person, the symptom becomes a disguised expression of the impulse so that there is some satisfaction, but it is also a form of self-punishment for the guilt involved in the impulse. The guilt-punishment mechanism is common in persons suffering from neurosis. Sometimes the self-punishment precedes the impulse expression, sometimes it follows and in other persons it will be simultaneous. These people also have ways of getting others to punish them, probably a technique they learned in childhood.

In the hysterical person, the impulses causing anxiety are those of love, sex and anger, with anxiety and guilt about these. The ego is not strong enough to completely control the drive. Repression has removed the impulses from the control of the conscious ego so that a sense of alienation from self is experienced. This means a lack of awareness of the internal conflict. Instead, there is an intense awareness of the symptom. It is as though the person is looking into a deep pool, but there is an opaque glass just under the surface through which he cannot see. His awareness of the symptom includes anxiety and suffering about it, which justifies his search for love in the form of attention and sympathy. These people frequent the office of the physician, pastor, and other helpers looking for some external remedy which will seem to excuse their ego from responsibility. In therapy they can be very demanding, and they try to set-up the therapeutic process so they are protected from pain of self-discovery. For this reason these unhealthy processes, along with other forms of defensive reactions, are both self-defeating and self-perpetuating.

In the initial interview these persons will make a strong bid for sympathy, while they carefully watch the therapist for positive or negative reactions. They may recite a long history of physical complaints, and of many visits to physicians with little positive results. These persons have a short fuse for certain kinds of situations, and can explode quickly and violently in anger, usually only verbally. If they have not had a medical examination recently, this should be insisted upon since defensive symptoms can become confused with real symptoms.

A young woman came to her pastor with a history of headaches going back to the age of six. She had had all sorts of physical studies, including neurological examinations. All were negative. She was an only child up to the age of six, when a brother was born. Her headaches began shortly after. She would complain bitterly about her long and continued suffering, but she also seemed indifferent to it. She did not want to give it up, but she felt she had suffered enough. The birth of her brother was only one factor in the creation of the symptom. A deeper factor was the kind of relationship she had with her parents, her desire to come between her parents and displace her mother in her father's affections. Since the pastor in this situation was trained to recognize symptoms of this kind but not to offer the depth of treatment demanded by this problem, he referred her to a psychotherapist.

Some persons come to the pastor suffering from phobias. There are many objects toward which people may develop an unrealistic and controlling fear. Whatever the object of the fear — an animal, the dark, going out on the street, or death, to mention only a few — there is a symbolic connection between that object and the impulse. The person is really afraid of the impulse, be it sexual, or anger, or something else, but he displaces his fear on an external object which also represents the wish. Thus, the object of the fear becomes a clue to the nature of the conflict, but the controls may be so strong that treatment becomes a long and difficult task. The phobia is a means of both impulse expression and control. The person may suffer from intense anxieties and may have his actions severely restricted. He may also use his phobias to control his family, or, if he is a strong leader, to control social, political, or religious groups. These persons never come into treatment, since they believe their fears are justified by conditions. Phobic persons often consult the pastor looking for easy and simple prescriptions for the cure of their anxieties. Some pastors fall under their control and try to give such solutions. Any mode of treatment dictated by the neurotic person will always be aimed at the perpetuation, not the removal of the symptom. These people really need their symptoms until they are able, with help, to work out the underlying problem.

A quite different group of persons who will consult the pastor are those who have lost control of impulse. With many the problem will be some form of impulsive sexual behavior, usually without guilt, but sometimes with the anxiety of getting caught. With others it will be the expression of some destructive impulse. Some of these people will be very passive and dependent, while others will react to an underlying passivity by being overly aggressive. Some will show very poor judgment and get themselves involved in all sorts of behavior with destructive results for themselves and others. Some of these persons are capable of only very superficial interpersonal relationships, but they are very smooth talkers and can seduce the pastor into sympathy or even approval when they do not need either. Sometimes the behavior of this group places them in the category of criminals. In all of them a sense of irresponsibility of various degrees will be observed.

In the process of evaluation the pastor will need to appraise the relative strength of the impulse being expressed and the ability of the person to control these impulses. He will need to appraise other qualities of the person, such as the capacity and desire for insight, the sincerity and depth of his desire to change his behavior, and the ability of the person to form the kind of relationship with another which is necessary for therapy.

On the question of impulse control, these persons use compromise for defense. They give up control of one impulse in order to control another which they perceive as more dangerous. Thus, a man may seduce women sexually in order to control an underlying and more frightening impulse to destroy or harm women. Or a person may engage in either sexual or hostile behavior in order to avoid experiencing a depression, or a sense of inadequacy or lack of love. Many persons talk about being very lonely, which indicates their own inability to form close human relationships. They are indeed lonely, but destructive behavior only alienates them further. The pastor will notice that such persons accept their behavior as belonging to them, as an expression of their ego, or, in more technical language, as ego-syntonic. This may make therapy difficult or impossible, since they may not want to change. They may only want to avoid getting caught. Some may seek therapy only out of a fear of being caught which might have disastrous results professionally or otherwise. There will be no real therapy unless the therapist helps the person to reject the problematic behavior, to experience it as undesirable rather than acceptable. There is also the need to evaluate the depth and strength of the underlying problem in relation to the individual's desire and strength to move into it therapeutically. Therapy for these persons may be a long process, and only pastors who are sufficiently trained should attempt it. Or a referral may be made to another therapist.

Depressed persons present a different problem in terms of pastoral evaluation. With these people impulses are controlled, but at the expense of great guilt and self-punishment. The conflict between impulses and a severely moralistic conscience is intense. The depressed person may speak of petty actions to which the guilt is attached, but this is the defensive maneuver known technically as displacement. The depressed person has the problem of control of hostile impulses. These impulses, originally directed toward persons for whom there is also love, are repressed and turned in against the self. It is as though the hated person is within the person, and is part of the self. But the ego is also trying to resolve the problem and get relief from the suffering. For this reason depressed people are often open to help through psychotherapy.

In making a pastoral evaluation, two kinds of depression must be kept in mind. These are the neurotic depression and the psychotic depression. Neurotic depressions, sometimes called reactive depressions, are a reaction to a real or fancied loss which greatly reduces the person's self-esteem. Psychotic depressions are the produce of inner pathological conditions and may be part of an illness such as manic depressive reaction or schizophrenia. The former responds much more readily to psychotherapy than the latter, which presents very difficult problems. As with all of the categories of personality disorder discussed in this section, the pastor needs to know a great deal more than can be presented in this volume.[7] The other side of the manic picture, the so-called manic phase, is rarely seen in pastoral therapy, since this person behaves as though his wishes were being gratified, and hence has a false sense of well-being. Here the controls have broken down to some extent. The pastor should know about these persons, since their tendency to be very active can be easily exploited in the work of the church to their harm, and also because they can become trouble-makers. They can be very difficult to handle administratively. Sometimes these people become supersalesmen.

Schizophrenic persons present a still different kind of problem in relation to control. Often they are sensitive, withdrawn persons seemingly naive but tending to confuse fantasy with reality, and often showing intense fear. They have a deep inability to trust, either others or themselves. They are deeply afraid of losing control of their impulses and feelings. They are very frightened of closeness or intimacy (hence the withdrawal), and to move toward them too rapidly or to offer them much intimacy may precipitate an anxiety reaction ranging from mild to panic intensity. This reaction is due to their fear of losing control, or to their fear of loving and being loved. Retreat into fantasy becomes a refuge for them because they can control their own fantasies, and hence it seems safe. If ego controls break down and a disturbance ensues, fantasies will then emerge in terms of ideas that cannot be logically understood. The language is deeply symbolic. Only pastors who have special training in the treatment of schizophrenics should work with them therapeutically.

A word is in order here about the pastoral evaluation of adolescents.[8] Often the problem of control is important, as youth may fear the loss of control of feelings and wishes that are emerging from within for the first time. Sometimes these young people behave as though they have no controls, when in fact they are quite rigidly controlled in ways not apparent to the casual observer. Some adolescents need help in loosening up some of their childhood controls so that ego growth is possible. Others need help in establishing some controls. Pastors who work with youth groups will readily observe these young people. But there is a real problem in the evaluation of adolescents. It is often difficult to distinguish between the adolescent who is experiencing the normal identity crisis and the one who is becoming schizophrenic.

Erik Erikson[9] insists that adolescence is not an affliction, but a normative crisis where there is increased conflict but high growth potential.

We have been saying that one question to be answered in the pastoral evaluation concerns the nature and extent of feelings and impulses. The pastor will make a mistake if he stops to give a lecture on this problem. He will therefore have to resist, except in those cases where this is a specific need, the tradition that the task of the pastor is to reinforce the conscience. There is usually rather the need to help people develop more mature consciences that do no harm either to themselves or their neighbor.

There is also a concern regarding the nature of the controls. There are controls that are congruent with the Christian faith and those that are incongruent. Some writers talk about this as the difference between ego-morality and superego-morality.[10] We think of it more in dynamic terms: the strength of the ego to make autonomous decisions and exercise autonomous control as over against the strength of unconscious aspects of the self bearing down on the ego, and exercising control through anxiety and guilt, and complicating it by self-punishing processes. The pastor will help each person evaluate his own feelings of guilt and anxiety, and discover the origins and the power of these in his life. Some people need help in developing a realistic guilt,[11] while others need help in alleviating excessive guilt. The pastor will examine deeply his own tendencies so that he does not seek to force others into his patterns or values—in other words, to control them. People may adopt his values, but this should be out of autonomous choice. The Christian conscience is one which at the minimum seeks no harm for itself or its neighbor, but at a higher level seeks positive good. It operates on the basis of the kind of love that seeks to bind persons together rather than separate them, a kind of love that with intelligence and imagination seeks genuinely human values. This is freedom from a legalistic conscience and freedom for creative human relationships.

OBJECT RELATIONS

The growth of personality is vitally related to the experience of receiving satisfaction from the external world for emotional hungers. On a primitive level, the need for food and the experience of being fed is a prototype for being fed on less physical and more spiritual levels. Those persons or things through which needs are satisfied are called objects; they are the objects of the drive for satisfaction. They include mainly other persons, but also objects such as the home, other institutions, the job, important ideas, and hobbies. Healthy object relations in infancy are primarily a matter of receiving satisfaction. In adult life, healthy object relationships require the ability to give as well as receive satisfactions. For example, parents are often called upon to give more than they receive from a child. At the same time they need a mutually satisfying relationship of giving and receiving from each other.

The beginning of object relationships is in infancy. The dependency and helplessness of the infant on a mothering person is fundamental. The needs of the infant for closeness, warmth, and security must be gratified along with the need for food. In early infancy there is a lack of differentiation between the self and others. Then the development of the sense of the self begins, and others are differentiated from the self. But the child has already felt the goodness or badness, or the mixture of his world. He develops feelings about the good self and the bad self, the good mother and the bad mother, on the basis of the quality of relationships, that have existed, along with his own fantasies.

Each stage of development makes its contribution to the process of object relationships. Patterns of seeking or giving (or the inability to ask or receive) become well established and persist into adult life. When these are pathological, it is the task of psychotherapy to seek to help the person modify them. For this reason the assessment of the person, in terms of his object relationships, is an important step in the beginning process.

The need to receive satisfactions for emotional drives is never outgrown. If the intensity of some needs is not modified, or the ability to give as well as receive is not developed, the person remains childish. The term *narcissism*[12] is often used to describe this; it is a level of self-love that uses others primarily or solely for self-gratification. There are persons who have learned to submit to the demands of others so thoroughly that they become willing partners in a childish relationship. The seeds of its own self-destruction are contained in this relationship, as is frequently seen in marriage therapy. Healthy object relationships at every stage are reciprocal. For example, a mother may feel intense satisfaction as her infant smiles at her and may respond with increased warmth. When such relationships are either neglected or overdone, the child's growth may become distorted, and he may expect similar relationships in his adult life. Unhealthy relationships may be reciprocal but may satisfy immature needs such as dominance, dependency or sado-masochism.

Various qualities of relationship[13] are derivatives of each stage of growth. To work this statement out in detail would require a book on psychopathology. In brief, the pastor needs to know the pathology as well as the healthy aspects of interpersonal relationships. Further, he needs to be sensitive to the manner in which a person uses objects or permits himself to be used by them.

Illustrative of the kind of object relations we have in mind are the need to control others or be controlled by them, or to relate to others without seeking to control or be controlled. The tendency to sexualize all relationships with the opposite sex, or to repress sexuality and seek only platonic relationships, or to use sexuality in mutually satisfying ways under appropriate conditions are other examples. Or there is the person who uses others to give him a sense of identity he has failed to achieve from within, or who operates on the need to rebel against others rather than working out conflicts in mutually satisfying ways. Others seek a sense of pseudointimacy to compensate for fears of real intimacy. These are only some of the possible descriptions of object relationships.

In healthy adult object relationships there is mutuality in the satisfaction of needs. There is give and take, an acceptance of responsibility and concern for others, a recognition of the individuality of others, and the ability to have positive feelings toward others which are appropriate. Others are allowed to have an identity of their own. The achievement of a solid identity is necessary in order to experience mutuality with others.

Becoming a mature person means outgrowing many of the childish ways of relating. The obstacle to this is that the childish ways give certain satisfactions that the person thinks will be lost if he changes. He cannot visualize what he would be like without them, and this is frightening. He needs living models of healthy adults to give him an image of what a person can be before he can achieve such a goal.

A crisis occurs when a significant person or object is lost. [14] The severity of the crisis may be an indication of the pathology of the relationship. There are also normal differences in intensity of reaction. The death of an aged parent, though difficult, is usually not as difficult as the loss of a child. The pastor is familiar with these circumstances, but he may not understand the psychological processes behind them. One avenue to understanding is to help the person explore, in a detailed manner, the nature of the emotional relationship with the lost one. Sometimes the threat of rejection is sufficient to set off a defensive reaction such as depression. Often the history of a person coming into therapy will reveal a recent loss that contributes to the present problem. Grief reactions may be delayed for years. For some the deprivation involved in a divorce or in the loss of a job presents severe crises. The work of mourning includes working through the shock and grief. New adaptations required by the loss must be made. If this grief work is not successful, some disturbance in interpersonal relationships will result.

There are some interpersonal relationships that predispose to object loss [15] because of the burden they entail. A woman whose relationship to her husband is largely a projection of ambivalent feelings toward her father is likely to place a burden on the husband emotionally. He will never know what to expect from her, and some of her actions will be highly contradictory. A person whose relationship is characterized by intense dependence may make the spouse feel smothered by demands. A person who projects his own self-image on another, and unconsciously seeks to love himself through the other, will eventually create severe tensions. Persons involved in a symbiotic relationship (where each gratifies deep needs in the other and also supports the immature patterns of adaptation and defenses of the other) will find the relationship potentially threatening because of the possibility of change of feelings. The other will then feel hurt, abandoned, and angry, and may have difficulty in finding a substitute object.

Ambivalent object relationships contain the seeds of dissolution. Persons who have had severe conflicts with parents in childhood, and who have strong images of "good" and "bad" parents,[16] may displace these feelings to another, a spouse for example. At times there will be a childish attempt to get or give a pampering kind of love, and later a response of intense hostility or provocation of hostility in the other in order to prove him bad. The spouse of the alcoholic often fits into this pattern. It should be emphasized that the motivation of these provocations is unconscious.

Sometimes object relationships are grounded on a vicarious experience in which a person seeks gratification of his own needs through another. A mother who is unable, because of her own anxieties, to accept an adult relationship with her husband may seek to live out her life through her child. It is impossible for the child to gratify all of the mother's needs. Such a relationship forces the child into either a dependent or a rebellious relationship. In either case, the mother's needs will not be satisfied and she will grow increasingly angry at the child and the father.

People always have some kind of object relationship with their bodies. Sometimes this is called the body image. We may deny the realistic importance of the body; we may overevaluate it; we may express our self-love or our self-destructiveness through it. Some may hide behind it, as do obese persons. Often women succumb to the pressures of advertising of cosmetics and clothing in the adornment of their bodies. Others reject this and make themselves up in a very unattractive manner. Some persons with an ambivalent attitude about themselves dress in a manner that makes a seductive appeal to the opposite sex, and become angry when there is a positive response.

The use of our bodies as a source of satisfaction of needs has numerous hazards. Through illness or injury our bodies may be weakened or deformed. A child crippled by disease may suffer from impaired ego development, that is, a deep sense of inferiority and dependence. A woman who loses a breast through surgery will experience this as emotionally traumatic. A man who prides himself for his physical stamina may feel a deep loss and become depressed as age depletes that strength. Some people become depressed at a gray hair or a wrinkle. The body, as an object, may suffer many changes and losses which place a demand on the ego for new adaptations.

An appraisal of object relationships is a very important part of therapy. The pastor needs to understand the difference between helping people become aware of their relationships and helping them change those relationships. The latter may be much more difficult. Awareness of the quality of a relationship is not sufficient to help people modify behavior when such behavior is grounded in intense childhood experiences. Some recently introduced methods of psychotherapy used by pastors aim only at awareness of relationships. Frequently such treatment is not beneficial, or may even harm the individual. While awareness of relationships is an essential part of the therapeutic process, there must also be an awareness and a working through of earlier experiences out of which the relationships grew.

The manner in which people respond to the pastor, either in general pastoral relationships or in the evaluative process, will provide clues for the understanding of their behavior. The pastor will have to use his judgment as to whether such relationships should be brought up and discussed in general pastoral relationships. Certainly discussion is mandatory in the therapy process.

There is another side. The pastor needs to be aware of the quality of relationships he forms with others, particularly persons seeking his help.[17] What kind of relationships are easy or difficult for him to handle? What are his blind spots? His need for closeness or distance, his need to provoke or avoid hostility, anxiety, or guilt in others, his need for vicarious emotional satisfaction, and other needs will interfere with the evaluative or therapy process. They may also handicap him in general pastoral relationships.

A healthy freedom to deal openly and tactfully with object relationships within the evaluative and therapy process is a requirement for the pastor. The aggressive or inhibited pastor will destroy the process or may harm the person. A tactful inquiry to the person, or a suggestion that he consider his interaction both to the person and to others, followed by further exploration can be helpful. Sometimes a therapeutic impasse will occur because the pastor fails to take initiative in inquiring about the nature of the interaction or fails to make an interpretation of behavior as he understands it.

The pastor needs to be aware of his own and others relationship to religious objects. For some pastors the church itself is an object of devotion, rather than a means through which people are served. This may occur when the pastor fears close personal relationships, and protects himself from others by emphasis on the organization. On the other hand, members of the parish may use the church in a similar fashion. They may, for example, give much time to church activities, thus avoiding close relationships within the family and within the church. The pastor may encourage this devotion while not realizing its deeper meaning.

The pastoral therapist must be concerned with the person's relationships to such religious objects[18] as God, Christ, religious beliefs, and the Bible. The meaning of these objects may stimulate questions in therapy or in various study groups. What kind of a relationship is desired with the object? What needs does the person seek to have met in this way? Are these needs actually satisfied, or is there a sense of frustration? How realistic are these needs, and the hope that they will be satisfied, or are they largely fantasy? Was the object satisfying on an earlier level of development, but not at present? What is the place of such defenses as

projection, identification, and displacement in relation to religious objects? Is there something about the relationship which
creates or releases guilt? Is the relationship to religious objects
characterized by mature or immature attitudes? Does the relationship promote, interfere with, or preclude closer human relationships? Does the person's devotion to religious objects make
him a better person, able to show more love and warmth to
others, able to produce the "fruits of the Spirit" (Gal. 5:22)? The
parables of Jesus contain many descriptions of both creative and
destructive object relationships. In the evaluative interviews the
pastor should seek information that enables him to make some
assessment of the person and the way he relates to religious
objects. If the pastor is observant he will be aware of these
factors in the behavior of many persons within the usual church
activities.

TIME DIMENSIONS

We move now to another aspect of pastoral evaluation. Life
has always had three time dimensions in the view of the Biblical
faith: past, present, and future. The existential psychotherapists
also make use of these categories, as do other forms of psychotherapy such as the psychoanalytic. For the psychoanalytic ego
therapist, such as Erik Erikson, all three are very important.
Other therapists have tended to stress the here and now to the
more or less complete rejection of past and future.[19]

Pastoral diagnosis or evaluation, since it is seeking to understand the whole person in his total environment with stress on the
functioning of the conscious ego processes, must take account of
the person's previous experience. This means some attention to
history as part of the evaluative process. History is a process of
individual experience within groups, such as the family, through
which there are many transactions that change both the individual and the group. History is grounded in biological processes, it
takes place through psychological and social processes, and its
real goal should be the development of the individual through the

assimilation of the values and the spirit of the group. That individual development is often distorted through harmful group processes and relationships is common knowledge. Indeed, out of this distortion comes the problems with which we deal in psychotherapy, as well as in other forms of healing. Pastoral evaluation, therefore, has to ask where the individual began, what he has been through and how he has responded to whatever his history offered him.

From the point of view of the individual, two processes are involved in the power of historical experiences in personal development. One is the development of recurring and self-perpetuating patterns and attitudes that go into the formation of personality. The other is the process of memory.

It is easy to oversimplify the question of personality development, and there is much that is not known about it. A sound theory is essential to good psychotherapy, but it must be flexible enough to change with new factual data. Study in this area is essential to the pastoral psychotherapist, indeed to the general pastor. The point to be stressed here is the cause and effect influences in personality growth, either toward health or illness. It is not only true that what a man sows, that also shall he reap; it is true as well that what is sown in a child, perhaps even before birth but certainly in infancy and thereafter, that shall he also reap. Psychotic or neurotic conditions do not blossom full blown in adolescence or sometime after. They have their origins in processes that begin in early infancy or by the time the child is six years of age. These processes are built into the personality with a rigidity that makes change difficult or, in some cases, impossible.

The idea that personality patterns and attitudes form a structure that can be relied upon brings anxiety to many persons who fail to see that this operates quite as much in the development of strong, healthy persons as in the unhealthy. Often this anxiety leads to a reassertion of the principle of freedom within the Christian faith, and the rejection of a causal process. This is a mistaken response. Actually we are dealing with two sides of a paradoxical condition within persons. Many personality patterns are developed through causal processes. In this, however, the organism has a choice or is in itself a determining factor. It is this ability to determine its own responses that constitutes its freedom or autonomy. It has functions which are autonomous, or self-determining. These are ego functions. This autonomy can be exercised (1) to discover the influences of past experience on present behavior; (2) to evaluate these influences in terms of their consequences for present and future relationships; and (3) to decide what to retain and what to give up. The more unhealthy a person, the more he is determined by external influences. The healthy adult has achieved a high level of autonomy. He has found freedom from controlling feelings and responses, and has learned to determine his own responses. Most forms of psychotherapy are predicated on the assumption that the person has at least enough autonomy to come for help, to cooperate in the initial stages of therapy, and to move toward an increase of autonomy.[20] Such increase of autonomy should be one of the goals of pastoral psychotherapy.

One reason some workers react against any emphasis on the history of the individual is that they have discovered that this is used sometimes to rationalize, and hence to justify, a present condition. "I am the way my parents made me, so there is nothing I can do about it." But this needs to be dealt with as a defense against change rather than a reason for denying the power of history.

To be alienated from one's history,[21] to feel cut off from a personal past, or to deny the one and only historical life process one has experienced, is to be cut off from the roots of one's personal identity. Identities that seem to spring out of the present, without roots in the past, are shallow and distorted. They cannot lead to real fulfillment, but only to regression and sickness. Such persons are like trees that have been submerged in water with only a few leaves showing; they soon disintegrate. Whatever the one historical process through which a person has come into youth or adulthood, healthy maturity requires that it be understood and accepted in both its strengths and its weaknesses, that its strengths be fulfilled and increased, and that its weaknesses be forgiven and overcome. The religious tradition through which a person has come is part of his total history. This also needs to be understood, accepted, and brought to fruition. The person who denies and rebels against any aspect of his history and refuses to come to terms with it will have identity problems, quite as much as the person who clings to outworn forms and practices of his past. In any assimilation of our historical-cultural experiences, it is the spirit and values of our past which are important, not its forms and practices.

The psychological process which binds us to our past is memory. Memory is an ego process and the way in which it is used or misused is one indication of ego strength. A person's earliest memories are usually significant, as they indicate something about his object relationships. The quality and dynamics of memory reflect the life style and emotional responses of the person. We often remember what we wish to remember, and forget what we wish to forget, or distort memory with fantasy of what we would have liked. The person who plunges into childhood memories with many details, but with no emotional value to the material is obviously repressing strong feelings and isolating intellect from feeling. The person who cannot remember periods of his life, who for example has no memories before eight years of age, or who blocks out memories between six and ten years, is unconsciously avoiding something painful. The person who remembers only painful experiences or who remembers something painful but overstresses its value, is using this to repress some more painful memories. These are known in the psychotherapeutic literature as "screen memories," since they screen out important material. The person who cannot remember much good about his past, but only experiences that create anger, may need to deny the love of his parents in order to justify his anger toward them. A person who permits himself to become obsessed with petty memories that seem to cause him pain far beyond their real significance is using this device to punish himself for guilt about something he does not want to remember. The kind of memory that is significant for the therapy process is not merely an intellectual recalling. It is rather a re-experiencing where the person re-lives the experience as though it were happening now. The past becomes present in consciousness. Some persons have the strength to do this early in the process, while with others it takes a much longer time and is a very gradual process.

Without excluding other time dimensions, pastoral evaluation should take into account the ways in which a person has taken his past into himself, the qualities of important figures in his past which he has introjected or incorporated into himself, the kind of responses he learned to make and still makes, the content of his memories, and the way he uses his memories. Evaluation is for the purpose of assessing the relation of present problems to past experiences and relationships, deciding what needs to be worked with and what should not be dealt with in the therapy, and the relation of the therapeutic skills and training of the pastor to the therapeutic task.

We turn now to a consideration of the time dimension of the present in pastoral evaluation. The questions here are: How has the person put it all together? What is he like now? How does he see himself now? What does he want from the therapist now? Why is he coming now for help to this particular therapist?

Religion and pastoral psychotherapy is concerned with wholeness. Many persons think of religion and the concerns of the pastor from a very limited understanding. Religion concerns ethical standards, they say, or a set of beliefs or "loving your fellow men" in a vague sort of way. It is none of these, yet all of these and much more. The much more is significant. Religion in the Biblical sense is concerned with the wholeness of life, not only man and his inner being but man in relation to his world and to God. Actually nothing is foreign to the Biblical faith. The pastor, therefore, must consider all aspects of the person. To do this he must often seek information from other helpers, such as a physician who works with some partial aspect of the whole man. He seeks this information with the permission of the person. Asking for such permission builds up a kind of confidence. It tells the

person that the pastor is not leaving anything out of consideration. The pastor will need the training and experience necessary
to evaluate the data in terms of the whole person, or to rely on
the opinion of someone more expert.

To illustrate: A man in his twenties consulted a pastor about his
dissatisfaction with the church and with religion. He was obviously
angry. But about what? Some of this anger turned out to be
residual from his relationships with his parents in childhood. Some
of it was attached to a lameness resulting from polio as a child. He
deeply resented his handicap and the fact that he could not be like
other boys. He turned much of his anger toward religion, the
church, and God. But much of his anger was displaced from his
parents to his polio. It was much safer to hate his lameness than
to hate his parents. And he could hate God — God was a long way
off, and God had come to represent the evil this man hated.

Data from memories of other aspects of a person's experiences
and relationships must likewise be considered. This would include
memories of the person's social and cultural relationships, from
the educational, sexual, and vocational areas and others.

Without minimizing the importance of transactional processes,
there is a danger of falling into a certain trap. The fallacy begins
by using an oversimplified cause and effect concept that asks
what the effect of the polio was on this boy's personality. If the
pastor is concerned with the inner life of persons, there is a more
important question: What did the boy do with his experience of
polio? What in terms of feelings and attitudes toward himself,
others, and life did he bring to the experience, and how did he
respond to it? For pastoral evaluation and therapy, emphasis
must be placed on the reality of the intrapsychic processes. The
intrapsychic reality not only is influenced by external conditions
and relationships, it influences these and often creates them
unknowingly. Many spouses project bad feelings on the other,
and then are in a position to blame the other for the problems in
the marriage. No matter what happens to us, our responses are to
a large degree determined by our own intrapsychic processes,
including memory, and wholeness requires that each person take
responsibility for these.

Another aspect of this is important for the pastoral evaluation. Experiences from any part of our external world translate themselves into the intrapsychic world in terms of gratification or frustration. Conflict will develop within the person if gratification is excessive or frustration too severe and without compensation. Overgratification of the need for love can produce as much guilt or anxiety as undergratification. Some persons want love very much, but are so afraid of it that they create relationships in which they do not receive it. They can then blame the other person for being unloving, while at the same time they feel relieved that they do not have to cope with a feared gratification. In pastoral evaluation the manner in which material from the external world is taken in and translated into gratification or frustration, into pleasure or conflict, into good or bad, is important. The questions have to be asked as to how the person has dealt with the conflict, what defense processes he has used, how he has coped with his problem, and how this has led him to perceive his world and make it what he needs to have it. This is all involved in trying to arrive at an estimate of how the person has put his life together. Neurotic conflict is a disturbance of the basic drive of the organism toward wholeness. Anxiety is an indicator of the conflict and not the conflict itself. It is important to estimate the level of the anxiety in order to gauge the intensity of the conflict. One importance of the history is that it will give some clues as to the nature and developmental level of the origin of the conflict, and assist the therapist in making his evaluation.

There are other clues to the inner life of the person, and the way he has put his experience together. One of these is the nature of his fantasy life, which often can be elicited by asking about his daydreams. Refusal to reveal at least some of these may be an evaluative clue also. Is the reluctance the result of lack of confidence in the therapist, or is it the result of extreme sensitivity and the inability to reveal? The kind of novels or movies an individual likes can also be a clue to his fantasy life. In addition, what he thinks of himself and how he feels about himself should not be neglected. Congruence or conflict in his feelings about himself should be noted. How has the person resolved his identity problems? Has he been able to accept his biological nature as a part of his identity? If a woman, does she accept or reject her femininity; if a man, his masculinity? The behavior of a person in the interview should be noted and included in the evaluation. The manner in which the person makes decisions, especially the decision about therapy, is important. The person who can take the initiative and indicate that he wants help is much stronger than the person who wants the therapist to make the decision for him. Before they can become good subjects for therapy, many persons have to be helped to move from the "it happens to me" attitude to acceptance of the fact that they are doing something to hurt themselves. A young woman who complains that "nothing ever happens" may be saying that she does not expect anything to happen in therapy, or that she does not want anything to happen to change things, or that she desperately wants something to happen, is scared it will, and is warning the therapist not to let it happen.

Religious faith and human experience is oriented toward the future. The quality of this orientation is either hope or fear. These hopes and fears have found various symbolic formulations. Depressed persons cannot hope, and they will seize upon various religious formulations, such as "the wrath of God," to express their experience. Other persons will have fantastic expressions of hope, such as "mansions in the sky." With these persons it is as though all needs are satisfied, and they will not seek help. Depressed persons will come since they want relief from pain. Others will come who have realistic hopes, that is, to resolve painful conflicts and find some satisfactions. Real hope grows out of the experience of finding sufficient satisfaction today to give assurance of satisfaction tomorrow.

Hope[22] then becomes an ingredient in pastoral evaluation for therapy. Real hope is grounded in the belief that realistic needs can be satisfied, that change is possible and desirable. Fantasy hope is grounded in immature wishes untempered by an understanding and acceptance of realities, immediate or ultimate. The nature of a person's hope can be an indication of the nature of the therapy he seeks, and where the therapy has to begin.

Real hope does not deny the destructive element in life. In life and in therapy self-destruction is often a crucial problem. Here a task in therapy is to help the individual to renounce his infantile desires and accept more realistic goals and values. Individuals whose hopes grow out of fantasy usually deny the destructive element in their experience and want some kind of magic answer. Hope that does not take into account and deal realistically with adverse and destructive elements in human experience is not genuine hope. How a person deals with his anger, hostility, and destructiveness is vital to any real assessment for therapy.

Hope is essential in the attitude of the pastor. The person will sense any hopelessness in the pastor, and also any superficial or false hope. Realistically based hope may not be as effectively communicated verbally as nonverbally, by helping the person discover such goals and also the denied or latent resources within him that can be put to use in reaching them.

There are two poles to realistically based hope. One is long-range, the ultimate possibility. The other is an immediate next step. Any distant goal is achieved by many shorter steps. For example, the complete remaking of the personality is a very long-range goal, if indeed a possibility. Helping a person grow by removing the emotional blocks to growth may be more realistic, but this will involve immediate steps. If the pastor settles on goals in a rigid manner, he will block the person. It is well for him to have goals in mind, but he must also sense the goals the person has set for himself, sometimes unconsciously, and must deal with them. Unrealistic goals are an expression of inner dynamics which become a therapeutic problem. Sometimes an impasse occurs in therapy because pastor and person are locked in a conflict concerning goals of treatment, or they are unconsciously in collusion about nontherapeutic goals.

Hope then needs to be translated into goals that take into full account the dynamics of the person, the extent and strength of his defenses, the areas in which adaptation is a problem, and realistic steps toward a more satisfying adaptation. Resistances must be seen as aspects of the person that are not in complete harmony with the goals, and must be dealt with as they arise. For example, a depressed person may want to overcome the depression but may not want to give up the unconscious purposes (controlling the family, for example) for which the depression is used.

Hope must be realistic in the sense of time. How long is the future? Of course, no one knows. The time required for persons to grow and change varies, and depends on what kind of changes are envisioned. Can the pastor show the patience that is born of hope, and can he realistically give the time? Under time pressure he may push too hard and destroy the therapy. Or he may waste time—for example, by not recognizing and dealing with an impasse or by not helping the person focus his communications on therapeutic issues. Somewhere there is a fine line between moving too rapidly and marking time, and this will differ from person to person. It is the task of the pastor to find that line in each relationship. This is why short-term therapy should not be defined so much in terms of a given number of sessions as in terms of the hopes of the person, the resistances against these hopes, and the pace of the movement. These judgments are part of the assessment or evaluation process. Rather than put a person under more pressure than he can handle, it is better to make a referral.[23] However, the manner of the referral should express hope, not hopelessness!

In summary, the present and future time dimensions involve how the person has put his life together, what kind of an inner life he has developed for himself and what kinds of hopes, expectations, and goals he has set for his future. The time dimension is not only a matter of deviation or of the calendar. It is a matter of the quality or meaning of that duration—what quality has been experienced, what quality is now experienced and what is hoped for. These enter into the nature of the organic wholeness a person has created for himself, the level of his developmental attainment, and his success or failure in differentiating himself from others and arriving at a viable sense of personal identity. The pastor will see many who are weak in one or more of these areas, whose wholeness is threatened by conflict, who face adult responsibilities with immature development, and whose relationship with others results in identity confilct. The pastoral therapist will make some estimate of the extent of these and of the intensity of suffering and defenses the person is experiencing.

MOTIVATION FOR THERAPY

This brings us to the important issue of motivation for therapy. Why is the person coming to this particular pastor at this time? What are his hopes and expectations, and how does he want the pastor to deal with these? How has he dealt with his pain in the past, and how is he likely to conitnue to deal with it in the therapeutic relationship? What kind of future does he hope for, and how is it to come about?

Sandor Rado[24] has developed some interesting formulations concerning motivation in psychoanalysis which are important also in pastoral care and psychotherapy. He relates motivation to developmental stages. The most primitive motivation is that of craving for magic solutions, representing early infancy. The pastor must do everything that the person desires, and he must do it by magic. This motivation involves deep dependency, omnipotence, and the need to control. The person feels helpless and tries to balance this with the feeling that he can control the forces of life through the magic of the pastor.

In addition to understanding this motivation in the person, the pastoral therapist must understand how this relates to his own inner dynamics. Highly intellectual and theologically sophisticated religion is often a mask for a strong need to give magical answers. Some pastors have not worked through their own desire to be omnipotent. This can be something of a vocational hazard in the ministry. The pastor may be motivated by a feeling of guilt lest he disappoint the person's expectations. He may feel that he must give the kind of help that is asked. He may also feel a strong need to be a popular dispenser of help; if so, he is likely to have certain magical formulae for use in every situation.

On a level of development above the magical, Dr. Rado finds a motivation of infantile dependence on parental figures. In infancy, mother realistically did a great deal for the person that he could not do for himself. Now he feels helpless and expects the therapist to do what he needs, not magically, but realistically in terms of the therapist's competence. He is in the stage of being led by the hand, not walking by himself. He has great dependency needs and a weak sense of responsibility or initiative.

Likewise, this may find in the pastor a need to have people dependent on him, to show his power, his superiority, to be parent to a child. If he has been trained in some of the manipulative therapies, he will find such persons eager subjects. But the dependency will not be outgrown, and though some symptoms may be changed, the person will not experience healthy growth into self-reliant responsibility.

The third level of motivation described by Dr. Rado, still higher on the developmental scale, is that of self-reliant cooperation. This person wants to learn how to help himself and will use the pastor to this end. This is an adult level of adaptation, and places the relationship on a realistic basis from the beginning. The mature pastor will welcome this kind of person as one with whom he can work and help. An immature pastor may find this kind of self-reliance a threat to his own omnipotence and his need for having others dependent on him.

The fourth level distinguished by Dr. Rado is the person who wants to learn and to make full use of his potential for growth. In the matter of potential it is evident that not all are born equal, so no absolute standard of growth can be applied to all. It is much more a matter of individual appraisal by the person himself with the help of the pastor separating unrealistic from realistic elements in the self-concept.

It is necessary to help persons achieve at least the third level of motivation before any real therapy can begin. If, with persons on the first two levels, help is given in terms of their expectations, some superficial adjustments may be made. But there will be little or no growth, and the person will require continued dependent support from the pastor. In some situations this is the best that can be hoped for. A skillful pastor can help some of these persons outgrow their dependency and move to a more self-reliant stance. This may take time, and will be done only through skillful interpretative processes. Noninterpretative therapies, such as a strict person-centered approach will be of little help here. Persons on the fourth level may find some growth regardless of the limitations of a given therapeutic approach. Uncritical therapists often accept this as evidence that their approach works with everyone.

In dealing with problems of motivation, there needs to be a full discussion and acceptance of the person's negative feelings about therapy and the therapist. This needs to be done with understanding. Interpretations of motivation can be done successfully only after a sufficiently strong relationship has been established. If the pastor falls into the trap of gratifying the person's immature motivations in the evaluative process, he may find it very difficult to move him away from these later. In this sense therapy begins with evaluation.

The pastor guards against any personal need to "sell" therapy, or to persuade or seduce another into therapy. His approach should be from the perspective of the person, where the person sees his problems and pains, the practical consequences of the problems, and how therapy may benefit the person. However, no promises should be made, as they may be defeated by the person. With the acceptance of negative feelings, there should be an attempt to deal with whatever is behind them. Some forms of therapy stop short of this. Misconceptions about therapy should be clarified, and strict honesty should prevail. The therapist should consider what is involved in accepting the person on whatever level of motivation he happens to bring, and work toward a more mature level. For example, a student may be referred by the dean, or a spouse may come because the other spouse requests it. The task of the pastor in the evaluative process is to begin to help the person move to a more responsible level of motivation in terms of his own needs. This may not always succeed, but must succeed if therapy is to take place.

Traditionally, the goal of psychotherapy has been that of helping the individual with his own problems and not trying to change his environment. His relationships with his environment, including other persons, has been considered to be his problem to be dealt with in his own way. There have been some exceptions to this. For years child guidance clinics insisted on treating the parents along with the child, but in separate processes. This has emerged today into family therapy where the entire family is seen together, and guilt is removed from one member as the identified patient. Many pastors and social workers have also tried to help individuals by manipulating their environment, for instance, by placing a child in a foster home or urging a divorce. Institutionalization is another form of environmental treatment. Environmental treatment in pastoral therapy should be highly selective, and perhaps referred to a social agency. The pastor should be careful recommending it for reasons of his own, such as a feeling of inadequacy. With some persons it is necessary.

In recent years another kind of environmental manipulation has been adopted by some psychotherapists, including pastors. This has picked up the emphasis on social action and reform, and some therapists have openly encouraged their people to work for various kinds of social action. A clear expression of this approach is to be found in Seymour Halleck's work.[25] Obviously, it is an approach suitable for only certain kinds of therapists and people. The pastor will have to decide for himself whether or not this is a suitable goal for him in his particular setting.

It should be part of the self-discipline of the pastoral psychotherapist to write out some kind of an evaluative summary and statement in concluding his assessment and in making his decision for future contacts with a person. The value of writing this out is that it gives an opportunity to collect and organize the data, to study it carefully, and to arrive at carefully considered judgments. Otherwise his work may be slipshod and his judgments based more on feeling responses rather than on a careful consideration of the facts. Feeling responses are part of the evaluative process, but careful consideration of the factual data offers a balance to what might be purely subjective judgments. Certainly written analyses and conclusions should be part of the records of any pastoral therapy center.

The criteria discussed in this chapter represent functions of the ego or self. As already indicated, there is still an important question to be considered. "How has the person put it all together?" This expresses concern for the whole person, the "psyche" of the New Testament. It is essential for the pastor to keep this in mind. Otherwise he may get so involved with one aspect that the whole person is lost. This is the hazard of the specialist. This question also involves the positive growing aspects of the person; it concerns ways in which the person has organized himself, his aspirations, values, and goals, as well as negative factors. It will include the nature of his commitments. It should help a person evaluate himself and discover some of his own needs.

In the next chapter we shall discuss therapy as a process.

NOTES

1. Gordon Allport, *Pattern and Growth in Personality,* New York: Holt, Rinehart and Winston, 1961; Gordon Allport, *Personality and Social Encounter,* Boston: Beacon Press, 1960; Leopold Bellak and Leonard Small, *Emergency Psychotherapy and Brief Psychotherapy,* New York: Grune and Stratton, 1965; Gertrude and Rubin Blanck, *Ego Psychology: The Theory and Practice,* New York: Columbia University Press, 1974; Heinz Hartmann, *Essays on Ego Psychology,* New York: International Universities Press, 1964; Emanuel F. Hammer, *Use of Interpretation in Treatment,* New York: Grune and Stratton, 1968, Ch. 11.The works of Erik Erikson should be consulted on the subject of ego psychology. They all deal with this problem. In addition see Edgar Draper, *Psychiatry and Pastoral Care,* Englewood Cliffs, N.J.: Prentice-Hall, 1965.

2. H. A. Witkin et al., *Personality through Perception,* New York: Harper and Row, 1954.

3. See chapter 7 on countertransference.

4. An excellent example of the mystic's perception of integration with God and self is Nikos Kazantzakis's portrayal of Francis of Assisi (*Saint Francis,*

New York: Simon and Schuster, 1962). See also Herbert Fingarette, *The Self in Transformation,* New York: Basic Books, 1963.

5. The theological term is *kenosis* (Phil. 2:7).

6. Erik Erikson, *Childhood and Society,* rev. ed., New York: W. W. Norton, 1963.

7. The books already referred to in the first reference in this chapter, as well as others.

8. Pastoral evaluation of adolescents cannot be done adequately if the family is excluded. Interpersonal and transactional relationships within the family can best be understood through sessions with the entire family, as in family therapy. Working with families has been one traditional approach of the pastor, and training in family therapy can be of great value to him. The following books may be helpful on this and on evaluation of adolescents in general. See John E. Meeks, *The Fragile Alliance,* Baltimore: Williams and Wilkins, 1971; Sherman C. Feinstein, Peter L. Giovacchini, and Arthur Miller, eds., *Adolescent Psychiatry,* New York: Basic Books, 1971; Committee on the Family of the Group for the Advancement of Psychiatry, *Treatment of Families in Conflict,* New York: Jason Aronson, 1970; John Spiegel, *Transactions: The Interplay Between Individual, Family and Society,* ed. John Papajohn, New York: Jason Aronson, 1971; Nathan W. Ackerman, *The Psychodynamics of Family Life,* New York: Basic Books, 1958.

9. Erik Erikson, Identity and the Life Cycle, *Psychological Issues,* Vol. 1, No. 1, 1959, p. 116.

10. E. Mansel Pattison, Clinical Psychiatry and Religion, *International Psychiatry Clinics,* Vol. 5, No. 4, Boston: Little, Brown, 1969, pp. 93–117.

11. Howard J. Clinebell, *Basic Types of Pastoral Counseling,* Nashville: Abingdon Press, 1966, pp. 224–242. It is unfortunate that Dr. Clinebell associates guilt with the confrontational type of therapy. This confuses the issue of the use of confrontation and also seems to imply that guilt must be handled by confrontation. The therapeutic problem in the case material given here is really that of resistance.

12. See previous references on narcissism, chapter 2.

13. Harry Guntrip, *Personality Structure and Human Interaction,* New York: International Universities Press, 1961; Harry Guntrip, *Schizoid Phenomena, Object Relations and the Self,* New York: International Universities Press, 1969.

14. George L. Engel, *Psychological Development in Health and Disease,* Ch. 26, Philadelphia: W. B. Saunders, 1966; Gregory Rochlin, *Griefs and Discontents,* Boston: Little, Brown, 1965; Sidney Levin and Ralph J. Kahana, eds., *Psychodynamic Studies on Aging,* New York: International Universities Press, 1967; Foundation of Thanatology, *Bereavement and Illness: Selected Readings,* New York: Health Science Publishing, 1973.

15. George L. Engel, op. cit., Ch. 27.

16. E. James Anthony and Therese Benedek, eds., *Parenthood,* Boston: Little, Brown, 1970.

17. Chapter 7.

18. See chapter 3.

19. Rollo May, Ernest Angel, and Henri F. Ellenberger, eds., *Existence,* New York: Basic Books, 1958; Karl Menninger, *The Vital Balance,* New York: Viking Press, 1963; Joan Fagan and Irma Lee Shepherd, *Gestalt Therapy Now,* Palo Alto: Science and Behavior Books, 1970; F. S. Perls, *Ego, Hunger and Aggression,* New York: Random House, 1969. The references in an earlier chapter to the work of Erik Erikson should also be consulted.

20. Andras Angyal, *Neurosis and Treatment,* New York: John Wiley, 1965.

21. Chapters 3, 4 and 5 of Erik Erikson's *Insight and Responsibility* (New York: W. W. Norton, 1964) are especially pertinent here.

22. Karl Menninger, *Theory of Psychoanalytic Technique.* New York: Basic Books, 1958; Ezra Stotland, *The Psychology of Hope,* San Francisco: Jossey-Bass, 1969.

23. William B. Oglesby, Jr., *Referral in Pastoral Counseling,* Philadelphia: Fortress Press, 1969.

24. Sandor Rado, "Relationship of Short-term Psychotherapy to Developmental Stages of Maturation and Stages of Treatment Behavior," in *Short-term Psychotherapy,* ed. L. R. Wolberg, New York: Grune and Stratton, 1967, pp. 67–83.

27. Seymour L. Halleck, *The Politics of Therapy,* New York: Jason Aronson, 1971.

Chapter 6

The Process of
Pastoral Psychotherapy

PROCESS AND CONTENT IN PASTORAL THERAPY

Pastoral psychotherapy, like any psychotherapy, may be viewed from the perspectives of relationship, process and content. In the past, greater emphasis was placed on content. Recently the emphasis has shifted to process, to what is going on within the person, within the therapist, and the dynamic interactions and transactions between therapist and person. In this chapter we shall deal primarily with process, but also somewhat with content. In the next we shall deal with problems of relationship.

Psychotherapy is an intervention in the life processes of an individual for the purpose of resolving inner conflict and promoting growth. The experience of fixation is central in this concept; that is, the idea that emotional conflicts block the normal growth of the personality and skews it in ways that distort processes of maturation and adaptation.

Therapy is frequently confused with other experiences that promote growth. A genuinely loving experience within the family, or a deeply accepting experience within the church, for example, may stimulate personal growth in those areas in which there is not a severe conflict. An analogy may be seen in the building which has beautiful architectural lines on three sides, but on the fourth side it is a hodgepodge of distortion and weakness.

An all too frequent observation has been the student who in theological[1] school showed signs of handicapping conflict but who relied on experiences within the family, within his profession, and within other relationships to produce growth, feeling that the conflicts and neurotic tendencies needed no attention. Then after fifteen or twenty years in the ministry the weakness in his personality shows up in terms of crippling depression or other neurotic behavior that severely handicaps him. Often the religious conversion process has been used in an attempt to resolve conflict. Our observation has been that very frequently it has resolved nothing, but has given the individual a new direction in which various aspects of the conflict can be worked out in activity. This can have unfortunate results. In other persons some growth is necessary before they find strength to deal with their conflicts. Still others are unable to utilize growth experiences because their conflicts and defenses prevent them from utilizing positive aspects of human relationships or psychotherapy.

We use the word *content* to indicate the facts and intellectual interpretation of those facts which are part of the communication process. "My mother was a wonderful woman," is content. If the therapist replies, "What did you find wonderful about her?" it is still content. However, underneath the words the therapist may detect a defensive attitude on the part of the person. He may need to idealize his mother to defend himself against his anger toward her. This is process. At the same time the person may need to defend himself against angry feelings he may have toward the therapist, and say, "You are really the greatest." In general pastoral care, many such compliments come to some pastors. Some encourage compliments. This is process. Underneath all verbal content communications, the life processes that make up the character of the person, the therapist, and their interactions find expression. This may be largely unconscious to the person, but the therapist must become aware of it and help the person to become aware of it. The task of the pastor is to sense what is going on in the interchange between himself and the person, and know when it is time to do something about it.

Process has to do with the immediate interaction or transactions between person and pastor, and it is a two-way street. The pastor should ask himself what is happening within the person, within himself, and between them. What process underlies the person's communications? the pastor's communications?

Another way of saying this is that the focus of attention should be on what is happening now in the therapy room. Perhaps the person is talking about his relationships with his mother when he was a child. What is behind this? Is it a serious attempt to understand this relationship, and how he has responded to it? Is he placing the blame for his present plight on his mother, and seeking to avoid responsibility? Is he talking about his mother because it is comparatively easy, but using this to avoid some more painful material? Is he telling the pastor that he must be a different kind of a "mother" to him, or the same kind? What happens if the pastor brings the discussion back to the present situation by asking what bearing the relation of the person to his mother has to present problems? Does the person avoid this by intellectualizing, by changing the subject, by ignoring the question, or by some other subterfuge? The character responses of the person will be manifest here, and they are a determining factor in therapy process.

Many other such illustrations could be given. The point is that underneath the content of verbal communications a process is taking place which expresses the dynamics that create the problem or symptoms for which the person seeks therapy. With proper timing, understanding, and skill the pastor must help the person discover these. In other words, in the therapy hour the person reveals the basic life processes, interactions and transactions,[2] conflicts, feelings, and defenses that create the problem which brings him to therapy. These should be the focal point of the pastor's attention and response.

TRUSTWORTHINESS OF THE PASTOR

Beginning with the first contact,[3] whether this be in the church, in an office, in the hospital, over the phone, or elsewhere, the initial issue is the ability of the pastor to communicate that he is trustworthy and the ability of the person to respond with enough trust to get the process off the ground. Lack of genuine trust on either side leads to a block in the developing process, or a kind of manipulation which is designed to preserve a sense of pseudo-security. It is as though the person is saying, If I can control you I will not need to be afraid of you. In such a process there will be no therapy.

The pastor in the parish has many contacts through which either trust or mistrust is developed. The manner in which he relates to his people in times of crisis, such as bereavement, or his attitude in the pulpit or in conducting the liturgy, his way of handling various administrative situations, and his casual contacts may inspire a sense of trust which gives the therapy relationship an excellent basis. Or the opposite may be true. This situation may be a source of anxiety or a creative opportunity for the pastor.

The pastor who works in a setting where the therapy relationship may be the first and only contact will have a different problem. A person who is referred to him may bring a measure of trust from the referring person. For some persons, the role of the pastor and what it symbolizes inspires trust. Some will be more cautious and will need several sessions in order to develop trust in the pastor and in the process. Others will not develop the necessary trust.

Trust means that the person feels secure in the relationship, believes he will not be hurt as others may have hurt him in the past, and is ready and able to work within the relationship. For the pastor to be trustworthy means that he is able to make real in the relationship the basic assumptions of his faith in regard to persons, particularly that the basic processes of life are trust-worthy and that man is endowed with a margin of freedom along with those dimensions of life in which he is determined. Without a measure of faith, there can be no pastoral therapy. In addition to this, the communications of the pastor must be of such a quality that they instill trust in him as a person. This includes both process and content of communications.

The pastor will have to sense when the question of trust needs to be brought out in the open and discussed in the initial interviews. Some persons find it very difficult to trust because they were not able to learn this in their early experiences of being mothered. Other persons are able to trust, and no discussion of the experience is needed. Others will be unable to trust enough to get the process of therapy off the ground until the issue is discussed. The slowness with which some persons develop sufficient trust to permit the process to move forward is one reason why the process with these people takes so long.

The motivation for therapy should be explored in the first session. The question here is what brings this person to this pastor at this time? The way to find the answer to this is simply to ask the question and listen carefully to all the nuances of the answer.

The problem of wanting to depend on the magic of the pastor, or on his expertise and authority will show itself, if present, in the first interview. It does not need a long discussion on the part of the pastor. The more the pastor talks about any issue, the more he moves toward intellectualization of his position, the more he gives the person the opportunity to build up defenses. The therapy process should be dealt with in terms of its motivation, not its explanation. The pastor can briefly state that he does not work this way, that it would not help the person if he did, and then wonder aloud why the person wants this approach. The question of motivation is thus raised, and the pastor will have to decide whether this is sufficient for the moment, or whether it should be pursued.

An illustration of this problem is seen in a woman in her forties, whose adolescent daughter was involved in drug usage. She wanted the pastor to give her directions for handling the daughter. As the session developed she also wanted directions for handling her husband, with whom she was in conflict in regard to the daughter, and also a younger son who was showing rebellion against the father and leaning heavily on the mother. At first she pleaded for this kind of "advice." Then she became a little belligerent, clearly indicating that she got angry if she did not get her

own way, and she was accustomed to controlling her family. The
pastor quietly indicated that he could not accede to her wishes and
wondered why she wanted this kind of relationship. She replied by
invoking the name of the pastor who had referred her, saying that
he had indicated that she would be treated as she requested. At this
point the pastor interpreted to her superficially how he saw her
problem and what he was prepared to do. He stayed on the level of
how he saw the family relating to each other, and asked for her
confirmation, which she quickly gave. This gave her some confidence that the pastor understood what she had been saying, and
was able to relate discrete elements to each other. He did not mention other elements he saw in her — her rigidity, her supermoralistic
attitude, her tendency to blame others, and her ill-concealed bit-
terness toward her husband. He indicated that he was prepared to
offer two approaches. One would be that of seeing her individually
in order to help her with the anxiety about herself and the family,
which she readily admitted. Her resistance to this took the form of
saying that if the others changed, her anxiety would be lessened.
The pastor wondered aloud if she did not have the possibility of
determining her own feelings rather than accepting dependency on
others. She first accepted this appeal, and then began to show
some ambivalence. Did this mean that she had to do all of the
changing? The pastor indicated that there was a real need for
family therapy, and what this meant. She replied that they would
not come, but that they had never really considered it. Since time
was getting short, the pastor indicated that the only decision
that was needed now was whether she wanted to come back for
another interview and talk more about what she and the family
wanted to do. She quickly said that she did.

This account not only illustrates the problem of control, but
another central issue. This has been described in the literature of
late as "contracting."

THE CONTRACT OR COVENANT

The word *contracting,*[4] is of course a legal term, but many pastors have taken a liking for it. It would seem that a better word

is *covenant,* a word with strong Biblical roots. It places the emphasis more on the quality of relationship between two people than on legalistic aspects. However, this word has fallen out of general use.

Whatever the term used to describe the process, it is the process itself and the skill of the pastor in handling it that is important. Here the pastor clarifies his expectancies from the person, and what he is prepared to offer, and what he is not prepared to offer. This needs to be definite to avoid misunderstanding. The frequency and length of interviews, the pastor offering his time and skills in the hope that the person can use them for the resolution of his problems, the responsibility of the person for bringing pertinent material to the sessions to the full extent of his ability are part of the covenant. Under no circumstances should the pastor promise a cure or a solution of a problem. The person can frustrate this and then claim that the pastor has not fulfilled his promise. The pastor should not raise extraneous issues, neither should he attempt to describe the therapy process in any detail. The manner in which he conducts himself in the first interview should be clarification enough. The important thing is not to sell the person on a description, but rather to offer a trustworthy person with whom he can share his problems.

One reason that such a clear understanding is needed is that once a relationship is established it is difficult to change. For example, if in the first interview the pastor gratifies dependency needs in the person by advice and suggestions, the person will insist these needs continue to be gratified. If the person discovers that he can control the therapy process in the first interview, he will insist on continuing control, and therapy will be destroyed. On a very simple matter, if the pastor allows the person to go overtime in the first interview, he is establishing a precedent for further interviews.

A clear and firm covenant or contract is the only basis on which therapy can proceed. This applies to the pastor quite as much as to the person. For example, the person has the right to definite appointments. The pastor who cannot offer this should not engage in therapy. There will be realistic reasons why appointments will need to be changed by both parties occasionally. At other times cancellations will be part of the resistance of the person, or perhaps the pastor, and must be dealt with as such. In part, the covenant is a commitment in terms of time, place, fee (if any), and the basic expectations and responsibilities of both parties.

After an interview or two the person should have a clear sense of what is required of him if he is to find some relief of his pain. Self-observation and self-revelation are fundamental, as only in this way can he come to an increased awareness of how he handles his feelings and how he relates to others. Any tendency to talk about others in a manner which implies or states that they are responsible for his condition is unfruitful and should be interpreted as resistance. He may need help in accepting responsibility for his own condition and feelings. He should be gently guided back to himself in a manner that encourages him to talk about his own motivation and defenses.

Self-observation or introspection and communication of thoughts and feelings to another freely may be difficult because the person may not want to know himself or be known by another. To be known or to know means that he faces a decision as to what to do about himself. He may want to communicate freely and not want to, and may need help in resolving this conflict. He may want relief from his inner pain, but also fear that revealing himself to another makes him vulnerable.

EMPATHY

This brings us to an aspect of the early process that is more to be demonstrated than discussed. By his attitude and manner, the pastor will demonstrate to the person that his concern is to bring understanding, resolution of conflict, and healing. There is no substitute for being genuine in this. However, this requires knowing the person in more than psychological or theological terms — that is, more than knowing *about* him, more than content knowledge. It means a direct kind of knowing, but with the full acceptance and affirmation of the other as a person. This is often called empathy,[5] the ability to feel what another person is feeling while maintaining objectivity. It requires an openness and sensitivity to others, the ability to be aware of how one would feel if he were in the shoes of another, the ability to know how one actually feels in the presence of another. The feelings of the pastor may be countertransference, and this will be discussed later. However, he should know himself well enough to know what brings forth certain feelings from him. The transactional process in therapy does not mean satisfying the feelings of the person, but it does mean understanding them and responding to them in a therapeutic manner. This requires a sensitivity to the process taking place beneath the verbal communication.

The pastor has a Biblical prototype for this kind of sensitivity. It is found in such passages as Psalm 139, where God is depicted as having a very close, intimate, and direct knowledge and understanding of man, a presence with men, not for the purpose of creating guilt and giving punishment, but for the purpose of redemption. Paul in his great hymn of love (I. Cor. 13) speaks of the experience in which the partial knowledge or understanding of the present will become a full self-knowledge or self-understanding, even as first we have been fully understood. Such empathetic knowledge and self-understanding brings a person to the awareness of inner resources which are not of his own making, but now become available for his appropriation. There may be a great difference between the verbal content of religious communications and the underlying processes of religious experience.

AUTONOMY

One of the inner resources is the autonomous use of the self in the process of therapy. A frequent question in the early interviews is, What do you want me to talk about? This indicates that the person has become accustomed to surrendering his autonomy to others, and wants to follow the same pattern with the pastor.

If this occurs, no healing will take place. A measure of inner autonomy is a God-given potential, a means of grace, and it develops only by being used. It is only by struggling to use himself autonomously in the interviews, and then learning through the process what the obstacles and inhibitions are, what one is like under autonomous conditions, and how the therapist and others are used for purposes of protecting the neurotic conflict, that self-understanding and the freedom to be increasingly self-directing is developed. The acceptance and affirmation by the pastor sets up a condition where the defenses[6] are of gradually decreasing necessity in the relationship. But they are still used because the person is responding to images and experiences from his past, which have become repetitive, sometimes projected on the therapist. This can be looked at with the aid of the therapist, but it must first be experienced by the person. The process of therapy might be described as helping the person experience alienated and repressed aspects of himself, and then bringing these back into the functioning of the ego. A sense of alienation is never alleviated in a vacuum, but only through the kind of experience we have been describing.

VERBALIZATION, SYMBOLIZATION AND AUTHENTICITY

Central to the process of therapy is the communication by the person of what he is experiencing, feeling, and thinking. Verbal communication, the ability to formulate one's experiences in communicative speech is an ability which distinguishes man from other animals, and which is essential to awareness and understanding. Communication also takes place in other ways, such as by posture, facial expression, bodily movements, vocal timbre, and manner of speech, such as slowness or rapidity, brokenness, false starts, disconnectedness, and silences.

The therapist also communicates, both by speech and by behavior. If he is bored, angry, frustrated, judgmental, impatient, indifferent, or if he is understanding, patient, gentle but firm, and possesses a sense of his own identity—all these get communicated along with any ideas he presents.

It cannot be overemphasized that communication in the therapy process is a two-way street, and that it is not complete until it is received, understood, and responded to therapeutically by the therapist. This does not mean that he has to respond verbally to everything the person says. He may allow the person to talk for a considerable time without interrupting him or making a reply. Indeed, if the pastor fears interrupting the person or if he interrupts him constantly, then the pastor should ask himself what is going on in him. On the other hand, the manner in which the pastor listens is in itself a form of process communication, therapeutic or antitherapeutic. The very passive, silent pastor may be communicating either his indifference or fear of the person, while the overtalkative pastor may be communicating his need to keep the person away from him because of anxiety. The person may give verbal or nonverbal communications, which are meant to bring such responses from the pastor. The task of the pastor is that of penetrating the circle of unhealthy or neurotic communications, and keeping the process on the path of understanding and growth.

This means that the listening of the therapist is aimed at catching the underlying meaning of the person's speech. A woman may talk about her desire for tranquility in her home and her need for peace and quiet, but with a quality in her voice and expression on her face that indicate that underneath there is anxiety and conflict. This is part of the individual's inner self which she wanted to avoid by talking about peace and tranquility. Underneath she is also telling the therapist that she would like peace and tranquility in the interviews. She does not want him to disturb her. As a rule, all behavior that the person brings into the sessions has some underlying meaning for the therapy process itself. A man who becomes very disturbed when he recounts experiences of rejection by his girlfriend last week and his mother previously may be asking the pastor to give him a kind of protective, comforting love. His weak, pleading manner may also be aimed at provoking the disdain of the pastor, as previously it had provoked the contempt of his girlfriend.

At times, the focus of listening may be changed. For example, focusing on tonal quality or modulation to the near virtual exclusion of content may be more revealing than the combination of both. The pastor must be very careful about reading into the person's words his own personal feelings and ideas. He must be sufficiently free from his own need to project that this is avoided.

This means that the pastor must listen to himself to catch feelings, defenses, fantasies, and motives in himself that may be reflected in his responses. Being aware of these is the best guard against expressing them, but no guarantee. He needs to ask himself whether his responses are being stimulated or provoked by the person, or whether they arise from something from within himself. He may have a need to protect others, or to control others, or to defend himself, or to be authoritative or withdrawing. Every pastor, even for the general work of the ministry, needs a deep understanding of himself.[7]

In recent years there has been a reaction against verbalization in psychotherapy and an insistence on techniques that encourage behavior that results in the expression of feeling. This has ranged from mild touching to nude contacts in a swimming pool. Sometimes there is an effort to break down defenses and encourage persons to express intense emotion in some form of behavior. It is held by some that no understanding, but only expression, is necessary for change. This seems to be only a form of acting out, of expressing the emotional derivatives of conflict in behavior for the purpose of avoiding insight and resolution. We believe that awareness can be and is expressed in communicative speech and is an essential part of psychotherapy. The experiencing of intense feeling in a disorganized, incoherent manner which results from a breakdown of defenses may be damaging to the person. An earnest attempt at understanding needs to be made. On the other hand, intellectualization as a defense is ineffective. The pastor must always respect the defenses of persons. Defenses should not be attacked or broken down until the individual no longer needs them. Then he will discard them himself and put something else in their place.

The reason for emphasis on verbal communication is to be found in the nature of life. All life needs and seeks a structure through which function is expressed. Words and formulations are the human way of creating an ego structure that embodies and sets forth the intangible forces and functions of the inner life.[8] The use of verbal structures is closely related to the development and use of the self. From the self-exploratory stage in psychotherapy, through the resolution of conflict and the making of decisions, verbal formulations play a central role. The repression or minimizing of the place of structure in the interplay between conscious and unconscious processes means that important aspects of the whole person are alienated from other aspects of which they are an integral part. Structure and function are two sides of one process.

There is a paradox in the nature of verbal formulations or symbols. Their function is to promote insight, but they can also be used to conceal insight.[9] This is true of all structure. It may become hardened and fixed and serve the purpose of avoidance and dissociation. Then the organism is crippled in its functioning. Witness the hardening of the arteries and the bone structure of the body and also the person whose inner life is shrouded in darkness through beliefs that are held in a rigid and defensive manner. Such rigidity and defensiveness is really the condition and the functioning of the self. It is a reflection of the inner condition.

Uncontrolled regression in which ego functions are temporarily set aside differs from "regression in the service of the ego"[10] in its outcome. Spontaneity in which the ego participates by observing, understanding, and synthesizing moves in the direction of wholeness. The use of verbal symbols in this process contributes to ego strength. Verbalization is an ego function which needs to be utilized for health. This, along with symbolization, is a capacity which distinguishes man from animals, and for the fullest self-realization it must be utilized.

Usually in psychotherapy verbalization begins on a descriptive level and moves to the level of insight or significant meaning. This is the value of the emphasis on the what and the how of experience before the why. Many pastors tend to push the why before they or the person knows just what they are dealing with and how it works. The what and how of experience are important as a basis for insight. But knowing how one feels needs to be honestly and openly examined to discover why one feels as he does and to make the decision to retain or give up such feelings.

The symbolic process leading to health is the same in psychotherapy as in life. It involves, for one thing, the constant attempt to expand the meaning of one's symbols in a manner which is accompanied by the growth of the self. The growth of the self and the expansion of the meaning of symbols are two sides of one process, which take place simultaneously. This is the reason why it is futile to argue which should come first. They come together. And they involve the whole person, thinking, feeling, and striving.

A second essential for the health and healing processes is that the authenticity of the symbolic formulation must be checked and rechecked. The meaning of the symbol must be changed when it is discovered to be inadequate or when it is wrong. Often within the church and within our educational system persons may accept symbolic formulations which are not genuine for their experience.[11] At other times genuine symbols may be rejected, or inadequate symbols may be used to conceal genuine experience. Ambivalence may become a problem. Many religious persons quickly accept the word *love* as an authentic symbol for them, but reject the word *anger* as something evil and therefore not within their experience. The love-anger ambivalence makes them very anxious. The alienated anger needs to be brought in and made a part of the self without anxiety. "Anger" then would become a genuine symbol for their experience, and self would grow through constructive handling of the anger, and the meaning of their formulations would expand. Greater health or wholeness would result.

When the process of verbalization is used to conceal meaning or where it is isolated from feeling, with feeling repressed, an unhealthy process exists. Here the therapy process aims at the gradual bringing into awareness the manner in which verbalization is used, defensively, inauthentically, and distortedly. With the increase of awareness comes the expansion of the meaning of the symbol and the simultaneous enlargement of the self. One reason traditional religious symbols have lost their meaning for many persons is because their unexpressed meanings are so incongruent with their creedal meanings.

Verbalization and symbolization has a cultural component. This may result in considerable difference in the words used or in the meanings given to common words, especially theological words. The task of the pastor is to be aware of his own meanings and to avoid projecting them into the situation. It is also to understand the meanings of the person in terms of his cultural and religious background.[12]

Genuine communication about the inner self and its struggles takes on a mood of reflection and meditation. It expresses the sense of increasing contact with oneself, especially with parts of the self which have been alienated. It is a search for truth about the self, truth here being a dynamic life process rather than a proposition. Unacceptable aspects of the self struggle to emerge into consciousness, albeit often in disguised and distorted forms. It is the task of the pastor to help the person pierce through the disguises and discover what is behind them. There will be a struggle here, as defenses are also operating to prevent the living process from emerging. The person should be instructed to reflect on himself and his experiences and report what comes to his mind. The pastor's interpretation of the communication should aim at penetrating beneath the symbols to their underlying meaning, thus assisting both in the growth of meaning and the expansion of the self. This means taking back into the self what has previously been rejected, or repossessing what has previously been dispossessed. The result in the person is a deeper sense of his own humanity, a new ability to be close to others in appropriate ways, and a broader sympathy with all men which is the basis for a sense of community. Being at one with himself, he can be at one with others.

THERAPY AS A RELIGIOUS PROCESS

This reflective, meditative, and self-revelatory process is essentially a religious process. It is the essence of genuine prayer and mystical experience.[13] That it may be carried on in a nonreligious context is the basis of Freud's concept of free association and its use in psychoanalysis. Psychoanalysis requires the presence and appropriate activity of an understanding therapist in order to help the person work through defenses and distortions. In religious words, this is the priesthood of the believer. The experience is at the heart of prayer and mysticism when these experiences are a genuine search for truth, that is, for that which is alienated from the self and the expansion of the self by "reunion with the separated." Prayer is often ineffective in dealing with neurotic conditions because the alienation, defenses, and distortions require the presence of another human being who demonstrates his deep acceptance and understanding of the person even while he works at unmasking the distortions.

The pastor who is disturbed by the question "Where does God come into this process?" is expressing his own lack of understanding of the religious process. Here God is thought of as an external Being who somehow penetrates the individual with healing power. There is a strong sense of dependency in this concept. Rather, God should be thought of as already present within any process in which self-revelation, the search for the truth about the self, or genuine growth toward love and faith are experienced. As the person becomes more aware of his inner strengths he understands that he is using resources which he did not create, that he finds them within. They are part of God's creation in the nature of man; they are also a means of grace and healing. The task of the pastoral therapist is that of helping persons discover the healing forces which God has placed within him, and then to symbolize that experience in ways which are meaningful to him.

The pastoral therapist should be aware that when he is dealing with the depths of a person he is participating in an experience of profound religious significance, and at appropriate moments communicate this to the person.[14] The secular therapist may or may not share this responsibility, depending on his personal faith and convictions.

SELECTION OF DATA AND GOALS

We move now into certain recurring problems in the process of therapy. These are the selection of the data and dynamics on which attention will be focused on resistance, interpretation, and termination.

The fulfillment of the covenant and the increase in the quality of life is virtually dependent on the clarity of goals in the mind of the therapist, and his ability to help the person work toward those goals. To do this the pastor deals with the material presented in a manner which contributes to achieving those goals.

One aspect of this can be illustrated in terms of the various stages of development. Two young women may present somewhat the same symptoms. They are disturbed and anxious as they face a commitment in love and marriage. Each has some confusion in her feminine identity and also some fear of intimacy, the one more than the other. One has a strong sense of responsibility for herself than the other, but still a measure of dependency on authority. This woman has a stronger sense of autonomy than the second, but is not entirely free from the authority of her parents. The first woman has some sense of competence in her work, while the second uses work and extravocational activities as a means of avoiding close human relationships. Each has some confusion and guilt about sexual feelings.

The above analysis is not so much in terms of the content of the conflicts as in terms of the dynamics of the personalities involved. In terms of the content of the conflict, the second woman is suffering from much more intense conflicts on an earlier level of development than is the first. These conflicts involve their mothers, but also their fathers. Because of the intensity of the conflicts, and the age on which they began, the second does not have the ego strength of the first. The pastor will need to decide whether he is competent and has the time to work on the conflicts in the early level, or whether he had better confine his efforts to problems at later levels of development. There is also the question as to what the person is prepared to work on. The pastor often has to be content to help a person with oedipal or later conflicts, and prepare for referral for deeper therapy later on if it is desired.

The pastor will have to think in terms of the level of development on which conflicts arose, the points of fixation or blockage of the developmental process, and the points to which the person has now regressed. The feelings which a person may express, or his ability to express certain feelings will be related to this issue. In other words, feelings themselves may be symptomatic of conflicts and will need to be dealt with in that light, rather than being taken as the problem itself.

On the other hand, there are issues involved in the way a person responds to the conflict, the ways in which he uses conflict, and what he has learned to allow conflicts to do to him. This means that there are certain goals for the pastor in terms of dynamics. These are very important.

We have already mentioned most of these goals, but we will restate them here. One is the individual's capacity for responsibility for himself, as over against dependency on others. Therapy involves developing responsibility regardless of the content of the conflicts. But this will be more difficult if there is severe conflict on the first two or three years of life than if the conflict arose later. Likewise, autonomy has been mentioned as a goal. This goes with responsibility but also has to do with the person's relationships with authority figures. Other goals may be expressed in terms of helping the person free himself from barriers or conflicts with trust, or with love and sexuality, and with aggressiveness. Some persons will need help in handling their impulses while others will need help in modifying a too strong conscience. All will need help on those qualities of ego functioning that are necessary for a high quality of mature living.

An illustration of how this all worked out in one situation is seen in a woman who came to a pastor with intense conscious anxiety and a number of painful physical symptoms for which physicians said there was no physical cause. Consciously she felt that her anxiety was her reaction to the attempts of a dominating father to control her even though she was in her thirties, married and with children. She understood the anger as her response to his attempts to control, which at times were cruel. She resisted any effort to help her see that her anger was also a defense against her feelings of love for her father about which she felt very guilty. She was searching for other persons who could somehow convince the father to call off his domination. Thus the question of her responsibility for the resolution of her problem arose early in the therapy. She needed others to make decisions for her, as her father had always done in childhood, but she had to learn to make them for herself. Throughout childhood she had maintained a passive stance toward her father, but now had to learn that her aggressiveness was a necessary protection. She gained strength to resist her father's control, even to defy him. Even though she resisted any attempts to deal with the love aspects of her relationship to her father, her warmth and affection for her family increased and her sexual adjustment to her husband improved greatly. She gained understanding that some of her anxiety was her response to her need to control her father for her own protection. She gained strength as she relinquished her desire to control him as unreal and futile, and gained confidence in herself that she did not need to be overwhelmed by him, but could determine for herself how she would respond to his attempted domination. Many deeper childhood conflicts were not dealt with in terms of their content. Work was centered on helping her understand the nature of her responses in her immediate situation and how she needed to change these responses. The pastoral therapist needs to be clear that his goals concern those ego qualities that are necessary for an improved quality of life.

EMOTIONAL CATHARSIS

We move to a consideration of emotional catharsis as a tool in pastoral therapy. Some persons come to the pastor in various states of emotional disturbance, and need the opportunity to vent their feelings to an accepting listener. A distinction should be made between the emotional disturbance which is due to a present, real situation such as a bereavement, and one which is grounded in underlying emotional conflicts and character structure. Many obsessive and hysterical persons, for example, enjoy bending the ear of anyone who will listen. Usually they talk about nothing but symptomatic material. At its best such talking is only a palliative procedure. At times it intensifies the sense of frustration since it cannot lead to any lasting results. For therapy to take place in conditions where strong feeling is due to underlying emotional conflicts, the conflicts must be brought up and understood. The cause of the tension is worked out in this way. Sometimes an emotional disturbance is so strong that some catharsis is needed before the real work of dealing with the underlying conflicts begins. Catharsis, by itself, brings only a temporary relief.

Some persons who come to pastors are suffering from a paranoid condition[15] of varying degrees of seriousness. They will want to talk about other persons who are mistreating them. They will show suspicion and hatred toward members of their family, toward neighbors, fellow employees, superiors, and others. They will resist efforts to get them to look at themselves, at what is going on within them, at the real source of the anxieties and angers which they are projecting on others, blaming them and thus avoiding responsibility for their feelings. These persons can consume endless hours of the time of the pastor to no avail. Expression of feelings that are symptomatic does not lead to resolution of conflict, growth, or new ways of living which are more satisfactory. There is a paradoxical situation here. Working through underlying conflicts and the feelings involved in them is necessary, but the expression of feelings which are only symptomatic and part of the defensive system does not result in change or growth.

The pastor needs to evaluate the strength of feelings in relation to the strength of controls. Sometimes expression of strong feelings is indicative of the weakening of controls and of resulting regression. Decompensation is the technical word here. In such a situation, anxiety on the part of the pastor will hasten the deteriorating process. The person needs to feel the strength of the pastor and to borrow some of that strength until he can again get control of himself. Anxiety on the part of the pastor often becomes the basis for giving bad advice.

A traditional recourse of many pastors in times of mutual anxiety is to pray with the person. When prayer is used in this kind of a situation it is usually with the implication of the need of an outside power to come in and take over the care of a helpless person. Emphasizing human helplessness and the need for dependency on an outside power in this kind of a human condition is essentially a reversion to the helplessness of infancy, and is debilitating to the already weakened and threatened ego. Pastors frequently observe this. It can be equally debilitating to give unrealistic advice or maneuver the person into a dependency on the pastor to supply solutions. The pastor's faith in the creative and redemptive work of God should give him faith in the inner resources of persons to deal with severe conflicts once those resources are mobilized and utilized. But many seek a more childish, not childlike, dependency.

On the other hand, prayer may be an internal resource for both pastor and person though this may not be formalized. Prayer, as we are thinking of it, is the deep, inner desires which are part of every human being, as these desires are evaluated and revised under the influence of an ego ideal, often spoken of as "the will of God." The evaluation of childish wishes in the light of more mature goals or of reality considerations, or the renunciation of a lesser satisfaction for the sake of a greater satisfaction, are part of the process of genuine prayer. Such prayer may be continuous, an ongoing struggle, sometimes carried on below the level of consciousness but occasionally breaking into consciousness. It may take place without being verbalized. It is an integral part of the therapy process. It leads to the kinds of relationships that develop inner strength and self-reliance. The tragedy of many lives is that prayer in the sense of unevaluated and untransformed wishes is gratified. Popular thinking understands this, for it has a phrase, "he asked for it." Therapy can take place only because people can wish, can become aware of and evaluate their wishes and consequences, and can find, often through struggle and pain, the transformation of childish and destructive wishes into motivation for a higher quality of life. This is prayer in its deepest sense. At times it may result in motivation to alter some aspect of external reality rather than conform to it.

There are times when a pastor must set limits on intense or uncontrolled emotional expression. One way to do this is to change the subject. Another is to inquire of the person what he hopes to gain from such uncontrolled expression. The pastor will have to sense whether the emotion is a response to a realistic situation that the person is fully aware of, such as a sudden bereavement, or whether it is due to an underlying neurotic conflict. He will need to sense whether it is genuinely a strong feeling under the control and service of the ego, or whether it reflects a weakness in the ego that requires that he set some limits. In the first, the ego will determine the context in which the feeling is expressed and will struggle to master it. In the second, the ego will be overcome by the feeling and will be unable to cope with it constructively. This is unhealthy regression.

Emotional catharsis then may help a person to reduce the pressure and, thus, make it easier to deal with the real problem. It may help him discover feelings and processes below consciousness, and may be handled in ways that strengthen the defenses and retard or prevent further breakdown. The pastor needs to carefully evaluate those present day techniques which aim at producing deep emotional expression artificially and prematurely. Deep emotional material should be brought out only when the person feels strong enough to do so autonomously, and where the relationship with the therapist is such as to give the necessary strength. Furthermore, catharsis is not sufficient in pastoral therapy because the pastor aims at helping persons understand the quality, meaning, and motivation of their experiences, not just temporary emotional relief.

RESISTANCE

Resistance arises early in therapy. The individual wants help, but for various reasons he places obstacles in his path to exploration and understanding. This may be conscious or unconscious.

The idea of resistance is not new to the pastor. Every effective pastor becomes aware of persons who profess to want to change, but the same old patterns continue to be lived out. The pastor may experience this within himself. He is also familiar with the Biblical evidence on this point. Biblically, two different phrases are used which are closely akin to modern psychodynamic ideas. They are "stiff-necked" (Acts 7:51; Jer. 7:26; 19:15) and "hardening of the heart" (Mark 6:52; 8:14-17; John 12:40 as well as numerous Old Testament passages).

Resistance is an attitude which basically closes the mind to exploring and understanding the nature of the problem; in other words, to insight. Resistance protects the defenses. In one incident (Mark 8:14-17) Jesus says to the disciples, "Why do you discuss the fact that you have no bread? Do you not yet perceive or understand? Are your hearts hardened? Having eyes do you not see, and having ears do you not hear? And do you not remember?" In Acts 7:51, Paul tells his hearers that they are "stiff-necked" and that they always resist the Holy Spirit. Resisting the Holy Spirit is usually interpreted as turning against the light, rejecting understanding, or truth, or insight. In dealing with resistances, the pastor is on solid religious grounds.

There are certain common kinds of behavior which would appear in any list of resistances. One of these involves communication. Some persons will offer a barrage of words with a rapidity and continuity which prevent the pastor from making any kind of a comment. This person is keeping away from himself and also keeping the pastor away from him. Others will sit in silence. Silence needs to be understood as it may be due to one of a number of reasons. But the stubborn, hostile, or awkward kind of silence is usually resistance. The person may have much on his mind but does not want to reveal it, or he may be repressing feelings so that his mind is blank. The pastor may be seduced by his own anxiety in the face of silence to talk too much, or to preach in order to have something happening.

One of the instructions to persons at the beginning is to speak freely whatever comes to mind. At times the pastor will become aware that a person is sorting things out, and of holding back things he does not want to reveal. False starts are one evidence of this. The individual will start a sentence, then stop, back up, start another sentence, back up and begin again. This needs to be called to his attention. He is probably moving into something which he does not want to say.

Resistances which utilize communication processes emphasize again that many persons do not want to be known, either by themselves or another. A person may say, "the hardest thing I have ever done is to tell you this." Another person may put up a barrier, "that is something I absolutely will not talk about." Others who begin with the notion that the pastor does all of the talking, and they do not have to reveal anything will quit rather than go through a process of self-revelation. Others may want a "profile" of themselves which they can file away and make themselves believe they have done something.

Again, the difference between communication as content and communication as process should be emphasized. The training of pastors is heavy on the side of content, and it is difficult for many of us to focus on process in the communication. Our process communications are as important as those of the other person. We may indicate indirectly an interest in one phase of his life. He may, therefore, feed us material on that phase, while avoiding real problems, or he may withhold material that needs to be discussed. The communication process needs careful scrutiny for resistances and defenses, as well as meaningful experiences.

Another form of resistance is often called externalization. It consists in placing the fault on something outside of the self. This is frequently met in marriage therapy. The spouse is at fault or in-laws. This has to be dealt with early in the process or therapy will not get off the ground. The person needs to have this behavior pointed out to him with the suggestion that he deal with his side of the situation. What is going on in him, what is he feeling, what is he doing to stimulate or provoke the behavior of his spouse? If the pastor gets sucked into the projections he gets into collusion with the person, and there will be no therapy. Though they want help, persons have an unconscious need to have their defenses confirmed by the pastor, as well as by others.

Dealing with resistances calls for a knowledge of the basic defenses and character structure on the part of the pastor. He must also have the ability to see and recognize behavior for what it is. If a person places emphasis on his high respect or affection for someone like a parent, the pastor should inquire about anger toward that person. On the other hand, strong expression of anger may in itself be a defense and resistance against a deeper conflict, such as wanting to be dependent on that person. Seductive behavior is an attempt to distract the pastor from the real problem, though it may also reveal a childish need to be loved.

The pastoral therapist will find persons using various religious ideas or behavior as resistance. A person may resist recognizing anger at a parent by quoting, "Honor thy father and thy mother." The pastoral therapist will have to see the defense in this, and perhaps reply by saying, "Yes, but we do not honor our parents unless we become honest about all of our feelings toward them." Or a person whose religion is very strong on the legalistic conscience may need to be told that his preoccupation with guilt serves as a cop-out from the real problem. The individual who insists that only God can help them needs to have his sense of helplessness gently challenged and some of his strengths, including responsibility for himself, brought into the open. The person who insists that his failures are the "will of God, and God controls my every breath" needs to be helped to understand how such ideas serve to prevent him from dealing honestly and realistically with a real problem which only he can resolve. The pastor is very familiar with the person who puts on an external show of religiosity in order to cover up glaring weaknesses. A moralistic attitude on the part of the pastor, condemning the person for his resistances will usually be harmful rather than therapeutic. The pastor needs to learn to speak so that his concern comes through as he attempts to help a person understand and remove block to progress.

It is the nature of most religious defenses and resistances that they are highly acceptable to the individual who uses them. This may be true of other kinds of behavior as well. A person may feel that his sexual behavior is quite acceptable to himself, but he is afraid of being caught and punished. Another person may use similar defenses but find them unacceptable to himself. Some find their temper outbursts acceptable and justifiable. Technically, these contrasting attitudes toward resistances are known as ego-syntonic and ego-dystonic. If therapy is to proceed, ego-syntonic or acceptable resistances must be made ego-dystonic or unacceptable. In theological language this means a person who does not feel guilt about some behavior must come to feel realistically guilty about it before he will desire to change. The kind of guilt referred to here arises from the realization that one is really hurting himself or others by behavior which he feels is acceptable to him. The aim of much preaching, especially those who aim at "conviction of sin," is to make sin ego-dystonic. Sometimes this results in a massive self-rejection which is relieved only through the assurance of God's acceptance. Thus, the situation is dealt with symbolically rather than realistically, and the process will become repetitive.

An example of ego-syntonic behavior is seen in a woman who reacted to a deep lack of maternal love in childhood by becoming overly absorbed with the children in her Sunday school class. The excessive satisfaction she received from these children were evidences of the projection of her own ego needs and childish self-love. She loved herself through them. She thought of herself as being a very superior teacher because of her intense "concern" for the children. Other teachers and a pastor confirmed this opinion.

However, there were problems. Some of the children rejected her bid for closeness. If a child would drop out of her class she would be hurt and depressed. Some mothers suspected her highly emotional attachment to the children. In the spring, when Sunday school disbanded for the summer, she became depressed. Her conflict was also revealed in the fact that she had married a man who did not want children, and this became a point of conflict in the marriage. They came into therapy because he had become involved with other women. He accused her of treating him as a child and said he wanted a more mature relationship with women. This she could not understand. Her own attitudes were so highly acceptable to herself, and reinforced by other persons, that she had no desire to change or even to explore the possibility that she needed to change and grow. Some of her feelings were too painful to be faced. After all, what is wrong with loving children? She did not see that the intensity and possessiveness of her feelings were a reaction to her anger for being unloved by her mother, and a consequent dislike of children.

Another form of resistance is overt behavior designed to protect the ego against pain and to avoid insight. This is usually called *acting out*. Sometimes the term *acting in* is used for similar behavior inside of the therapy session, and *acting out* for behavior outside. Either way, it is overt behavior that grows out of the therapy relationship and is aimed at blocking attempts of the therapist to help the person gain insight into painful conflicts. It is aimed against the therapist.

Acting out in the therapy session may take many forms. Some of these are openly seductive. The person may prefer some direct satisfaction of frustrated childhood needs rather than to work at gaining insight into those needs and into ways of change. Sometimes a person can be threatening as a way of scaring the pastor off painful topics. Constant raising of questions about the therapy process itself may be ways of avoiding the purpose of the therapy. Persistently trying to change the time of appointments, cancelling appointments, calling in sick after a session in which painful material started to emerge, trying obviously to please rather than to work on issues, neglecting to pay the fee, talking about experiences with much phony pain and then with a superior air asking, "Now, tell me what I should do about all that." In short, any overt behavior which seeks to block the movement toward insight is acting out.

Outside of the sessions, people may revert to behavior which is symptomatic of their problem, rather than face the problem in the sessions. Thus, a young man who had a penchant for seducing older women would repeat this behavior after a session in which painful material in relation to his father and mother started to emerge. Another person had a pseudo–heart attack in such circumstances, and would feel very humiliated and subdued when the doctor would not admit him to the hospital because "there is absolutely nothing wrong with your heart." A man who was resisting marriage therapy made a physical attack on his wife between sessions, then returned in a mood of grandiose self-confidence that it would never happen again, and he would not go further in therapy. Grandiose self-confidence that one has full control of himself and will never take another drink is a favorite mode of acting-out resistance in alcoholics.[16]

It should be noted that resistance has its healthy aspects, as well as its unhealthy aspects. A person with no resistance is a person whose ego functions have broken down and who is therefore at the mercy of his impulses. This is a psychotic process. On the other hand, resistances that are too strong and rigid make therapy impossible. Breaking down resistance suddenly by forceful confrontations or pressures may put the individual at the mercy of his impulses before he has built up sufficient strength to deal constructively with them. Some of this strength will come from the relationship to the therapist, and sufficient time must be given for this to take place. On the other hand, unless some move is made to interpret the resistances early in the therapy and continued, the person will come to feel that he is getting nowhere and will discontinue.

Later the subject of transference[17] will be discussed. Some workers feel that all resistance is transference. This implies a broad concept of transference which would hold that anything brought into the therapy hour is the utilization of previously learned responses and has some relationship with the person's previous experience and habitual ways of responding. The value of seeing such maneuvers as resistance is simply that this focuses attention on present use of defenses, whereas the transference concept focuses on where they came from in the first place. Each of these perspectives are essential aspects of therapy. It is necessary to focus on what is happening in every stage of therapy between person and pastor, and to deal with both the constructive and unhealthy aspects.

How should resistance be handled in pastoral therapy? First, it should be recognized as such by the pastor. This calls for a knowledge of psychological defenses, and a sensitivity on the part of the therapist to what is going on. Without such recognition resistances will be ignored, or they will be taken as the real problem rather than symptomatic. The focus of therapy should remain on what the person is actually experiencing, the underlying fantasies which motivate behavior, its roots in his previous experience, and its consequences.

Second, resistances should be pointed out in a manner and with a timing the therapist feels is appropriate for a given person. Of late, confrontation has become the stock-in-trade of many therapists. Confrontations are necessary, but they should be realistic, accurate, and pertinent to the situation at hand. They should not be outlets for the anger or countertransference of the therapist. Calling attention to what is taking place between the person and pastor includes focusing on the actual behavior, on its actual consequences, with some wondering as to where it comes from. Early in therapy the person probably will not be able to deal with the last question, but it will set him looking into himself, his real feelings and fantasies.

Sometimes a third step is clarification. The person may need some help in understanding just what is meant. All comments on the part of the therapist should be short and brief. Long dissertations should never be given; they invite more defenses.

Encouraging the person to talk about his experiences and his feelings often brings clarification from within. This is the best kind.

A fourth step is that of helping the person discover hidden aspects of his motivation. This is really the work of therapy. Helping the person discover what he is doing in terms of resistance may remove that behavior in the therapy hour, but unless there is a deeper understanding of the motives and fantasies behind the behavior, the change will not be permanent. This has been the weakness of many encounter techniques.

A young couple came to marriage therapy after a rather long experience in a group where both were told repeatedly that they were controlling each other and persons in the group. There was truth in this, but the implication was that now that they know it they should do something about it. They were stymied in this. Actually they were both very frightened of their positive and negative feelings (love and anger) and they were very controlling of themselves, as well as of each other. The intimacy they craved could not be achieved. The controlling aspect was a symptom, not the real problem. It was their way of maintaining inner security. Both had fantasies of themselves as too weak to cope with the demands of the other, and of their own desires for tenderness and warmth. This would mean giving up more of themselves than they were ready to give up. The group had taught them that they could express a kind of superficial anger, but it was unable because of its inherent limitations to release their warm, tender feelings for each other. These factors were deeply hidden, and needed long exploration which the group avoided, but which made some form of therapy necessary.

A fifth step in dealing with resistances may be that of repeatedly calling the situation to the attention of the person. An indication of the strength of the ego will be the promptness or slowness with which a person gives up resistant behavior in the interviews. He will need help to understand that therapy involves dealing with his innermost thoughts and feelings and longings, and anything that gets in the way of this defeats his best purposes. The pastor will need to exercise patience and may need to bring to the surface the struggle which the person is experiencing in dealing with himself, and to offer encouragement in terms of possible beneficial results to follow. In this way the resistance and its motives will be worked out. Theologically, the Christian pastor has known that while a person may make superficial changes in himself quickly, real progress comes through gradual struggle with inner obstacles within a redemptive relationship. This has been known in some circles as "growth in grace," and in therapy the grace must be mediated through the therapist.[19]

INTERPRETATION

Like other aspects of pastoral psychotherapy, interpretation is something of a natural for the pastor. He is supposed to be an expert in the field of theological interpretation, and does much of this in his preaching. Some of it may be pertinent, but it may also miss its mark. Theological interpretations in sermons are usually quite general. In therapy they must be specific and personal. In either case, something of the attitudes and feelings of the pastor are communicated along with the ideas. The openness or defensiveness of the congregation may be more variable and more difficult to determine than that of an individual in therapy.

Other factors influence this communication process. One of the dangers of the pastor is that he will carry his sermonizing habits into the therapy office, and for the most part they are not appropriate there. The therapy function has much to teach the preacher.

The purpose of interpretation is to aid the process of therapy. In the early stages it will center on blocks or resistances to the process and later move to defenses. The standard rule is always to begin with conscious, observable material and gradually move to deeper material as the person is able. Interpretation should be couched in the concrete language of experience, rather than psychological or theological generalizations. It should be aimed at helping the person understand experiences which he does not seem able to understand by himself. It should deal with ego processes such as perception and reality testing, the nature and strength and weakness of controls, the defenses which are used against conflict and anxiety, the quality of a person's relationships with others, and the consequences of his behavior. In a sense, interpretation is offering the ego functions of the pastor, including his knowledge and understanding, for the use of the person. The ego of the person is helped to do its work.

Another way of looking at interpretation is to see it as making connections between experiences which the person is unable to make. Defenses create blind spots, and these need to be clarified. Interpretation seeks to bridge the gaps in understanding, to help the person understand how the various aspects of his experience, which he has separated are really related. It seeks to give meaning to experiences which are not understood by the person. In this sense it is prophetic. Interpretation differs from intellectualization since it seeks to help the person become open to his own inner feelings rather than be defensive. The defenses of a person should always be respected, while the pastor seeks to help the person deal with underlying feelings so that he will no longer need the defenses.

Some pastors make too few interpretations, following their own passivity, or a consciousness of lack of knowledge, or because they are trying to use a noninterpretative method. The person may then feel lost, without any adequate guide in his struggles, and may feel the pastor cannot help him. Other pastors may make too many interpretations. Instead of giving minimum assistance to the ego, they give maximum assistance, or they take over the ego functions of the person. This creates dependency and blocks healthy growth. Interpretations need to be made sparingly, they need to be timed in terms of the attitudes of the person, and the pastor needs to have considerable evidence to support his interpretation. Interpretations should never be argued or forced. If the person rejects them, they should be withdrawn and reconsidered by the pastor. Perhaps they are wrong, perhaps the timing was bad or perhaps they were given in a manner which makes them objectionable to the person. In the long run, the interpretations which the individual makes for himself are the most helpful, and he should be given ample opportunity to help himself. Obviously, the motivation, the level of self-reliance, and the ability to be curious about himself, to observe himself and report to another what he sees and what it means are important elements in the pace in which the person learns to make his own interpretations. But very few people, if any, ever get over all of their blind spots.

Interpretation may cover three general areas of experience, or in terms of personality structure, three levels from surface to depth. The first of these is the level of conscious experiences, those areas of life where one is aware of unhappiness and dissatisfaction, though he is not aware of the reasons for his failure to make satisfactory adaptations. For example, in early interviews a woman may talk about her problems with her mother, with her boss, with her husband, and with some friends. She may see these as discrete experiences, in no way related. Their relation needs to be clarified, and by listening carefully the pastor may sense an underlying theme arising from within her. For example, she might be very demanding and is finding all of these people resisting her demands. In a noncritical way, this might be pointed out or a question raised about it. Does she understand this tendency in herself? Does she see it as a problem? Or she might be very submissive, but deeply resenting this, projects her anger on them. She might be fighting within herself and projecting her conflicts in her relationships. The pastor could begin by asking what connections she sees between her various unhappy relationships. If she sees none, the idea should not be pushed but the conversation allowed to continue. Perhaps in the next interview she will report seeing some connection in terms of similar patterns of relationships made in dogmatic and critical manner then the interpretation is likely to be rejected, and the relationship weakened. She may make demands on the therapist in order to make him prove that he is not like others. If submissive his interpretations may be accepted verbally, but the unconscious resentment will prevent any real acceptance or real change in behavior.

As a general rule, conscious material should be interpreted before unconscious. It will strengthen the person's confidence in the therapist if connections are pointed out between conscious material which he may not have seen before but is now ready to see. Often in the beginning sessions questions can be raised about conscious material which the person is not ready to face.

The next level of interpretation is that of dynamics. When the therapist goes beyond the idea that the person seems to be demanding in his or her relationships to the question as to what this means, what feelings may be behind it, and how it operates in his or her life, he is getting into dynamics. Resistances, feelings and defenses, and various ego functions are part of the dynamics. Some persons at the beginning are ready to move into this; others take longer, and some will drop therapy when they see this is what it means. They want cut and dried answers, not explorations. With some persons the discovery of the how of their behavior is enough to bring about a change; with others, a deeper step is necessary. Why? Certainly one aspect of the process that needs some interpretation is any impasse that develops between the person and pastor. Needless to say, the pastor should also investigate the contribution of his own attitudes in creating such an impasse.

The why of behavior, the third level of interpretation, moves more deeply into feelings, defenses, origins, and the core conflicts and fantasies of the person. This is a slow process, and many pastors will not move into this depth. Here the psychogenesis of symptoms become important. The manner in which the person's character and symptomatology became structured from childhood, the quality of important childhood relationships, the manner in which the person brings past experiences and relationships to bear on the present and the reasons he does this are important areas for exploration. The extent to which a pastor may go into these things depends on his training and on the need of the person.

Much has been written in recent years about the value of insight. To be effective, insight must have a comprehensive quality about it. A person may have certain insight into the origins of behavior, but still want to hold on to it because of the gain in the present. Or another person may explore in great detail his hostility toward a parent, but not find this effective until he explores his love feelings toward the same person. Or another person may confuse insight with intellectualization and hold on to feelings which create problems. Another person may have a passive attitude toward himself and life, and expect things to change without any effort on his part. The pastor may give the impression unwittingly that therapy makes the change rather than being a process through which a person is aided in making his own changes.

The test of insight is how the person uses it in his everyday life, and it is not difficult to explore this. If symptoms are being overcome, relationships improving, the emotional life more satisfying, ego functioning more effective in terms of daily adaptations, the quality of his life improving, then positive results are being achieved. This requires an alertness on the part of the pastor to what is going on in various aspects of the person, without emphasizing any one aspect. One form of resistance is to stress what the pastor seems interested in to the neglect of other aspects. This is a form of person-pastor collusion and results in a dead end.

It should be emphasized that there is an experiential counterpart to insight. Interpretation best serves its therapeutic purpose when it assists the person to recover some lost or repressed function of himself. Thus, a person whose aggressiveness has been repressed through relationships with adults from childhood needs to rediscover this part of his real self in a manner which makes it available to him in his daily adaptations. Some approaches which emphasize feeling and minimize understanding may make him aware of this repressed aspect by techniques which aim at breaking down his defenses. Without understanding the defensive and repressive forces, as well as the impulse to be aggressive, and without examination of his immediate situation he may give expression to his aggressiveness in ways that make for maladjustment and more problems. Therapy has to involve the whole person in his particular life situation, and not just part of him.

Part of the material for observation is the behavior of the person in the office. When this becomes a matter for interpretation is a matter of judgment. We are thinking of such bits of behavior as whether the person moves his chair toward you or away from you. Does he casually light up a cigarette or does he show anxiety about it? Does he hold his coat on his lap or does he hang it up? If a woman, does she sit seductively, and so on? The manner and content of the response to the question as to why the person has come is important to note. Clarifying the presenting problem may be an important work of interpretation on the conscious level at the beginning. The pastor is constantly thinking about the deeper meanings of conscious material, but needs to be certain that the material itself is understood and clarified before moving into deeper meanings. He also learns that he hears and observes things which are not appropriate for interpretation until later in the process.

For example, a young woman took the chair farthest from that of the pastor for the first four interviews. In the fifth interview, she seated herself in a chair closer to that of the pastor. It was noted by the pastor as evidence of reduction of anxiety and the development of a stronger trust. But it was not commented on by the pastor since other things seemed more important. It did signal a readiness on her part to begin the real work of therapy, and this is what really mattered. Interpretation should never be made in order to demonstrate the pastor's knowledge.

How should interpretation be done?

First, no interpretation should be made out of the thin air. The pastor should have adequate data of an experiential nature to support his interpretations. This means that they should not be made too frequently. It is better to make a few good interpretations than a frequent number of poor ones. Timing is very important in terms of the person's readiness for the interpretation. They should deal with material which is conscious or near the threshold of awareness. The pastor should be aware of sudden, emotional insights on his part and check them carefully, as they may be more counter-transference than a realistic view of the person.

Second, interpretations should always be made in a tentative manner, allowing the person the opportunity to confirm or deny as he chooses. Often questions are an effective form, provided they allow the person the freedom of determining his response. Such a question as "I wonder why you do this, or what is behind your behavior, or what purpose it serves for you?" can be helpful. The person needs a sense that he is working on his situation with the assistance of the therapist, and not vice versa. This removes some defensiveness. No one wants to feel that another knows more about him than he knows about himself. Brevity is an aspect of tentativeness. Long speeches may reflect confusion in the pastor, or a desire to show off his knowledge, or to persuade the person. They stimulate defensiveness. The language should not be in the abstractions of theology or psychology, but in the language of experience; language which has some emotional value for the person. Figurative, concrete language[20] that may carry emotional value can be very helpful. The pastor who knows his Bible well can use some insightful phrases effectively with some persons at times.

Third, interpretations should never put a person down or devalue him. The person needs to be appreciated, his self-esteem protected, and the positive elements in his struggles and defenses recognized. All defenses serve positive purposes as well as negative. What would this person be like without his defenses? He would probably be a defeated and perhaps deteriorated human being. It is an art to be able to show our appreciation of the person's struggles and goals, while pointing out the harmful consequences to him of his tactics. His willingness to struggle against his anxiety is admirable, but he is mistaken in his methods. Or his need to control his anger serves a purpose to him, but can he understand why he is angry, and the price he is paying for the way in which he is controlling it. We may assume that the person is doing the best he can at a given time with the strength which he has. The pastor should ally himself with that strength and only question the person's strategies and techniques. The pastor needs to examine carefully any tendency in himself to devalue the person. Sometimes this is called reductionism, where something which is valued highly is reduced to a mere psychological mechanism or other concept less valued by the person. Sometimes a person will react against an interpretation where the word "sex" is used, but can accept the idea if the word "love" is used.

CLARIFICATION AND CONFRONTATION

Sometimes in the process of therapy interpretation has to be preceded by clarification and confrontation. Clarification is simply the attempt to explicate the issues and feelings. It is an attempt to make the communication clear, perhaps by asking for the meaning with which the person is using a certain word. Sometimes communications are confused, and the person seems to be saying two things. He may be expressing ambivalence, or may not be, but the therapist needs to be clear as to just what the communication is. It tends to destroy confidence in the pastor if he operates on the basis of a misunderstanding and then has to backtrack. Sometimes the person may want to cause such confusion as a means of resistance.

Confrontation[21] is somewhat different. It is interesting that this word has come into the language of therapy even though in its primary connotation it implies hostility and aggression. When this is the case in therapy it is a sign that faulty attitudes are present in the pastor. Likewise, the pastor who uses confrontation as a stock-in-trade would profit by an examination of his countertransference feelings. It may well be that he is chronically hostile. The pastor who is afraid to confront the person may have a reverse problem, fear of his own aggressiveness or fear of losing the love of the person.

Some approaches in therapy encourage confrontation, if not the open expression of anger on the part of the therapist. Such approaches usually ignore or do not understand the meaning of the inner processes of the person, especially defenses and other ego processes. Or perhaps the therapist is keeping his attention on the conscious meaning of the symptom, while not considering the deeper, unconscious meaning. On the other hand, pastors who adopt a consistently confronting method will, upon self-examination, usually find that it fits into their own processes and that they use it in many other aspects of their ministry.

When is honest confrontation,[22] gently but firmly bringing the person face to face with his evasiveness or resistance, desirable? When the person seems to need encouragement toward self-observation and exploration of his symptoms, not just recounting symptoms. An obsessive person, for example, will go on endlessly about the suggestion that he look at his motivations and at consequences. Or when a person is definitely resistive and evasive and needs to have this called to his attention. Or when he introduces confusions, or moves from topic to topic, or talks continuously about others in order to keep away from himself. Bringing a person face to face with his behavior or attitudes should be done in a firm but kindly manner, and usually some interpretation of the behavior needs to be made at the time or shortly after. Confrontations should follow the flow of conversation, utilizing what the person brings and not seek to distract or control him. A sensitive pastor will also time his confrontations and interpretations so they come when the person is most open to them. It is a sign of a genuine working relationship when the person replies in some such words as, "Yes, I have had that in the back of my mind but didn't want to say it."

REGRESSION

There is another phenomenon in human life which plays an important part in therapy. The phenomenon we speak of now is known as regression. For many it is thought of as a defense mechanism. It is, however, more than that. It is closely associated with its opposite movement in life, growth or progression. These two concepts attempt to describe the movement of life energy from earlier stages of development to later ones, or the reverse. But it is not just the movement which is important; it is the context in which the movement takes place.

Regression can indeed be used as a defense mechanism. This occurs in all of us, to a greater or less degree, when under the influence of fatigue, illness, or intense emotional conflict we want to give up, be taken care of, comforted and even babied. The excessive use of alcohol is a form of regression. The ideas of the schizophrenic express regression to early infantile states through verbal symbols. To understand them one must experience for himself a kind of regression. What would he mean if he entertained such ideas? All neurotic symptoms have in them the element of regression; that is, of behavior that expresses conflict between impulses and repressive tendencies on an earlier stage of life. It is the regressive behavior of some persons that brings them to the pastor, for instance, the man or woman who has suddenly become unfaithful to the spouse, who demands the right to freedom and happiness, and who seems to have reversed his previous patterns of behavior. Regression is a phenomenon in most marriage conflicts, though not all infidelity is due to regression. Any behavior has to be understood within its context. Behavior which has a strong element of acceptance by the person, yet which is out of keeping with acceptable norms of adult behavior is likely to be regressive. The element of acceptance grows out of the fact that the behavior expresses childish wishes which earlier were kept under rather rigid control, but now are owned as part of the self.

Society has its accepted forms of temporary regression. The man who has to stop at the bar on his way home and have a drink or two with the boys, or the persons of either sex who have to do this on every Friday night in order to let down for the weekend, the behavior of some persons away from home which is so different than their respectable behavior at home, parties and various kinds of celebrations in which inhibitions are down, certain religious activities in which the individual surrenders his control to a supposedly supernatural power, and even sleep — all of these may be seen as temporary forms of regression which act as safety valves for repressive forces, and establish some equilibrium within the person. But the emphasis here is on the temporary nature and the acceptability by a group.

It should be recognized that no human being is strong enough to adapt to his world and find a high quality of life consistently. Tensions range from the strains of daily life,[23] which all of us face, to severe inner tensions arising out of long standing conflicts. The greater the inner tensions the greater the problem of adapting to the ordinary world will become. On the other hand, sometimes persons caught in a group crisis or disaster will be able to submerge their own tensions and act very constructively.

Certain psychological processes are to be found in all regression. The person's capacity for reality testing is weakened to a greater or less degree. Primary process thinking in which wishes, desires and strong feelings and fantasies predominate, control behavior. The person who engages in various kinds of objectionable behavior while feeling that it will make no difference to his family or on his job, or whose capacity for critical evaluation of himself is set aside, is an illustration of this. Sometimes primary process thinking is rationalized as being due to the voice of God or control by some other power. Ego functions of control are taken over by the impulses and fantasies. Sometimes this results in uncontrolled speech and the pouring out of material that the person is unable to deal with. This is best handled by suggesting that the conversation stay with present reality problems. Sometimes there is very strong and unreasonable anger expressed, and the threat of violence becomes intolerable to others. One function of the ego is to perceive danger from the environment and act accordingly, but in regression this ability is weakened or set aside altogether. Sometimes regression will involve the whole personality, as in a psychosis. At other times it will involve only a part of the personality, while the person functions in a normal manner in other areas.

Thus far we have been talking about forms of regression which are induced by the need to find relief from intense anxiety and conflict. But we have also indicated that the regression impulse is the opposite of the impulse to grow or progress. There is much that is not understood about the movement between these directions. Religion has long known and utilized the principle of retreat in order to go forward. This has taken regression out of a rather mechanistic understanding and placed it in a purposive context. Jesus pointed out to Nicodemus that he needed to be born again, and Nicodemus was confused. On another occasion he told his hearers that unless they became as little children they could not enter the Kingdom. In other words, they were to go back to a previous stage where growth had stopped and grow up again in a new way. The disciples could not endure the tension of Gethsemane, so they regressed by going to sleep and drew a question from Jesus. The experience of St. Paul on the Road to Damascus had many elements of regression, but it resulted in a forward movement and growth. Retreats are a standard form of activity in many religious groups. Meditation, if practiced deeply, involves regression for the purpose of moving ahead. Likewise, mystical[24] experiences may contain regressive aspects because the mystic himself is regressed, but for the purpose of reorganizing and reintegrating the person. Moving back to where life has stopped growing has long been recognized by religion as a valid principle. The explanation of the mushroom growth of small groups in the church may be found in part in the need of many persons to undergo a regressive experience within a group context.[25] Certainly this has occurred in many groups with a variety of results. It is one of the challenges to leadership in small groups.

One psychotherapist who was concerned with the idea of purposive regression is C. G. Jung.[26] He made regression and progression a fundamental aspect of his theory of human energy. He defined progression as the daily advance of the process of psychological adaptation. He stressed the gradual rather than sudden nature of progression. He spoke of a need to attain a basic attitude inducive to adaptation, and then gradually making this attitude effective in actual adaptations. How often we hear people speak of exactly this problem. He spoke of the fact that the attitude may be permanent, but that there is a constant need for new applications and adaptations because of the demands of the environment and also of inner change.

Jung saw regression as consciousness coming face to face with unconscious processes, or what he called the soul. Some of his ideas are congruous with modern ego psychology. The ego not only has the problem of adapting to the external world, but in regression it is called upon to make some adaptation to the inner world. This is the focal point of pastoral therapy, the inner world, its values and meanings.

Progression and regression take place in persons as a natural process. For growth we face the necessity of adaptation to our world. But regression brings the necessity of adaptation to our inner world. We cannot escape either. Adaptation in each direction is something of a simultaneous problem. This is close to the Biblical insight that the kingdom of God is within us, but it must also be translated into the external world. Misunderstanding on this point has resulted in conflict between proponents of therapy and those of social action.

Jung's ideas on progression and regression are somewhat similar to Ernst Kris's concept of "regression in the service of the ego."[27] Kris interprets artistic production as the result of the artist's ability to regress to feeling and fantasy levels of his being, and then to create artistic forms that express and communicate his inner experiences.

GROWTH AND CHANGE

Pastoral psychotherapy should be seen as an endeavor at developing the creativity of persons. This would mean that the pastoral therapist should expect some regression, but should try to help the person use this as a basis for further ego growth. This means that he helps the person clarify his intention to grow or progress, to understand his resistances, his reason for the regression and to set goals for himself that require the integration of his inner and external worlds, including his religious or ultimate view of his world and of life. This will include a realistic view of his own potentials and limitations and the opportunity for development in the real world. One of the struggles the person will experience is that required to give up some of his narcissism and the desire to force his narcissistic needs on to others. In place of this he will need to discover that he can find a deeper satisfaction of his own needs by learning to help others find similar experiences. He neither has to control nor allow himself to be controlled. This is one of the meanings of genuine trust and love in terms of either psychological maturity or religious understanding.

Progression or the re-creation of the self requires more than reasoning about one's goals and intentions. Here the dependency needs of both person and pastor may face a test, as the person may ask for a verbal religious system to which he can conform and the pastor may want to give this. This is confusing structure with function, symbol with reality. The creation and re-creation of the individual requires the constant laying hold on the basic impulses, desires, and urges of life, the source of real power in life, and in discovering symbols which simultaneously express that inner energy and the realistic values in the outside world. This has been the genius of religious symbols when used for the purposes of insight and creative expression. When not used creatively they promote the goals of unhealthy regression. Through the various functions of the pastor the individual may become acquainted with various symbols and their meanings, which in religious history have served an integrative function in other persons. These are resources from which he may choose. If he attempts to create his own symbols he may end up with "private" symbols, completely unrelated to his culture and to the real world, and become psychotic. The task of the creative individual is to use the symbols of his culture and his religion as the expression of his own authentic meaning integration, and not as the empty forms which are so prevalent in our culture and which lead to regression.

It should be recognized that we are describing a kind of change in human life which religion has tried to produce, but which it has little understood. Likewise, the psychological sciences on which modern psychotherapy is based has no complete understanding of this. The change from mistrust to trust has been called by one writer "the miracle of faith." The faith of the pastor, if genuine and authentic, plays some little part. There is a redemptive element in suffering that is accepted and partially understood. Beyond this religious insight has spoken of factors operating which are beyond the control of either the person or the pastor, but available for their purposes. Both know that neither can take credit for the miracle of creation and growth. Religious insight has found explanatory power in the symbol of the Holy Spirit. When the symbolic structures of religion are utilized to gain insight into the self, and into authentic values in life, and thus to serve the purposes of growth and creation of the person, then the human ego finds fulfillment. There is mystery in this, just as there is mystery in why a seed dropped into favorable ground begins to grow and matures into a plant, the possibilities and limitations of which were determined from within the seed itself.

The process of pastoral psychotherapy, when effective, leads to growth and change. There can be no cure without change. The problems which bring people to a pastor grow out of feelings and attitudes that are faulty and produce pain and misery. Only through a relationship in which autonomy is a large element can the individual work out his own destiny as a person, a "psyche." Religion has encouraged people to expect this change quickly and without much effort on their part. This is a mistake. Some sudden and spontaneous cures do occur, but we do not know how to produce them. For the most part, real change comes slowly, and with effort at working on those parts of our selves that are causing us pain. God has placed the potentiality for change within us, but we have to accept our responsibility in bringing it about.

We move now to a further consideration of the pastoral therapy relationship.

NOTES

1. Robert J. Menges and James E. Dittes, *Psychological Studies of Clergymen: Abstracts of Research,* New York: Thomas Nelson and Sons, 1965;

Margaretta Bowers, *Conflict of the Clergy,* New York: Thomas Nelson and Sons, 1963.

2. John Spiegel, *Transactions: The Interplay Between Individual, Family, and Society,* ed. John Papajohn, New York: Jason Aronson, 1971.

3. Bruce Hartung, "The Initial Call," In *Toward a Creative Chaplaincy,* ed. Lawrence E. Holst and Harold P. Kurtz, Springfield, Ill.: Charles C Thomas, p. 15.

4. An instructive discussion on contracts is found in Karl Menninger, *Theory of Psychoanalytic Technique,* New York: Basic Books, 1958, Chapter 2.

5. C. B. Truax and R. R. Carkhuff, *Toward Effective Counseling and Psychotherapy,* Chicago: Aldine, 1967, pp. 82–143.

6. Anna Freud, *The Ego and the Mechanisms of Defense,* New York: International Universities Press, 1946; Henry P. Laughlin, *The Ego and Its Defenses,* New York: Appleton-Century-Crofts, 1970; New York: Jason Aronson, 1979.

7. This topic will be dealt with more fully in chapter 8.

8. Theodore Thass-Thieneman, *The Interpretation of Language,* 2 vols., New York: Jason Aronson, 1973.

9. Carroll A. Wise, *Religion in Illness and Health,* New York: Harper and Row, 1942.

10. Ernst Kris, *Psychoanalytic Explorations in Art,* New York: International Universities Press, 1952.

11. Paul Tillich, *Systematic Theology,* Vol. III, Chicago: University of Chicago Press, 1963, p. 123 ff.

12. John Spiegel, *Transactions: The Interplay Between Individual, Family, and Society,* ed. John Papajohn, New York: Jason Aronson, 1971.

13. Evelyn Underhill, *Mysticism,* New York: Dutton, Inc., 1961, pp. 44–69, 167; Herbert Fingarette, *The Self in Transformation,* New York: Basic Books, 1963.

14. Don Browning, *Atonement and Psychotherapy,* Philadelphia: Westminster Press, 1966; Thomas Oden, *Kerygma and Counseling.* Philadelphia: Westminster Press, 1966.

15. See chapter 8.

16. See *The Big Book of A.A.,* Alcoholics Anonymous, rev. ed., New York: Alcoholics Anonymous World Services, Inc., 1966, pp. 540–552.

17. See chapters 7 and 8.

18. Thomas Oden, *Contemporary Theology and Psychotherapy,* Philadelphia: Westminster Press, 1968.

19. Leon H. Levy, *Psychological Interpretation,* New York: Holt, Rinehart and Winston, 1963; Emanuel F. Hammer, *Use of Interpretation in Treatment,* New York: Grune and Stratton, 1968.

20. Emanuel F. Hammer, op. cit., ch. 22.

21. Gerald Adler and Paul Myerson, *Confrontation in Psychotherapy,* New York: Jason Aronson, 1973.

22. The New Testament interpretation of confrontation may be summarized in the phrase "speaking the truth in love." Only a genuine, authentic love as exemplified in the New Testament is meant. The danger with confrontation is that so often it is done in anger (Eph. 4:15).

23. It will be noted that we have not discussed "crisis counseling" in this book, just as we have not gone into other specialized phases of psychotherapy such as marriage therapy. The reason for this is that we have been presenting an overall view of pastoral psychotherapy which is applicable to many forms of human problems. In any case, the pastor must know how to adapt himself to the therapeutic needs of the person and do what the condition of the person calls for. Knowledge of special areas of human problems such as "crisis" may be helpful in that. For those who want to read on "crisis counseling" the following may be helpful: Gerald Caplan, *Principles of Preventive Psychiatry,* New York: Basic Books, 1964; H. J. Parad, ed., *Crisis Intervention: Selected Readings,* New York: Family Service Association of America, 1965.

24. Evelyn Underhill, op. cit., 298 ff.

25. For an illuminating discussion of the experience of regression in the teaching of languages see Charles Curran, *Counseling and Psychotherapy,* New York: Sheed and Ward, 1968. In supervising advanced students in pastoral psychotherapy it is evident that the ability of the student to permit himself or herself to regress is central to his teachability. It is also evident in seminary classes where a student's reception of new ideas is accompanied by hostility at the professor or by exaggerated dependence. For a discussion of regression in psychoanalysis see Karl Menninger, *Theory of Psychoanalytic Technique,* New York: Basic Books, 1958, Ch. 3.

26. C. G. Jung (1928), *Two Essays in Analytical Psychology* and *Practice of Psychotherapy,* in *Collected Works of C. G. Jung,* New York: Pantheon Books, 1954.

27. Ernst Kris, op. cit.

Chapter 7

The Therapy Relationship

THE WORKING RELATIONSHIP

The relationship between pastor and person is the necessary ingredient in all pastoral ministry, and crucial in pastoral therapy. It is the basis for the process, the interaction and movement, and the manner in which dynamics and content are used. Its importance has led some to place almost exclusive stress[1] on it to the exclusion of other aspects. This results in the avoidance of process and content, and it tends to place an overemphasis on conscious feeling. It thus helps the person to avoid what is behind the feeling and reduces the therapeutic value of the experience. This faulty emphasis should not lead to a minimizing of the central function of the relationship.

We have already[2] dealt with certain theological aspects of the pastoral relationship. There can be considerable disagreement on this, since a theological understanding of the pastoral relationship depends on the general theological stance of the interpreter. We have indicated in chapter 1 the Biblical basis for the healing ministry. Any genuine pastoral relationship ought to be therapeutic or healing; that is, it should contribute to the wholeness of the person. It is only as the pastor is trained in the essential processes of therapy that the general pastoral relationship can become a basis for a therapy relationship.

The pastor in the parish is quite familiar with the necessity of having an effective working relationship with people. Most failures in the pastoral ministry, as well as in other forms of ministry, are traceable to faulty working relationships. These may be produced by factors in the people or in the pastor, or both. Often they are handled, as are many conflicts, in relationships by blaming the other person, rather than each side investigating the contribution it is making to the problem. The working relationship is very important on any level of pastoral care.

The working relationship[3] is the result of conscious attitudes and understandings in each party. It is the real person-to-person relationship—real because it is genuinely felt and responded to appropriately by each person. In therapy and often in the parish there is also a relationship where unconscious, childish, and distorted feelings predominate, whether these be of an affectionate, angry, or guilty nature. This, in psychoanalytic terms, is called transference. Transference, as we have seen, is essentially the displacement of feelings and attitudes from previous relationships and from general character patterns to pastoral relationships. We will first deal with the working relationship and then with the transference relationships in pastoral therapy.

The working relationship is based on the healthy aspects of the person responding to the healthy aspects of the pastor. The healthier both parties, the freer the working relationship is from problems. But people, being human and sinful, always have problems. We shall discuss attitudes of pastor and which seem essential to an effective working relationship.

It is necessary for the pastor to bring to the therapeutic or working relationship a genuine concern and respect for the individual as a person. The most distorted life is still deserving the respect and dignity of a human being. The person and his problems require acceptance. Being able to understand the hurt of the person and being interested in learning about him should contribute to a sense of common humanity in the pastor. Before God each stand in the same need (Matt. 25:34–45). The person is hurting in a manner which can be alleviated by human intervention, and this the pastor may attempt to do. This means that his essential goal is one of helping a person find healing, of removing or reducing the conflict, of encouraging the person to find growth and fulfillment. In this task, as we have said, the pastor must be concerned to allow the healing forces within the person to become operative. These healing forces include the trusting, loving, rational, willing, and decision-making potentials of the person. Healing does not take place by making persons subject to external authority, such as the church, the pastor himself, or abstract theological or moralistic principle. The basic Christian ethic is a love which does no harm to its neighbor but rather seeks to do good. People are sick because the development of such a mature experience of love has been blocked. The pastoral therapist is dedicated to helping persons gain insights into their experiences so they may make responsible decisions as to the future course of their lives. A relationship with a pastor holding these attitudes will help the person develop a sense of personal worth as a human being.

The central problem of the pastor in his therapy relationships is his identity as a person and a pastor. For example, trust is a basic quality of the working relationship. The pastor whose own identity contains distrusting and doubting elements will find it difficult to establish a working relationship grounded in trust. Unless a person can feel secure in opening himself to the pastor, nothing will happen. The person may return for a number of interviews, but will not be able to work on his problem. The pastor who is confused about his own identity will react to his anxiety toward a person by either being dogmatic and moralistic or openly uncertain. Either will be inwardly felt by the person as weakness and untrustworthy. Fitting the person into some preconceived structure, such as theological or psychological abstractions is one way of expressing uncertainty. It misses the individual and his hurt. Or the pastor may unwittingly indicate that he feels inadequate to deal with the person's situation. If this is an honest feeling it needs to be brought out, discussed frankly and a referral made.

Having learned to trust the loving, integrating, and healing forces within himself, the pastor quietly inspires such trust in some measure in the first interview. This is done more by how he speaks than by what he says; by his manner and bearing rather than his credentials; by a deep sense of security in his own humanity rather than in any verbal profession. A living profession of faith is much to be desired.

Autonomy is another quality of the working relationship which is related to the identity of the pastor and the ability of the person to accept it. Autonomy, like trust, is a condition of healthy existence. To the extent that the pastor has not developed autonomy, he tends to block it in others. The opposite of autonomy is authoritative control. This may be rationalized as being for the person's good. There are very few persons so sick that they have to be controlled by another. On the other hand, there are dependent persons who will seek help from the pastor because they feel he will gratify their dependency needs. There is no resolution of conflict or growth in this process. The need for dependency may be the central problem which needs to be resolved. If so, the gradual coming into a position of self-reliant autonomy may be a slow process, but it needs to begin in the first interview by allowing the person to decide what he is to bring into the session. Here he becomes autonomous to a degree, but it may have a marked effect on his life.

The pastor must be inwardly able to give such an autonomous relationship. This depends on the degree of autonomy he possesses or whether his decisions are made in a manner which aims at counteracting his own rebellious or dependency needs. Again, this kind of relationship is created in the actual process between the individuals, not through abstract discussion. The person should take a measure of responsibility for what happens in the therapy process from the very beginning. If he cannot do this, the reasons need to be discussed. For some persons this is a slow process with resistances present which must be dealt with. The therapy process and relationship needs to be seen as a prototype of a healthy relationship in the larger world.

Another quality of the working relationship is mutuality. Basically, this is a relationship in which the pastor and person accept themselves and each other as colleagues in a joint enterprise. This requires establishing an atmosphere of working together. The pastor should not give the impression that he is ahead of the person. If anything, he needs to remain a small step behind the person, letting him take the lead and responding to whatever he brings in a manner designed to increase health in the person. The pastor faces the issue as to what is a therapeutic response to what the person is bringing. It is the person's privilege to reject any responses without argument from the pastor. Perhaps later he will come to understand and accept what was said to him. Perhaps later the pastor will discover he was wrong. The pastor grants the person the same rights and privileges which he wants to enjoy himself. As a successful therapy process goes on, the pastor and person may have the satisfying experience of arriving at the same idea simultaneously. This shows they are emotionally together.

The working relationship moves along a pattern of change and growth which may differ from person to person. In the beginning, there is a dependence on the pastor for an atmosphere in which the person can do his work, for encouragement when the going gets hard, for needed confrontations, clarifications and interpretations. The working relationship helps the person to deal in a more open and healthy manner with himself and his own conflicts. As this process goes on, dependency on the pastor decreases and the person does some of these things for himself. He learns to observe and communicate to himself as well as to another. His need for the pastor lessens gradually. This is part of a growth process which is marked by increasing strength and self-reliance, both attributes of health. Here the pastor must possess the wisdom to let go.

What does the person bring to the working relationship? First, a need, a hurt with which he wants to deal. Second, he brings himself as a person and the pastor must accept this and know how to work with his kind of a person. This means that along with his hurt he brings his anxieties, his defenses, his habitual ways of responding to others. These may be problems to the pastor, but they are what the person has to bring, and the pastor must work with this or make a referral. Third, the person must bring some measure of positive response to the acceptance of the pastor without too much anxiety about it. Fourth, he must bring a willingness to work at self-understanding and insight, and to accept the processes of therapy. Persons who seek to define or control the therapy processes will do so to protect their own defenses, and no change will take place. Fifth, the person must bring some measure of trust, and the ability to make at least a minimal commitment to the pastor and the process. Sixth, he must bring a measure of autonomy and responsibility, at least enough to get the process started. And finally, he will have to bring his potential for becoming a growing, loving, and decision-making person. He will also bring his own limitations as far as the process is concerned, and the pastor will have to accept these, but hopefully work toward expansion of his capabilities for trust and autonomy.

TRANSFERENCE

We move now into the transference relationship. In brief, it is the displacement of feelings, attitudes, and responses from previous relationships and experiences on to the pastor. These displacements may be strong or weak, positive or negative, or both.

An example of transference is when the person comes to feel toward the pastor as he did toward a parent. The transference of such feelings is an unconscious process, and modifies the person-to-person relationship sometimes in a confusing manner. These may be unsatisfied feelings of love or anger toward a parent from childhood, and if so they will partake of certain childish qualities, one of which will be a strong need for immediate gratification. This need may be carefully rationalized. The person feels his love is self-justifying and deserves gratification, and becomes angry if it is frustrated.

Another kind of transference will grow out of the person's habitual way of responding. For example, the habitually passive person will respond passively to the pastor, the dominant person will attempt to dominate, the con man will be the con man, the guilt-laden individual will want to pour out his guilt almost endlessly if permitted. The pastor who is familiar with the various possibilities of character[4] structure will have little trouble in sensing what persons are trying to make of him because it is their habitual way of responding.

This can also be looked at from the vantage point of interpersonal or object relationships. The pastor will meet persons who constantly seek or use him for their own purposes. Or the individual who makes himself subservient or who controls others by appealing to their sympathy. Then there will be the individual who controls others by his aggressiveness or by some form of acting out.

The pastor needs to become aware of what people try to make of him and how he responds to different persons. Transference attitudes bring the past into the present relationships. The there and then becomes the here and now. Understanding what is happening in the interview will help the pastor handle it, and will give the pastor insight into how a particular person deals with others. For example, a businessman who begins by telling how powerful he is in his business, how he gives orders and others obey, is unconsciously telling the pastor that sooner or later he will be giving the pastor orders. He may also be telling the pastor indirectly what is wrong with his marriage, why his wife has left him or his children are in rebellion. On a deeper level he is telling the pastor something about his relationship to his parents, and the attitudes of persons with whom he identified as a child. This later information may not be pertinent in the present moment. The important aspect of the present is the transferential elements that are operating, and how they will influence the therapy process harmfully if not dealt with adequately. A good principle for the pastor is to understand that everything which a person brings into an interview has something of a transferential character about it.

The past is in the present, and will determine future responses unless its influence is modified.

It is important for the pastor to understand that transferential relationships may occur in the parish with persons who are not in a therapy relationship. Indeed there needs to be some displacement of trust from previous relationships before people will come for therapy. The opportunities for this are very numerous in the parish. The feelings people develop as they listen to the pastor preach or conduct worship, a funeral or a wedding, or as they interact in a committee meeting or other parish activities may have a great deal of displacement. If these are positive feelings, they will not present problems unless they are excessively strong or "sticky." If they are negative feelings then problems can arise. Pastors are particularly good targets for displaced sexual or angry feelings in frustrated persons.

The professional position of the pastor should not be neglected in considering displacement in the parish. By this is meant the fact that beyond his own person the pastor symbolizes a great many meanings. The pastor's own sense of his symbolic meaning is important, and he will communicate this to others. What it means to him to be a pastor, to be ordained, set apart with authority to preach and administer the sacraments, to be the pastor and leader of a congregation which is often referred to as "the church family," will not be hidden from others though may never be spoken. The pastor as a representative of God, Christ, or the Church draws much feeling of a substitutive nature, its character often being influenced by how the pastor presents himself in the light of these meanings, as well as by displacement. If being a representative of God leads a pastor to be dogmatic and authoritative, he will draw positive feelings from dependent persons who need and want authority, angry feelings from those still in adolescent rebellion, and he will be discounted by persons who have developed healthy feelings about real authority figures. If he is inclined to be "gushy" in his expressions of love, concern, or acceptance of others, he will find strong attachments coming from those who need such relationships.

In recent years many pastors have tended to downgrade their symbolic meaning because its negative aspects have been so apparent while the positive aspects have not been appreciated. The result of this downgrading is that many persons have lost a profound sense of security and religious strength. On the other hand, other pastors have a highly elevated concept of their symbolic significance. The pastor as a person can never entirely separate himself from the symbolic significance of his office and what people need to make of him, as this is related to what his office really signifies.

The problem with transferential relationships in the parish is that it is very difficult to deal with them. The pastor may not even know they exist. In the therapy process they are much more available for discussion and interpretation. A clue for such relationships in either situation are excessively strong feelings. The pastor has powerful religious symbols for the constant interpretation of himself, his office, and all of the objects of religious devotion, so that many persons who participate deeply and sincerely in the various means of grace may outgrow many of their childhood responses and move toward more mature relationships. Unfortunately there will be those whose sickness is too deep and rigid to permit growth in these ways, and some kind of therapy will be necessary. With many who have some freedom for growth, the process can be accelerated by therapy. Pastoral therapy is particularly helpful for those who feel frustrated in their religious lives and are unable to break through it otherwise. The time is here for study and research in the use of psychological understandings and knowledge of interpersonal relationships in the work of the pastor other than formal therapy.

To enumerate all of the possible positive or negative relationships that can be experienced in the pastoral ministry, completely unconscious to both parties though perhaps not to observers, would require a full-length work on personality growth and dynamics. We can only summarize some of the more frequent kinds of relationships and at the risk of some repetition. A very common one, in part stimulated by the attitude of the pastor and

in part by the symbolic meaning of his office are infantile omnipotent fantasies. The development of fantasies of omnipotence
from early infancy and their displacement through parents to
pastors and God is not infrequent. In this mood a person will
expect the pastor or God to perform a magical act which will
relieve him of his problems. He wants a miraculous cure which
will require no effort on his part. The frantic attempt of such persons to control everyone, even God, is sometimes missed because
of their appeal for sympathy. The attempt to control lies in the
fact that they try to dictate what the help shall be and how it shall
come. They want reality to adapt to them rather than seeking for
themselves a healthier adaptation to reality. In religious terms
they are unable to accept the real meaning of the will of God.

Another kind of feeling frequently met in pastoral care and
therapy is that of childhood dependency, on the one hand, or
persons who react to their dependency needs by becoming excessively independent. A young woman who expected her parents to
extricate her from serious problems and yet who was defeating
them at every turn, told the pastor in the first interview, "Nothing
ever happens." She did not see that she blocked any significant
movement. She was telling the pastor that nothing was going to
happen in the therapy process either. She would block him.

The pastor who is familiar with Erikson's eight stages of ego
development[5] will find these concepts a fruitful source of understanding of transferential relationships. Not that the pastor
applies the concepts to persons. He rather seeks to discover what
is going on between himself and the person and uses them to
understand. We have already indicated how persons engrossed in
a trust-mistrust conflict will bring this into the pastoral relationship. Can they trust the therapist? Likewise, persons involved in a
conflict with autonomy, or whose shame and doubt of themselves prohibits them from using their autonomous processes
effectively, will quickly reflect this in a therapy relationship.
They will keep their good and bad feelings in a state of irrecon-
cilable tension and will project these feelings out to other persons
where they continue the conflict. This will have to be dealt with in

the therapy by suitable interpretations, and by the pastor helping the person explore why he is either a good guy or a bad guy at various times.[6]

The meaning of love and intimacy for the person will be reflected in the relationship with the therapist. These feelings may be associated with shame and guilt, and be very hard for the person to deal with. On the other hand, if therapy proceeds successfully, a stage may be reached when the individual may issue an invitation to the pastor for sexual activity. The pastor's own feelings are important here. If frightened he will create more guilt and anxiety in the person. If he participates he will also create more guilt in the person and destroy the therapy. His task, as in all of these relationships, is to help the person understand both the impulse and the guilt, to evaluate the desire realistically and to turn the desire toward more appropriate expressions. Needless to say, exploration of the person's relationships with parents are also indicated in order to understand fully this situation.

Transference feelings may exist in mild or in more intense forms. Pastoral therapy, usually short-term, does not tend to produce the classical transference neurosis of psychoanalysis. In the classical transference neurosis the person acts toward the analyst as though the analyst were one or both of his parents, repressing or expressing positive or negative feelings accordingly. This situation is produced through what has been called the "blank screen" attitude of the analyst, or "an attitude of benevolent neutrality." The person is able, under these conditions, to project himself on the screen in both his positive and negative aspects. The pastoral therapist, usually working in a short-term process, is more active than the analyst, and hence may not encourage a full blown transference neurosis. But he may get it anyway, and as we have indicated above, he may get it through his pastoral relationships outside of therapy. Sometimes he will get a partial transference by his way of being active. For example, an interpretation given with a fair degree of certainty may bring the response: you sound just like my father. The pastor is not being as authoritative as the father, but the person hears them

as similar. Often the opposite occurs, and the activity of the
pastor in intervention will block transference feelings. In such
circumstances the feelings about the parent may be brought out
and discussed, but not as displaced on the pastor. The task of the
pastor is to help the person understand how earlier relationships
are influencing present relationships.

Another influence toward a strong transference is dealing with
dreams and associations to dreams. Dreams are the language of
the unconscious, as are associations. The individual is offering
something of his repressed self to the pastor for consideration,
and this involves the relationships experienced as part of that self.
The language of religion, in its highly symbolic forms, likewise
encourages the expression of unconscious processes and feelings,
and this is one reason that transference reactions are not uncom-
mon in general pastoral relationships. In a highly liturgical service a worshipper may experience some of the helplessness of
childhood within the security of the symbolic system and community experience with the priest being a strong father figure. In
churches using less formal liturgy, the personality of the pastor
may have more influence in a symbolic manner. If he is authoritative, punishing, or consoling he will bring transference feelings
accordingly. There is a real need for research in this area; but
such activity would also bring many anxieties and charges of
"psyching" religion. An understanding of what actually goes on
in people during various religious experiences is a neglected basis
for the creative development of liturgy and its use. Otherwise the
use of liturgy may encourage displacement without resolution
and release.

In the light of this discussion of transference, it should be
emphasized again that many feelings the person has toward the
pastor are essentially realistic; that is, they are the product of
the person-to-person relationship. Before the pastor jumps to
conclusions in regard to transference, he should look at his own
conscious attitudes and style. Self-understanding on the part of
the pastor is essential here.

The problem of dealing with past or present in the therapy process and relationship has already been discussed. Here it needs to be related to transference phenomena. Simply stated, this says that the past is living in present relationships. Any therapy process, beginning with present situations, is bound to touch deeper aspects of the person. Here we meet history, personal and social history. The pastor, with his training in the historical processes of religion, should find this easy to understand. In an effective therapy relationship the past is manifesting itself in the present. These dimensions of persons are an integral part of the whole, and they are influencing the person's outlook on the future. No person has found a flexible and adaptable sense of identity until he has come to terms with his past and understands how it operates in the present.

In dealing with transference feelings, the basic principles of intervention and interpretation should be observed. The primary principle is to begin with conscious, actual relationships in the therapy situation. These should be carefully explored and understood before past relationships are dealt with. Usually it is better for the pastor to wait until the person consciously introduces material from his past. However, the pastor needs to understand what is going on from the beginning, and to recognize that he is constantly dealing with transference material whether it is openly discussed or not. The important principle to keep in mind is that the person must clearly re-experience aspects of his childhood, and the feelings and needs in himself which were repressed. This means that part of himself that has been alienated from his ego functions are brought out of hiding. For example, a person whose fear of a parent created a repression of autonomy or love must re-experience that fear within the therapy relationship, work through the fear with the pastor and allow the emergence of autonomous or love needs. Only then can interpretation be really effective.

COUNTERTRANSFERENCE

The phenomena called countertransference is equally important in pastoral therapy. This is the other side of the relationship.

It is the displacement of unconscious attitudes in the pastor to the person, attitudes which are inappropriate in the pastoral or therapy relation. These attitudes may grow out of the character structure of the pastor, or they may be provoked by the person. They may be of varying intensity, and positive or negative in nature. Here we are dealing with what we make of ourselves and offer to others in response to what they bring to us.

There seems to be much confusion around the issues of transference and countertransference[8] today. Some therapists claim they do not get transference and avoid countertransference by dealing only with so-called objective material. Others seem to take their own responses as objective and valid criteria by which to judge the person. If they are angry at the person, that is the person's problem. If they experience sexual feelings toward the person then the person is interpreted as being seductive. Perhaps the person is seductive, but there is still the question as to why the response of the pastor and what it does to the person. A deep self-understanding, accompanied by the ability to be genuinely honest with himself, is a major safeguard for the pastor. This should be a continuous process. Another test of countertransference, though not infallible, is whether the person elicits a similar response from other people. Does the man who stimulates anger or excessive concern in the pastor also elicit these feelings from his wife, children, the boss, and others? The feelings of the pastor can be a reasonable guide to the dynamics of the person only when those feelings are reasonably free of a contaminating countertransference or displacement. Setting our feelings up as something of an infallible guide may be an expression of our own narcissism. On the other hand, the ability to feel with the person is necessary for empathy and understanding of the person. Feeling with the person in a way that leads to a therapeutic action is one thing. Feeling toward the person in a way that leads to antitherapeutic action is something else. If a pastor is uncertain or confused in such matters, he should seek consultation with another pastor or therapist who can help him untangle his feelings and decide the best course of action.

One manifestation of antitherapeutic feelings toward a person is the presence of a block or impasse in the process. If this happens it is either because the person and pastor are in collusion unconsciously, or because they are locked in a struggle around conflicting feelings. An example of collusion would be the pastor who himself is inclined to overintellectualize his feelings permitting the person to do likewise without interpretation. So long as they both enjoy intellectualizing, the therapeutic process is blocked. Or the pastor who argues that his interpretation is correct, or that the person must follow a certain course of action, either of which are rejected by the person is evidencing some countertransference. The result may be that the person does not keep the next appointment. When this happens, careful exploration should be made of the attitudes of the pastor in the last interview.

Any kind of acting out on the part of the pastor is the expression of unconscious attitudes, though perhaps rationalized. A need for being too close to the person emotionally or too distant, a strongly sympathetic or critical attitude, a gratifying or a punishing attitude, a need to assure the person that he is loved, a tendency to allow the person to be inappropriately dependent, or to be excessively passive or aggressive toward the person are illustrations. Sexual acting out and the acting out of anger are more gross illustrations.

Many more illustrations of the expression of displaced pastor attitudes could be given. These would include an anxiety to have treatment continue or to have it stop. Either way subtle means may be used unconsciously to communicate to the person what the therapist desires. In the supervision of pastors such material may show up on a tape, or simply in the way in which a session is reported. Overemphasis on or resistance to particular aspects of the person's problems, wanting to do the work of the person for him, not giving him sufficient understanding and support, listening intensively to some kinds of problems but going to sleep when others are discussed are other illustrations of displaced attitudes.

Some displacement is a normal phenomenon and not necessarily a sign of neurosis in the pastor. Displacement of this kind occurs in many human relationships. The displacement of good feelings may enrich human relationships, provided they are expressed appropriately. It is when negative or harmful feelings are displaced, or that positive feelings become too strong that relationships are hurt. Such displacements are very prominent in the marriage relationship, and the pastor should be familiar with the concept of projective identification.[9] One criterion for evaluating any kind of displaced feelings is their intensity; the more intense and insistent usually the more displacement. On the other hand, genuine feelings may also be intense.

Countertransference feelings may be experienced in any pastoral relationship. Here the evaluation of the person-to-person relationship as distinct from displaced feelings may be difficult at times, but needs to be made. In preaching, administration, conducting funerals or weddings, in calling and in other contacts, both the conscious and the unconscious attitudes of the pastor may be expressed. People may encourage this by asking for the satisfaction of dependency needs, or for verbal punishment, or for some other healthy or neurotic manifestation from the pastor. Many of the difficult problems of pastoral relationships are experiences of countertransference and need to be understood as such.

TRANSFERENCE AND COUNTERTRANSFERENCE IN THE EXPERIENCE OF FEMALE PASTORS

It will be evident that this chapter has been written largely from the point of view of the male pastor. With the increased number of women coming into the ministry, attention needs to be given by those women to the quality of emotional relationships they experience. This should really be a subject for intensive study by women pastors who are intensively trained in the field and who have examined their own possible transference reactions through personal psychotherapy. Here only certain general comments will be made.

First, the same general principles will apply. On the level of person-to-person relationships, the attitudes of the woman pastor will be an important factor, but the attitude of other persons will be equally important. If the woman pastor is aggressive, as she is likely to be, she will immediately find a negative reaction in persons who do not like aggressive women. A kindly type of woman pastor will be very appealing to some persons, but not to others.

On the transference level, the quality of response will be determined by the same factors which operate with male pastors. Because of relationships with their mothers, and also for cultural reasons,[10] some women will react strongly against women pastors, while others will be attracted to them. The same will be true of men. A woman pastor will experience the same kind of sexual seductiveness from men that a male pastor experiences from women. Women who have homosexual tendencies will be attracted to women pastors unless they are reacting against their homosexual feelings. It will be easy for some men and women to seek a dependent, mothering relationship from a woman pastor.

On the countertransference side, unconscious feelings of the woman pastor, both about herself, her profession, and men and women will need to be understood. Some women pastors will be more attracted to men, just as some men pastors are more attracted to women. Some women pastors will be frightened of men, or perhaps more accurately, frightened of their feelings for or against men. Women pastors with homosexual feelings may find themselves either attracted to or repelled by other women.

Some women pastors have been heard to talk as though they intend to ignore the sexual issues in their relationships with others. They say they are persons and intend to deal with others as persons. But there are no persons who are not male or female. The gender issue will not be resolved by pastors of either sex by ignoring it. Such denial is defensive, and sooner or later the defensiveness gets in the way of helpful relationships.

We have been talking largely about women pastors in the parish. Nothing we have said should be taken to mean that women should not be in the ministry. It just means that there will be

certain problems of relationship which need to be understood so
they can be handled constructively. It will not be difficult for
women to do a better job at this than men have done because they
are more intuitive, and may feel the need to pay more attention to
it. For either sex, adequate training on this level is needed in the
seminary. Women who enter the pastoral psychotherapy field
should have become aware of their own person-to-person (including gender) responses, as well as their possible countertransference reactions through their own personal therapy.

SUMMARY

In summary, the responses of the pastor of either sex may be
understood either as motivated from within or as being stimulated by the person. If motivated from within, they may be
either genuine person-to-person responses, or they may be
countertransference. If stimulated or provoked by the person
they are probably also countertransference. On the other hand,
the attitudes of the person may also be conscious, person-to-
person characteristics, or they may be transference. Because of
the tension under which the person finds himself, and the necessity for him to bring data into the interview, many of his feelings, if not all, will contain transference elements and should
be understood as such. It is not always necessary to interpret
these in terms of past experiences. However, focus should be on
whatever is happening within the therapy session, how the person
is feeling and behaving, and what this indicates about his conflicts
and defenses. The need to attack defenses is countertransference
on the part of the pastor. The pastor should rather help the person
focus on the experiences and feelings behind the defenses. When
the person is ready he will give up his defenses. There is no
substitute for constant focus on what is happening between person
and therapist in their interaction in the interview. For the pastor,
part of this must be on what he is feeling within himself.

The pastoral relationship has within it possibilities for great
good, but also for ineffectiveness and even harm. To the real

person-to-person qualities and the transferential qualities of the relationship must be added a third factor, a sense of the reality of what the Gospel requires of both pastor and person. Sometimes this is explicit; quite often, implicit but effective. The needs of the person may combine with the needs of the pastor or an ecclesiastical body to create a distorted and even pathological relationship,[11] and this can be rationalized by theological concepts. The Gospel, grounded as it is in a profound understanding of the nature of human life, as well as in a revelation of God, offers a sound basis for creative and redemptive relationships where the condition of honest self-understanding and desire for growth are present. There is no question about the need for correction of the symbolic meaning of the pastor held by some persons and groups. The pastor can assist in this process only as his motivation is self-honesty rather than defensiveness, and as he is moving toward the integration of his own sense of his symbolic meaning with the New Testament ideal.

Another transference phenomenon in religion should be mentioned. It is that God is often used as an object of transference or displacement. Feelings of childish dependence, for example, may be displaced onto God, and then we will expect God to do all sorts of things for us. If we will analyze the feelings and attitudes expressed in our prayers we may find large elements of childish dependence. Childish dependence is expecting God to do for us what we can do for ourselves. Or we may displace anger toward God. Or we may expect God to be an indulgent father, rather than expect us to take responsibility for ourselves. The examination of theological ideas may reveal how we are using them to rationalize some displacement that should be outgrown. To do this we have to look underneath the idea to the manner in which we use it. For example, the idea of the will of God may be used to express mature personal and religious attitudes or it may be used to express childish attitudes. In pastoral psychotherapy we are more concerned with the life processes revealed in the use of religious ideas than in the content of the idea. Our service to others may mean changing something in ourselves that is hindering progress toward wholeness in self or others. Again, pastoral psychotherapy is being a healing person to others by permitting them to deal honestly and autonomously with their own condition.

In the next chapter we will indicate some of the specific problems encountered in persons suffering from various pathologies.

NOTES

1. See Carl Rogers, *Client-Centered Therapy,* Boston: Houghton-Mifflin, 1951.

2. See chapter 2.

3. Many books deal with the therapeutic relationship, or therapeutic alliance. Among them are Roger A. McKinnon and Robert Michels, *The Psychiatric Interview in Clinical Practice,* Philadelphia: W. B. Saunders, 1971; Carl Rogers, op. cit., Robert Langs, *The Bipersonal Field,* Jason Aronson, 1976; Gertrude and Rubin Blanck, *Ego Psychology: The Theory and Practice,* New York: Columbia University Press, 1974; C. B. Truax and R. R. Carkuff, *Toward Effective Counseling and Psychotherapy,* Chicago: Aldine, 1967; Ralph R. Greenson, *The Technique and Practice of Psychoanalysis,* New York: International Universities Press, 1968. The therapeutic or working alliance is the basis for any therapeutic work.

4. See the next chapter. A discussion of transference and object relations is found in Harry Guntrip, *Schizoid Phenomena, Object Relations and the Self,* New York: International Universities Press, 1969. A discussion of transference in relation to marriage therapy is Bernard L. Greene and Alfred P. Solomon, "The Triangular Transference Reactions," *American Journal of Psychotherapy,* vol. XVII, No. 3, pp. 443–456, July 1961.

A description of transference relationships likely to be found in various pathological conditions is to be found in MacKinnon and Michels, op. cit.

5. Erik Erikson, *Childhood and Society,* rev. ed., New York: W. W. Norton, 1963.

6. The liberal churches, particularly, having gotten rid of the devil, need another symbol of evil, and the pastor often serves for this. The pastoral counseling department in a liberal seminary is likely to be symbolized in the same manner.

7. J. G. Ranck, "Religious Conservatism — Liberalism and Mental Health," in *The Minister's Own Mental Health,* ed. Wayne Oates, Great Neck, New York: Channel Press, 1961; G. D. Stern, "Assessing Theological Student Personality Structure," *Journal of Pastoral Care,* vol. 8 (1954), pp. 76–83.

8. Some reliable discussions are: Karl Menninger, *Theory of Psychoanalytic Technique,* New York: Basic Books, 1958; William U. Snyder, *The Psychotherapy*

Relationship, New York: Macmillan, 1961; E. A. Grollman, "Some Sights and Insights of History, Psychology and Psychoanalysis Concerning the Father-God and Mother-Goddess Concepts of Judaism and Christianity," *Americal Imago,* vol. 20 (1963), pp. 187–209; A. Godlin, "Transference in Pastoral Counseling," *Theology Digest,* vol. 9 (1961), pp. 78–83. A discussion of transference from the point of view of client-centered therapy is to be found in Carl Rogers, *Client-Centered Therapy,* Boston: Houghton-Mifflin, 1951.

9. For a discussion of projective identification as related to marriage problems see Bernard L. Greene, *A Clinical Approach to Marital Problems,* Springfield, Ill.: Charles C Thomas Co., 1970.

10. For a discussion of cultural factors in the transference relationship see John Spiegel, *Transactions, The Interplay Between Individual, Family and Society,* ed. John Papajohn, chapter 10, New York: Jason Aronson, 1971.

11. An example of this is when the pastor feels pressured, either from within himself or his ecclesiastical body, to enforce rigid standards of belief, practice, or ethics.

Chapter 8

Specific Problems in the Therapeutic Relationship

The need for an accurate description of the symptoms of a person grows out of the fact that symptoms reflect underlying conflicts, feelings, and defenses. Thus, when symptoms are grouped into the various diagnostic categories, a kind of short-hand understanding of the person is available to the pastor who understands the dynamics of symptomatology. While therapy is focused on the person, the various diagnostic categories give some understanding of what is going on in that person. This chapter will not be an exhaustive discussion of the various categories, but it will show the need for a grasp of such information by the pastor.[1]

THE DEPRESSED PERSON

Many depressed persons consult the pastor or sit in the congregation with a sad look, seemingly asking for help, but also ready to reject any help that may come. The normal effect of this on many pastors is a lowering of their mood. They experience a sadness, a minor depression in the presence of a depressed person. This may lead to a frequent popular response—the giving of encouragement, figurative backslapping, and similar techniques designed to make them feel better. If they feel better, the pastor feels better. Depressed people may use these methods on themselves. Some smile continuously to cover their sad feelings. Some are inveterate jokesters. Indeed, some of our best comedians have been depressed; in their attempt to feel better they learned to make others laugh, and in making others laugh they feel better.

Depressed persons have other characteristics that may elicit nontherapeutic responses. They want to avoid being hurt, but they hurt themselves and provoke others to hurt them. They are very controlling but appear weak. They make excessive demands but make themselves appear unworthy; they crave love but are afraid and guilty about love; they are very dependent but reject suggestions; they want help but often alienate the helper. The pastor must learn to deal openly with the many ambivalent attitudes of the depressed person.[2]

The response of the pastor will depend on his own emotional makeup, and possible experiences with depressed people in his childhood, for example, a parent. He may feel a challenge to his own power and effectiveness. His sense of omnipotence, or the mistaken attitude that somehow religion always has the answers to depression because it removes guilt, may be shaken. He may respond by being overprotective or oversympathetic.

The pastor may feel a sense of frustration in working with depressed persons, and may respond to this with guilt and anger. Responses to appeals for help which are rejected can create anger. Conflicting tendencies in them need to be recognized in an understanding manner that creates self-respect.

Occasionally, the pastor may feel bored and indifferent which are expressions of unrecognized anger. He may stimulate a person to make him feel better, and feel he has accomplished something. If the pastor feels the anger of the person, he may react with anger or withdraw emotionally. The ambivalence of the person needs to be dealt with simultaneously, with understanding and not in a punishing or critical manner. The person needs help in discovering how he blocks himself.

There are several theological problems that may be confusing in relation to depressed persons. One is the guilt experienced by these people. The inexperienced pastor may find that attempts to bring a sense of the forgiveness of God only intensifies the guilt feelings. This is because they are experiencing pathological guilt, not real guilt, though some real guilt may be involved. The pathological guilt is due to deep, unconscious conflict in feelings.

On the other hand, the pastor may be consulted by a person who feels very depressed because of something he has done, or something which has been done to him about which he has deep, unrecognized anger that is creating his depression. One way of distinguishing between pathological guilt and depression and depression and guilt arising out of an event is to take a careful history. Was the person depressed and did he suffer from guilt feelings before the event? Or did these feelings develop after the event? A pastor having taken a careful history of a man and finding that the depression was a number of years standing, referred him to a professional therapist. The man told the professional that he was depressed because the day before his wife told him she was leaving. Actually, he knew that she was leaving because of the very unsatisfactory marriage due to the long depression. This indicates the need in careful investigation, and it also illustrates how depressed persons may manipulate and control a therapist so that possible therapy is destroyed. In situations where the depression seems to be the reaction to an event, there still remains the question as to why the individual chooses to become depressed rather than to adapt in some other manner.

The appeal of the depressed person to the omnipotence of the pastor may involve his theological concepts. Unconsciously, the pastor may feel some support for his own sense of omnipotence in the concept of the omnipotence of God. He may feel unconsciously that he shares in the omnipotence of God. Not only is the power of the pastor being threatened, but also that of God is being questioned in a subtle way by the depressed person. The pastor may respond to this by using an inspirational approach. This is particularly true in sermons. Out of his own depression the pastor may preach very inspirational sermons, and draw many depressed persons to his congregation who are looking for something to lift them. Or the pastor may overdo the "shepherding" concept somewhat in vogue today. Depressed people seem to invite this but do not respond well to it. As a matter of fact, the shepherding image needs to be translated into another figure, since it is rejected by many moderns who resent being symbolized as sheep. The use of this symbol, even though it is very Biblical, may also say something about the attitudes of the pastor.

In dealing with depressed persons, the pastor needs to be clear on the theology of suffering, as well as the psychology of masochism and self-punishment. There is such a thing as realistic suffering and pain experienced because it may lead to a constructive, desirable end. There is also the self-inflicted punishment of the depressed person, where either self-punishment or the enjoyment of suffering for some pathological end is the motive. The former seeks some realistic change. The latter makes suffering an end in itself or a means to a perverse goal. Theologically, all suffering is often identified with the sufferings of Christ, which tends to confirm the omnipotence of the depressed person without any sense of release or change or no experience of resurrection. Sometimes during Holy Week the sufferings of Christ are dealt with in a manner which encourages the overidentification of the depressed person with Christ, again without curative results since the nature of the sufferings are very different.[3] For the reverse reason many persons find themselves depressed during the Christmas season when the advent of love is being celebrated, since they are unable to experience love and enter into the joyous celebration. Theologically, distinctions need to be made between constructive and pathological experiences of suffering just as they need to be made between constructive and pathological experiences of guilt.

The task of the pastoral therapist is to bring to his relationship with the depressed person an understanding of the various and complex aspects of human experience. While he supports the healthy aspects of the person, he brings his interpretative skills to bear on the depressed ego. This means exploring the individual's oversevere conscience, and the guilt and punishment process within him, as well as other dynamics, particularly the introjection of anger. This must be done gently but firmly. The person needs to be given the feeling that he can suffer as much as he wants to; the therapist will not interfere with this. He will, however, seek an understanding of both the reasons for the suffering within the feelings and experiences of the person and also of the consequences. He will seek to create a feeling of self-esteem in the depressed person in a genuine manner, but not in an artificial manner. He will try to help the person see where he blocks himself, but leave him free to remove those blocks when he feels able. Interpretation should center on the immediate situation, particularly on feelings of frustrated love and feelings of anger. Psychogenetic factors should not be neglected. Often the pastor can use the behavior of the person in the therapy hour to illustrate where his problem lies, that is, in the sense of loss of a loved object and in the person's inability to express angry feelings toward that object.

Angry feelings against the therapist will occur and should be responded to with understanding and with the assurance that it is all right to be angry, but it needs to be explored. The pastor will need to sense whether the angry feelings are toward him as a person, or toward him as a symbolic figure or both, and to explore these possibilities with the person. The real crux of therapy with depressed persons is to help them withdraw their anger from themselves, and deal with it in relation to their need for self-punishment. Catharsis as such is of little use. The discovery by the person as to how he has handled his feelings of anger, how these have created guilt and depression, the reasons for his inability to experience love, the harmful consequences of his responses of himself, and his potential for moving on to better ways of handling his problems is essential to the therapy process. The cognitive element is important in such therapy, but the experiential aspect is fundamental.

If the pastor will listen closely to the depressed person, he will recognize a dual fear, the fear of death and the fear of life. Pathological and existential factors seem inextricably interwoven in these fears. The pathological factors need to be interpreted. The existential factors need to be clarified and understood. What is needed is an experience with a person which demonstrates in a gentle manner the fallacy of these fears, as well as what Tillich[4] called the courage to be. The courage to be does not deny the existential realities of evil, suffering, and death. It absorbs these into itself and makes a profound affirmation of the essential goodness and meaning of life in spite of them. This means that the pastoral therapist must have mastered, to a good measure, his own existential fears of both life and death. Theological rationalizations or ideas of immortality are not what is needed here. Only a living faith that expresses itself quietly in human relationships, that is not afraid in the presence of the life and death fears of another, but can gently encourage their exploration, can bring genuine healing of the depressed person. The quiet faith of the pastor that life is worth healing even though that process lies through the valley of pain, communicates strength to the person. The courage to be implies the willingness to open oneself to the experience of love, both in terms of receiving and giving the use of one's potentials in creative aspects of living. The danger of the pastor is to lapse into a pseudooptimism which verbalizes a courage which is not experienced. The opportunity of the pastor is to possess a faith deeply grounded in trust which makes creative experience possible in the face of the many threats to life. This is genuine religious faith. This is the courage to be in the face of all denials of the meaning of existence.

ANXIETY AND PHOBIC ATTACKS

These somewhat differ but similar reactions will be discussed together. They are seen frequently in the office of the pastor or on the phone, whether in the parish or in a therapy center.

Anxiety[5] can be experienced in varying degrees, including intense panic, symptoms of distress such as a rapid heart rate, nausea, sweating, heavy and rapid breathing, diarrhea, dizziness. Sometimes the panic is so great that the person becomes sure he is going to die.

The phobic reaction is experienced more in anticipation. There are many situations which become the objects of phobias. Children usually go through a stage where they will have phobic dreams of wild animals or some other danger. Phobias are anxiety reactions focused on a particular object, and the fear is anticipated only in relation to that object. Anxiety reaction is a more generalized response which may not be attached consciously to any object or situation.

Pastors themselves are subject to anxieties and phobias. Sunday morning anxiety attack followed by Monday depression is sometimes experienced. One pastor experienced anxiety when about to preach because his impulse toward exhibitionism collided with his conscience and his knowledge of what would happen if this occurred. Anxiety can be experienced by anyone who is in a situation where he might fail, a student taking an examination, for example. Some persons avoid certain aspects of church life, such as the Holy Communion because of anxiety. Some pastors experience intense anxiety when called upon to visit a sick person. These manifestations are all symptoms of inner conflict.

Like depression, anxiety may be pathological or it may be rooted in the inherent threats involved in being human, or a combination of these. Many persons avoid the thought of their own death or the possible death of a loved one because of the anxiety such thoughts stir up. Yet everyone needs to come to terms with the possibility of his own death. Tillich[6] analyzed existential anxieties as those of fate and death, of meaninglessness and of guilt. The answer to these anxieties is genuine religious faith or the courage to be. Many people have been misled by those who advocate repeating verses of Scripture or certain prayers, or participating in other religious acts as a cure for anxiety. These may have a suggestive influence on certain types of persons, but they do not resolve the real issues. Only coming to terms with the source of the anxiety can do this.

The anxious person feels faced with a threat to his existence. The threat may come from within him or from the outside, and he feels helpless and passive in dealing with it. If an inner threat the term anxiety is usually used; if an outer threat, the term fear. The fear of death or of some other harm to himself or to loved ones may be part of the picture. Such persons make strong appeals for help, but the usual kind of reassurances are useless. Anxiety about death may be existential or it may be symbolic arising out of inner conflict. In either pathological or existential anxiety the cause of the panic may be displaced to a symbolic object. This may be vague or specific. Thus, a woman who feels her husband withdrawing his love from her may displace her anxiety to her children, or a person who is suffering from anxiety due to sexual or hostile impulses may displace this to many other vague or specific fears.

The pastor will soon learn that describing this process intellectually does little good. The person is undergoing an experience of helplessness which is deeply emotional. The above description of the dynamics of anxiety is somewhat oversimplified as far as the pathology of severe reactions are concerned. The pastor should have a thorough understanding of all of the processes involved so that he can understand what is going on in the person. For example, there will also be repression, denial, and usually a preconditioning to anxiety due to earlier experiences.

The pastor will need to consider the possibilities of his own countertransferences. These will depend on how he has handled his own anxieties. In his desire to help, which itself may become anxiety, the pastor may confirm the person in his anxiety and helplessness by unreal and premature reassurance. An attempt to alleviate the person's sense of helplessness until the underlying causes are dealt with will fail. The pastor may then feel frustrated and angry, indications of countertransference. The pastor's desire to have others dependent on him may be a reaction to his own feelings of helplessness. He may be sure, however, that the person will test him and seek out his weaknesses.

On the positive side, there is no substitute for a deep sense of confidence on the part of the pastor. Such confidence should help him relax and listen attentively to the person. He needs to sense empathically what the person is experiencing. He should be alert for denials and displacements, and also for reaction formations. The anxious person may try to make himself look very righteous with no forbidden impulses. Listening carefully will give the person the opportunity to ventilate his thoughts and feelings.[7] The attempt to understand on the part of the pastor will help the person seek understanding. Any support or reassurance which is then given will be grounded in an assessment of the strength of the person, not his helplessness. If there are real fears present, the pastor may respond helpfully to these. The task of the therapist is to help the person learn how he can deal constructively with his own neurotic anxieties by first working out their causes.

The major therapeutic action in panic states is to encourage the person to talk about his present life situation, the conflicts involved in it, the nature of the fears growing out of it, the inner conflicts which he experiences, particularly conflicts between impulse and conscience, and to encourage him to take responsibility for his feelings. The task of the pastor is to interpret gently and gradually what he believes the person is struggling with, but only after he has sufficient evidence on which to base an interpretation. The reasons for the person's passivity in the face of danger, rather than aggressive dealing with the situation may need to be explored. In many situations the person's background will need to be explored in order to deal with long-standing anxieties and psychogenetic material. Adult anxieties and panics may have a direct relationship to childhood fears and threatening relationships. This does not mean that present experiences are minimized. It does mean that anxieties from the past may be living in and influencing present experiences, even though the relationship is at first obscure and only vaguely symbolized. The exploration of both past and present experiences must be done in detail, not allowing the person to pass them off by vague generalizations. This reliving may be a new kind of experience for the person, and in itself can be ego strengthening.

HYSTERIA

Anxious people often become hysterical. The popular conception of hysterical behavior is that the individual becomes

uncontrollably upset at some occurrence. The pastor may see this
behavior at a funeral or even a wedding, or he may be called at
three in the morning by someone who demands immediate relief.

There is much more than this to hysterical persons. Usually
they are attractive people, and make themselves so because it is
part of their seductiveness. They dramatize their communications
and punctuate it with much body language. They are very emotional, but the feelings they express are usually defensive feelings
against the underlying pain which is the real problem. This pain is
a feeling they are not loved, accompanied by a hunger and a
demand for love. They are also afraid of love because of what it
represents in childhood relationships. They have not resolved
their childish love relationships with their parents, and hetero-
sexual love is usually more than tinged with yearnings, frustration, and anger toward the parent of the opposite sex. In their
seductiveness they often choose a marriage partner who is too
absorbed in his own problems to satisfy their needs. In addition,
in their need to protect themselves from love they often select a
partner who is incapable of giving them the love they both crave
and fear. Thus, the frustrations of childhood are continued, but
with the complications of adult relationships.

The pastor will find these persons to be dependent, clinging,
and suggestible. Indeed, they are the people on whom suggestive
types of therapy work to relieve symptoms temporarily, but not
to resolve inner conflict. They are continually in search of peace
of mind, but seem helpless to attain it. In their helplessness they
will appeal to the pastor.[8] They also appeal to friends for advice,
and have ways of getting contradictory advice, which is really
what they want. There is a strong element of guilt and self-
punishment, which often leads to the continuance of a detrimental relationship such as marriage. They are very self-centered,
indulgent, and given to exaggerations. Usually they have a way of
communicating to the pastor subtly the advice they want him to
give, and which they do not intend to take.

Hysterical persons make strong identifications. This gives the
impression that they are many-sided; they are really living after a

number of models and do not know exactly who they are. Thus, their identities are confused, and they may alternate between rather mature attitudes and childish attitudes. It is difficult for them to let themselves become completely involved in therapy. They want to discuss others rather than themselves. They may give a deceptive impression of their insight, seeming to have much more than is true. They often have more insight into others than into themselves. They will make heavy demands for extra attention, such as phone calls.

The pastor can easily be misled by the apparently strong positive transference these persons make easily. They seek gratification for their dependency. They have friends who gratify these needs, and they have an image of the pastor which places him in the same role. Subtly they will communicate this. Or they may seek to invoke punishment from the pastor, and again this fits into certain pastoral images. If the pastor does not gratify these needs for dependency and childish love, anger will result. They will feel both loved and hated, and will respond with ambivalence. To deal adequately with such persons the pastor, whether in a parish or in a center, will need a thorough understanding of them and a deep insight into his own reactions and relationships.

For example, the pastor will need to understand his own responses to the person's seductiveness and dramatization, to his helplessness and dependency, to his demands, manipulation, and anger. These tendencies may be encouraged, indulged or punished, or may be met with coldness and aloofness. They are protective devices. They should be interpreted at the opportune time. The pastor may find the person quoting him or misquoting him to friends or other professionals, such as physicians, or checking up on him. The basic problem here is the person's mistrust, and the pastor will need to examine his own reactions to such mistrust, as well as help the person to talk about it. The pastor should be very slow in believing how other persons are represented to him.

Being very comfortable within himself helps the pastor to deal with the ambivalences and acting out of the hysterical person.

This will make it possible for him to help the person bring out both sides of a problem, so he sees clearly the how of his responses before the question of the why is raised. But the behavior and its underlying motivation must be interpreted, not gratified nor criticized. Understanding needs to be expressed toward the person's real pain, his need for love, his fear of love and his guilt about love. The person must be allowed to make his own decisions by the simple device of quietly declining the responsibility of making them. The person's need to have others accept responsibility and make decisions for him must also be interpreted.

The acting out of the hysteric must be dealt with in an open, confronting, and interpretative manner. Such acting out can be understood as the seeking satisfaction for impulses and needs rather than understanding them. The acting out behavior is used to keep the conflict repressed and avoid insight. In other words, it is a defense, and hence will be justified by the ego. The hysterical person is inclined to act out sexually or in anger, but often deny themselves the very satisfactions they are seeking. Thus a woman may act out sexually outside of her marriage but find herself unable to enjoy this behavior. Guilt prevents the enjoyment of either the sexual or the anger components of the behavior. It should be obvious that sexual acting out between the pastor and the person can be very detrimental and should be avoided. The sexual problems of the pastor should be dealt with in his own therapy.

Hysterical persons who "convert" their problems into physical symptomatology sometimes appeal to a pastor after being to a number of physicians, faith healers, and assorted helpers without results. The pastor should first insist on a physical examination by a competent physician, with a report from the physician to himself. If the report is negative, usually the best procedure in therapy is to minimize the discussion of the physical symptoms, not listening to long recitals of complaints, but moving into the person's emotional conflicts. As these are resolved, the need for the symptoms declines. Indeed, sometimes the establishing of a relationship with a therapist brings a marked diminution of symptoms. This should not be mistaken for "cure." The under-lying problems still remain, and if not resolved the symptoms will return.

THE OBSESSIVE-COMPULSIVE PERSON

The obsessive-compulsive[9] individual is both interesting and difficult for the pastor. Much of his behavior can be understood as an attempt to allay anxiety and find security. He both craves love and is frightened by it. His apparent need to conform to definite standards of belief and action may appeal to the pastor until he discovers that this is used in a very manipulating, control-ing manner. The obsessive is highly controlled by his conscience and in turn wants to control others. He will hold his views of right and wrong rigidly, and will be so intent on doing what he considers his duty that the pastor may be seduced into using him in many church responsibilities. This person finds it difficult to relax and can easily become what has been called a "workaholic." With all of this he is definitely out of touch with his own feelings. He is very frightened about either giving or receiving love, but is constantly seeking it by his good works. He finds it hard to trust, and is so inwardly controlled that he surrenders his personal autonomy. Thus, he is deeply unhappy and dissatisfied. His con-stant activity and upholding of narrow standards of behavior does not bring him the love he seeks. This person often uses relig-ion to support his demands on himself and others. The helping professions are very attractive to such people, as they give opportunity to work out their compulsive needs with professional justification.

If these tendencies become a full-blown neurosis, the person will complain about unwanted thoughts intruding into his mind that he cannot prevent. Thus, in the act of making love, a woman may go over her store list or a man think about something he has to do at the office the next day. One function of such thoughts is to prevent the closeness that the person craves but also fears. Or the person may feel compelled to commit certain ritualistic but nonsensical acts, such as checking the kitchen range a number of times, checking the doors to make sure they are locked. Or he may develop elaborate and unique rituals of his own.

One of the major defenses of the obsessional person is to avoid feelings by intellectualizing. He develops a more or less elaborate intellectual system into which he tries to fit himself and others. This keeps him away from his own feelings and those of others. He takes a cold, austere, and rigid attitude and his thinking is usually heavily weighted with ideas as to what he or others ought to do. Sometimes he acts as though his thoughts are omnipotent, that others somehow will conform to his thoughts without the ideas ever being communicated. This is a high level of manipulation and control, as well as magical omnipotence. At all costs, feelings must be kept under rigid control which means not even allowing them to emerge into awareness.

The obsessive person is highly ambivalent. He craves affection and closeness, but is very frightened by it and tends to withdraw or become angry when others seek to get too close. This reaction is the basis for many problems in marriage. He has strong ambitions and desires, but is afraid to take the risk in working them out. If he attempts to express feelings or desires, he becomes anxious and retreats into his intellectual system.

The pastor who sees these people either in the parish or therapy center will need to have a firm understanding of his own emotional processes. If he is somewhat obsessional, inclined to intellectualize, he may be seduced by the person into an abstract discussion. This is exactly what the person wants, since it avoids the roots of his problems, that is, his feelings. He wants help on his own terms and not at the point of his real problems. If the pastor dislikes or is irritated by the intellectualization, he may become disturbed by the person's refusal or inability to deal with his real feelings. Or the pastor may feel secure in the person's intellectualizations and encourage them. Suddenly he may find himself in an argument with the person or attempt to deal with him by rational means.

The overintellectualizing process leads many persons to be attracted to certain professions such as the ministry and teaching. These professions seem to give justification for the process, especially teaching. Theology or science as intellectual systems should be void of feeling and strictly objective. We know today that theological, ethical and scientific systems often are grounded in deep unrecognized feelings. When such persons become advisors or counselors for others, they proceed on the assumption that a well organized system is needed, and they proceed to give it. This completely ignores the deep emotional and motivational processes in human beings. It may help already obsessional persons to further rationalize their existence, but it does not promote growth or health. The glaring fault of our educational system is that it does not give sufficient and adequate attention to emotional factors in both teacher and student. It is a hazard of theological education that it tends to encourage obsessional processes, or it stimulates other students to rebel against adequate and legitimate intellectual processes. Such a division is usually apparent in a student body. Either direction distracts the pastor from the deep emotional and relational roots of spiritual life, and they both tend to lead to professional bankruptcy after some years in the ministry.

We return to a positive approach to pastoral therapy with obsessional persons. The pastor cannot avoid these people. They are in the church as well as in all other organizations. Organizational structures appeal to them and give them security. The pastor will have to deal with them administratively if not in therapy. He needs to understand them and himself in relation to them. If therapy is needed or desired, he will have to know if he is adequately trained for the task, and if not make referrals to other resources.

Either therapeutically or administratively an easy, relaxed attitude is essential in the pastor. His emphasis should be on understanding. In a kind, firm manner he should avoid being controlled by obsessive persons, but communicate an acceptance of them.

Therapeutically, the task is to try to help the person become aware of his feelings, and thus remove the isolation between feeling and intellect. The pastor must demonstrate that he is not afraid of feelings, either his own or those of the person. Sometimes the obsessional is helped by being told that the pastor himself would be angry or anxious in a given situation, though this should not be overdone.

It will help if the pastor uses concrete language in his communications to these people. Abstractions tend to lead them into more intellectualization. When they use abstract terms he should translate them into concrete terms or ask them to do so. Philosophizing and theologizing should be avoided. Questions such as "What did that experience mean to you?" should be changed to "How did you feel in that situation?"

The pastoral therapist must deal openly and honestly with the ambivalences of the person. He should first seek to clarify both sides of the ambivalence so they are apparent to the person, and then help the person see how he blocks himself and his life by not being able to choose one side or the other. Making decisions is difficult for these people, since it means accepting one alternative of the conflict or finding a compromise. The anxiety connected with decision making needs to be brought out, as well as the fear of risk-taking the person will have. This will be rooted in the conflict between anxiety and trust. The trust the pastor shows in basic life processes in himself and in the person will be of great help.

Assisting the person to evaluate the consequences of his behavior will be a major step in the process of change. A person who cannot make a decision about a job is blocking his own progress because of his fears, and may be saying that he really wants a third alternative. A person who cannot do his part in resolving a marriage conflict may need help in seeing that the situation is as he wants it in spite of the pain involved. Two obsessional persons in a marriage may join in a collusion that is very self-defeating and painful, but insist that all of the change be in the other person. The consequences of such behavior needs to be clarified, bringing the person face to face with the decision as to whether he wants to continue it or not. In this process the person will need help in expressing and working out his fear or feelings, to resolve his doubts and take risks in making decisions, and to learn to use his capacity for autonomy.

We have said little about compulsions. Compulsions spring from the same emotional processes as obsessions, except they demand action of some kind rather than thought. The classical handwashing compulsion is well-known. It is accompanied by ideas of uncleanliness, guilt, and anxiety, and its aim is to undo conflicts and guilt in regard to anger or sex. There are many other compulsions, some common and others unique to the person. A rather unusual one was in a young woman who felt compelled to pick up any glass she saw along the street and eat it. The aim of compulsions is to allay anxiety and create security. The security they create is false.

Compulsions develop into rituals of various kinds. Life has to be lived in certain specified ways. There is a stress on order, on details, and the necessity of being correct and perfect. It is as though an outside power were in control. The autonomous functions of the ego, such as choice, decision making, and evaluating actions are surrendered to the authority of internal demands of an oversevere conscience in conflict with wishes. There is a strong magical element present in rituals. The person feels that particular acts will accomplish something otherwise beyond his control. He is both being controlled and seeking to control his own fate. Sometimes the conflict becomes a veritable life and death struggle. The individual is frightened at forces which make for both life and death, that is love, sex, and anger, and these must be controlled at all costs. If they get out of hand both he and others may be destroyed. When such a person talks about a fear of death he may consciously mean physical death, but the roots are deeper than this and involve the death of the self. The compulsive and obsessive person suffers from a deep sense of alienation from others. He cannot experience a sense of intimacy or closeness because of anxiety connected with his conflicts and because of the immaturity of the ego. Alienation means death, or in Biblical terms the wages of sin (alienation) are death. There are very profound aspects to a religious understanding of such experiences.

All of these dynamics may be expressed in rituals, including religious rituals.

In the light of this is understandable why compulsive and obsessive persons become deeply involved in religion. They are involved in the essential struggle between life and death which is central to religious faith. They also find religious rituals dealing with these struggles appealing, or sometimes they create rituals of their own.

Basically, rituals are a group way of doing things. There are all sorts of rituals not only in religion, but in business, law, education, medicine, family life, and personal existence. They are necessary to people living and acting together. They may also become compulsive acts.

Religious rituals include acts of worship. The whole gamut of life and death feelings — anger, hatred, rage, love, tenderness, sex, faith, guilt, anxiety, growth, fulfillment, pain and suffering or joy, despair, closeness, alienation, a sense of self or personal identity or a loss of self — may be a part of the religious struggle and worship from time to time. The real purpose of religious ritual is to bring the conflict to the surface and deal with it creatively. A creative solution may not be what practical men would approve, and religious faith has often been called impractical.

The neurotic person distorts religious rituals to fit his private and concealed purposes. These purposes grow out of his individual dynamics which may have many features in common with existential conflict. But the major difference may be in the level of consciousness or awareness of the components in the struggle, and in the goals of the neurotic process. These goals are to use religious ritual for the perpetuation of the neurotic conflict, for self-punishment and for control. Ritual is, thus, used in the service of neurotic need, not in the service of the ego for creative, life-giving ends. Creative religion constantly faces the task of purging itself of magical elements brought into it by neurotic needs. When religious ritual is used in a way that overemphasizes form and underemphasizes feelings and strivings, it becomes neurotic. A cold, impersonal funeral service is like death itself! On the other hand, the use of ritual which encourages the excessive expression of feeling, and defines the feelings a participant must have and the order they must occur, and prescribes the exact form of the outcome is also being controlled by neurotic processes.

In pastoral psychotherapy detailed attention to obsessions and compulsions should be avoided. Overemphasis on the symptoms only avoids the real issues, and the pastor should not become a party to this. Rather the conflicts and anxieties in the life of the person need attention. The deeper insecurities and adverse consequences of the behavior need to be brought out at whatever pace the ego of the individual will permit. Attempts to get these persons to relax may be futile or be turned into a ritual of relaxation which in itself creates more compulsiveness. Giving assurances of a religious "cure" must be avoided. The real meaning of faith — that a person has the courage to take risks and face up to his own inner problems — needs to be made clear. Healthy religion requires constant adventure, risk taking, search for new insights into self, and new relationships grounded in trust and love. Childish dependence that demands that one be rescued should be discouraged. These persons, and many others, need to be helped to understand that all anxiety cannot be eliminated from life, that some anxiety is part of existence, and that our God-given potentials need to be used in courageous living that overcomes anxiety. The pastor's own ability to give persons an experience of closeness and trust will help them to free up their own potentials.

Every pastor has to determine whether he has the ability and training to help compulsive persons therapeutically. If not, he should be prepared to make a referral. He still has to deal with them within the parish.

THE PARANOID PERSON

The pastor in the parish will be well acquainted with individuals with paranoid characteristics, and they are seen rather frequently in therapy centers. Some persons with these tendencies are very antagonistic to religion and the church — they see these as one of the aspects of life which threatens them. Others look to religion and the church for support against what they consider to be the oppressor or the enemy (Psalms 23:5; 59:1; 71:13; 86:14).

Paranoid feelings are to be found in most everyone at times. They may range from feelings that one is being treated unfairly to full-blown delusions of persecution. They may also range from a feeling that one is not fully appreciated for his real value and worth, that one is not loved, to feelings that one is a great person but others do not recognize this. In the paranoid response there is a large element of suspicion. The pastor may have difficulty in checking on the reality basis of the suspicion. For example, a woman may complain that her husband is unfaithful, which he actually may be, or this could be the projection of her own inner wishes and fears about herself. She may want to be unfaithful and is projecting this unacceptable part of herself. The psychological mechanism employed is projection, the placing on others of feelings and ideas that we reject in ourselves, the tendency to blame others for our own inner problems as a way of shifting responsibility from ourselves to them. Projection is seen frequently in marriage problems. The classical Biblical illustration is in the story of Adam and Eve. The object on whom the projection is made is usually hated as a serpent.

The person who uses the paranoid processes has the feeling that he has never been loved, is not now loved and never will be loved. He may expect to find love in the pastor, but if the pastor seeks a close emotional relationship the person will withdraw. This person fears closeness; he has been hurt in infancy by persons close to him, and he does not want more suffering. No matter how much he seeks gratification of his needs, he feels others will defeat him. His need for love, thus, is turned into anger and hatred. He wants to hurt others but fears this will only result in being hurt more himself. He makes strong demands for love, but has to reject it because of his fear. In many ways he will test out the pastor, whether in general pastoral relationships or in therapy.

The pastor may feel frustrated as he finds the defenses of the paranoid person rigid and inflexible. He may be tempted to argue or rationalize the person out of his ideas, only to find his best attempts ending in failure. He will find the person very logical; grant the main promise of the paranoid system and other ideas follow very logically. He can build a very water-tight system in which he seems to have great confidence. He can pile detail on detail to support his ideas. On the other hand, he reveals a marked incapacity to deal with his problems realistically. He expects others to solve his problems by changing the situation. The pastor should observe this, as it will become an important factor in the therapy.

The observant pastor will note that these persons will feel hurt at any interpretations he may make. They may say "You are putting me down," or "You're making me feel worthless." They need to feel this way and use the interpretation to bring feeling of hurt to the surface, and to indicate that the therapist made a mistake. Actually they are revealing feelings of guilt. The pastor should not apologize, but rather seek to help them deal with their feelings of being humiliated or hurt.

The pastor must stay a bit behind these persons and never get ahead of them. He should deal only with information they give him. Otherwise they will feel that the pastor is reading their mind and will become angry. The idea that others control their minds, or others are putting ideas into their heads, or they are being controlled by some electronic device, is frequent among these persons in extreme states.

The pastor, either in the therapy office or in general pastoral relationships, may feel irritated and angry at the provocations and testing which these persons give him. Unless he is aware of this and has control of his anger, he may express his irritation directly to them or he may withdraw from them and create a stalemate. Calling their attention to their behavior, citing a number of instances may be helpful if done in a calm, understanding, and reassuring manner. The need is to be open with them, demonstrating that their behavior can be dealt with without hurting them. This indicates that the pastor is not afraid of them as would be indicated either by attack or by withdrawal. These

people will respect strength if it is expressed in genuinely benevolent ways. The pastor will need to be alert for a direct attack on
him, and on his ability and on his truthfulness. They will play cat
and mouse with the pastor, leading him to feel that they are in
agreement, only to find a new attack being made either directly
or indirectly.

These people will tend to act out their feelings. In this way they
may cause the pastor considerable trouble in the parish, even to
the point of making false and serious accusations against him. If
they act out their feelings of power and omniscience, they may
seek to control the pastor even to the point of dictating what he is
to say in his sermons. Often they will not face the pastor directly
with these actions, but will work indirectly through a group or
through letter writing. If they act out their feelings of hatred they
may write "poison pen" letters, or they may make verbal attacks
on the pastor in a church gathering, or they may embarrass him
by becoming his unsolicited champion against someone else in
the parish. They may also make direct physical attacks causing
injury or even death.[10]

It should be emphasized again that any kind of acting out is a
discharge of fantasy and feeling for the purpose of avoiding
insight into it. In the therapy relationship an attempt must be
made to help the person understand this, and to understand the
feelings and fantasies which are being expressed. This may be
more difficult or impossible in the general parish situation where
the pastor is the object of the acting out. Quiet confidence and
strength, and a calm setting forth of the facts in the proper
circumstances are the pastor's best approach. The paranoid individual may take advantage of any show of weakness. Firmness
but kindness are necessary. In any case, the pastor must avoid
becoming an ally of the distorted ideas of the paranoid person,
just as he must avoid playing the role of an attacker.

We have pointed out that a characteristic of the paranoid
system is that if the major premise is granted, then the deductions
follow quite logically. The same can be said of many theological
systems. Does this means that such systems are unhealthy

distortions of reality as is sometimes claimed? This is a large problem with many facets that are out of place in this discussion. However, certain points may be made. First, any philosophical or theological system that is held firmly may have some elements of projection in it. Projection is one process through which man's inner and external worlds are related, and through which the nature and purpose of life are formulated. The question is what is the content of the projection? Is it constructive or destructive? Does it help the individual to adapt to life in a manner which increases his fulfillment and well-being and that of others. A second consideration is how the system is used by the person. Is it used to gain insight into himself and the nature of his experiences, or to avoid insight? Is it used for purposes of personal growth or to protect childish feelings that need to be outgrown? Does it take into account a realistic sense of the interdependence of all living things, or does it promote a childish dependence which destroys self-reliance and autonomy? Is it held rigidly, or is it subject to change, revision, and development? A third consideration has to do with the denial of truth of theological systems or of religion. There are many reasons for this. One is a feeling of counter-dependence. Dependence is viewed in a childish way, something which no mature man could acknowledge. So it is felt that we must declare our independence. But in this world no man is fully independent. The issue is between childish dependence, adolescent independence, or a mature kind of interdependence. No man is sufficient unto himself. Many who deny the truth of religion on the grounds that it is projection are merely using another psychological mechanism, denial, and are trying to create a position which in itself is illusory. When man seeks to deny his interdependence on all living things, and the dependence of all of life on a superhuman power he is putting himself in a position in which only anxiety, despair and self-destruction are logical ends. A fourth consideration is that the essence of religion is not in intellectual systems but in a living faith, actively lived out in human relationships in which the lives of the believers and of others are enhanced. This is part of the meaning of love. The nature of our organismic life is such that love is the life-giving force while hatred and self-containment destroy. The essence of religious faith is not to be found in intellectual systems, but in a life lived out in a manner which expresses vital faith. The genuine pastoral approach to religious beliefs is to try to understand the persons who hold them.

THE PSYCHOPATHIC PERSON

A pastor was consulted by a young man of twenty-eight years, well dressed, a smooth talker, very polite and deferential, obviously bent on making a good impression and securing help. He was married and had a good position, even though, as the pastor has observed, he had changed positions several times. He seemed to be quite anxious. This centered on the fact that he felt he was about to be caught in some behavior that he had been practicing for ten years. He indicated that the behavior itself did not seem to be a problem ot him, it was only that now he might be apprehended. His behavior was seducing women, always married women, usually older women and often the wives of a superior in his work. This was the case now; he felt this superior was getting suspicious about his relationship with his wife. He feared that, if caught, the husband would beat him badly or cause him to lose his job. He did not feel guilty over the seduction. His anxiety was about being caught.

The pastor felt sympathetic and wanted to help the young man. As the story unfolded it became apparent that the seductive episodes were always preceded by a period of depression and anxiety. In these periods the man felt weak, small, powerless. As the seductive process developed he commenced to feel strong and powerful, like a real man. Clearly the seductions were a way of acting out his inconscious conflicts and resolving his bad feelings. He felt he had a right to do this, that the world owed him pleasure, and that he was justified in taking it. As for the women, he was sure they were not in love with him but enjoyed sex with him. He certainly was not in love with them. Indeed, he seemed to have little concern for them, never considering the trouble they would be in if caught. His attitude toward his wife was about as casual. He showed no deep or continuing relationship with anyone, men or women. Relationships existed to give him what he needed at the moment, to exploit as he wished. He had already lost several jobs because of this behavior, but had learned nothing from these experiences except how to explain matters to his wife so she felt the company was responsible.

This pastor was dealing with a person who is sometimes labeled a psychopath, sometimes a sociopath, and sometimes a character disorder. Whatever the label, it indicates a person who habitually acts in a manner which preserves a deep sense of alienation from others while yielding him the pleasure or freedom from anxiety which he desires. These people are grandiose—they feel that they have a right to do as they please without suffering the consequences. Indeed, they can jump off the pinnacle of the temple without getting hurt, as the angels will take care of them (Matt. 4:5-7). They have a deep sense of immediacy. The past or future does not matter; they must have satisfaction of their needs at once. There is no reality testing, no postponement of satisfactions. If they think about the past it is to find persons or experiences on which to blame their predicament, not to get understanding.

One of his motives in coming to a pastor (or any therapist) is to have a loophole if he is caught. He can then explain that he realizes he has a serious problem and is attempting to do something about it. In our culture this softens many people toward him. Feeling grandiose, he will feel that he should have special treatment. He is an expert in selecting women who play up to his grandiose, pseduomasculine image, and do not understand that underneath this there is a very low self-esteem that they are salving.

These persons are often of high intelligence and are experts at intellectualizing. They do not want to deal with their feelings, except ersatz feelings. Their genuine feelings are too painful. They do have anger and can use this in a manner that defends their behavior. They are also experts at denial, often denying behavior for which they are in trouble, but confessing something that happened years before. They will readily accept, on an intellectual level, interpretations the pastor makes of their behavior. Then they will come back to the next session and explain themselves in terms of that interpretation but show no change in character or behavior. In this way they turn the therapeutic techniques into defenses. The pastor must break through their rationalizations, and denials, and confront (not attack) them with the motivation and consequences of their acts to themselves and others. He must help them see that, like Esau of old, they will not die if they do not have the bowl of stew immediately (Gen. 26:29-34). Abstract interpretations are useless here.

The pastor may come to expect that the person is using him for his own narcissistic ends, just as he uses others. He may find himself feeling that the person can be cured, or perhaps he can be converted. Many of these persons have gone the conversion route, but very few have had permanent results. Again, religion is used as a defense, not as a source of insight and change. Some of them use religion as a way of exploiting others. The pastor may also discover that these people have difficulty in forming a deep relationship with him, as they do with others. They will degrade and use the pastor as they do others.

These persons usually come from a very ambivalent family background. On the one hand, they were overly gratified at times and then frustrated. They lack adequate masculine and feminine images. Emotionally they are really little children demanding immediate satisfaction. The overgratification in childhood has confirmed them in their narcissism and grandiosity; the frustration has made them angry and bitter. They do not seem to have a conscience, but it is rather that they have strong defenses against feelings of guilt. Most f them have been at least emotionally, if not physically, seduced by the parent of the opposite sex while feeling rejected by the parent of the same sex.

There are emotional immaturities in all of us to a mild extent, which leads us to be irresponsible at times. The pastor must know what and where his are or he will get entangled, especially if the person is a member of the opposite sex, or if he has a homosexual problem.

These persons make up the group often called addicts. Addictions are the habitual demand for a special form of pleasure in order to avoid threatening feelings about oneself. Problems are resolved by a pill, or a drink or another form of irresponsible behavior. Ego control is surrendered to the addictive agent. Alcoholics, drug addicts, work addicts, play addicts, food addicts, and others share the impulsive need for gratification as a means of allaying anxiety or depression. The selection of the behavior is influenced by the nature of the conflicts, but it begins in the oral or infancy stage of development. Persons with sexual addictions may place an especially high value on oral sex. Intercourse will be a physical act devoid of meaning. They are inadequate on the level of mature sexuality, where whatever the form of the activity, it is used for the purpose of enhancing and deepening the relationship.

As in all work with people, the pastor should understand his responses to the person with a character disorder. He may, for example, respond with a sympathetic feeling that blinds him to the motivations of the person. If so, he will play right into his hand. The pastor may accept the version of the person that he is something of an innocent victim of his own impulses, and cannot be held responsible. If the pastor becomes too concerned to help the person, he becomes an easy target for deceit and defeat. Or the pastor may see only some aspects of the person's behavior, but be blind to others. Or he may get into an unconscious collusion with him. This would lead him to enjoy hearing about the person's behavior in detail, but missing the motivation for the behavior. Or in extreme situations, he may be tempted to act out with the individual. Overidentification with the person is antitherapeutic regardless of the form in which it is expressed.

Another form of overidentification is a guilt response in the pastor. He may feel guilty about some of the same kind of impulses that disturb the person. This may lead him to punish or to reject the person. A pastor who has a strong need to succeed in his work, who finds it hard to accept failure, may become angry or moralistic.

A firm, realistic approach is needed with these people. The first stage will involve helping the person to feel that his behavior is undesirable and unacceptable by stressing the consequences to himself and others. This will result in anxiety and depression which must then be dealt with for what it is. Acting out may occur, as the person will want to follow his habitual way of allaying anxiety. This has to be dealt with realistically — that is, interpreted as resistance, as not necessary, and as harmful to the therapy. If the pastor passively allows the person to "get away" with his behavior there will be no therapy. Meaningful communication and the attempt to gain insight and to grow will be blocked. The issues must be brought into the therapy process, not acted out. There is also danger of the therapy being aborted because of the anxiety, and this has to be faced openly. It may be rationalized by the person by saying that he is cured and needs no more therapy. The pastor must understand what is really going on, that the person is denying and avoiding, and displacing, and bring this to his attention along with possible consequences. The pastor must be careful not to be deceived by the individual's easy and affable reassurances. The process of therapy is that of helping the person outgrow his extreme narcissistic and grandiose orientation and be able to accept himself and others as people of worth, not to be manipulated for his own ends. The pastor must present him with a relationship in which self-esteem and other-esteem plays a large part and in which manipulation is not condoned. He must demonstrate his own reliability and consistency, and that he is working for the real interests of the person.

THE SCHIZOPHRENIC PERSON

The person who is suffering from a schizophrenic reaction is frequently seen in the church, in the pastor's study, and in the pastoral therapy center. Such persons range from being mildly disturbed to extremely disturbed, often requiring hospitalization. In the parish the incipient young schizophrenic person will be seen, along with those suffering from acute disturbances and chronic conditions. Many of the latter find a place in society where their adjustment problems are simple, and they get along fairly well. The schizophrenic individual often gravitates to the church in search of security or because of religious elements in his experience.

The pastor may also become involved with the families of these persons, who may show great anxiety concerning them and at the same time feel helpless in dealing with them. The families are always involved[11] in the illness, but usually they have no insight into the condition or their part in it. While they seem to want help for the youth, they may not want to change the family patterns to which he is trying to adapt by his symptoms. They want relief from their pain but do not want to change the family constellation.

Adequate diagnosis is a necessity and may be a problem especially with young adolescents in this condition. Erik Erikson[12] has pointed out that individuals experiencing the normal crises of adolescence often look and act as though they are suffering from a schizophrenic reaction. A constructive solution to this crisis must occur before the individual can move on to the next stage of ego development and enter into a relationship of real intimacy with others. This is what the schizophrenic youth does not do. His attempts at intimacy result in a pseudointimacy which is not satisfying.

Psychotherapy with these persons is a long, tedious process and should be attempted only by those who have adequate training. The average pastor can be supportive of the person and his family, and can guide them into the care of competent professionals. But he needs to understand them and also his own reaction to them.

The first observation that the sensitive pastor will make is that the ideas, behavior, and emotional responses of these people are strange and perhaps bizarre. Usual responses are absent. Their responses and statements may seem to come from nowhere, and are likely to be irrelevant to the situation. Emotional responses are inappropriate; the person may laugh when talking about something sad. Strange religious ideas may be felt as a challenge by the pastor, who will then want to correct them. This is in error.

The reason for this is that the responses of these persons reflect their inner condition. One inner problem of the schizophrenic youth is that of alienation from self and from others. This is the opposite of the experience of intimacy. The sense of distance may be great. Anton Boisen,[13] who himself suffered several acute episodes of this illness, interpreted it as due to the sense of isolation which arose from the sense of guilt. Others would reverse this formula and see the guilt as the result of the isolation, which itself is experienced in early infancy and results in an incomplete and unsatisfying experience of the self at every stage of emotional development. The result is a withdrawal from the world of reality into the world of fantasy. The ideas of the individual must be understood as emerging from his fantasy life, and hence they sound strange to a person who is more reality-oriented. Ego controls such as reality testing are weakened so that ideas and behavior from a deeper level emerge. These ideas and behavior root in a deep affect disturbance and can be understood as a defense against that disturbance.

The establishment of a therapeutic relationship with the schizophrenic person is quite different than with others. With these, the transference material is likely to come out before a working relationship is established. This is due to the weakness of the repressive forces of the ego. The material will be disguised and distorted, and expressed in symbolic ways that may not make sense rationally. The danger of the beginning pastor is that he rushes in with interpretations before the person is able to understand or accept them. More alienation may result. The person is putting distance between himself and the pastor and is withdrawing into the safety of his own world. Closeness is threatening.

The sense of alienation or isolation of these persons may be expressed in many different ideas and forms of behavior. Out of the severe identity problem will come anger and hostility, which threaten to destroy the person or lead him to fear he will destroy others. He is not sure of his ability to control his strong destructive impulses. He may express them in bizarre ideas about himself, such as being a great person with a mission to reconcile the world. His purpose may be to save the world, to solve all its problems, or to overcome some great evil. These feelings are often projected on the cosmic level, where they take on a strong religious character. The person, for example, may insist he is Christ.[14]

The development of a working relationship with such persons is a real step in therapy. It means that there is sufficient ego strength to cooperate at least on a minimum level. This requires gentleness and understanding on the part of the pastor.

In the therapeutic relationship the pastor may experience a deep dependency on the part of the person. This will be in conflict with his sense of mistrust, and the ambivalence will find expression in reaching toward and pushing away. Love and hate conflict may emerge. He may experience with the pastor a fear of others and also a need for others, including the pastor. There will be a movement toward his alienated self and then away in fear. The confusion of identity will be marked and perhaps also the identity of the pastor. In my role as his student, Anton Boisen frequently identified me as his son. Because of these ambivalences many of the remarks of the pastor may be misinterpreted. They will be heard in terms of the inner condition of the person, not in terms of the more rational point of view of the pastor. He desperately wants closeness, even to a symbiotic relationship, but he also dreads it. The pastor must not move toward the person too quickly or eagerly. He should always speak of both sides of the ambivalence simultaneously, bringing them together in a manner which enables the person to deal with them constructively.

The countertransference of the pastor is most important. He needs to learn to deal with processes or relationships, rather than the content of the person's ideas, and also his own feelings, his irritations and frustrations. The pastor needs to show his interest in the person and his conflicts, but not to the extent of increasing the anxiety and hence the symptoms. The conflict should not be intensified. The person does not need more anxiety. Neither will it help him to reflect back that he is anxious; he knows that.

If the pastor's need for a close relationship is strong, or if he seeks a quick intimacy in response to the obvious need of the person, the person will be frightened. If the pastor needs too much distance, the person may experience a feeling of abandonment. The pastor must have a deep understanding of himself to avoid extremes.

The dependence-independence conflict may confuse the pastor depending on whether he likes people to be dependent on him or not. Too much dependence may confuse the person's sense of identity and of worth; too little denies the strength he needs. The pastor may feel a conflict within himself and move in both directions which will further confuse the individual.

The pastor should be alert lest he be drawn into a power struggle with the schizophrenic person. This can be an issue in the administrative affairs of the church, as well as in therapy. The schizophrenic will demonstrate a common human trait in extreme forms, that of reacting to a sense of inner weakness with a strong need for power and control of others. Usually this is expressed in a passive manner. In this way he feels safe, but it is a pseudo-safety and constantly has to be reinforced. Because he is threatened by his own angry feelings or his feelings of love, he will seek to respond passively and may attempt a kind of stubborn, passive control of the situation that is difficult to deal with. If the pastor touches on some threatening feelings he quickly changes the subject. He may simply state his position and wait for everyone to conform to it. In this way any healthy self-assertiveness is repressed along with threatening feelings. He gives the impression of inadequacy and powerlessness, but in a passive manner he controls the situation. This is an attempt at independent self-identity.

The pastor may respond to the passivity of the person by moving in to direct his life or to try to stimulate more aggressiveness. Either approach may be a mistake, as it further threatens the person and increases the reaction which it was meant to alleviate. Any aggressiveness shown by these people may likewise be a challenge to the pastor, as it will usually move in some unhealthy direction.

The person needs help to develop a sense of confidence in his ability to control both love and anger. This can best be done as the pastor indicates by his manner that he is not afraid of negative or positive feelings. The strength of the pastor will be communicated to the person largely in nonverbal ways. A gentle approach is necessary here, as gentleness is always an expression of strength. A weak person demonstrates his pseudostrength by being overpowering.

The pastor will need to understand how he himself handles the world of reality in relation to his own fantasies in order to deal with this problem in the schizophrenic person. The world of fantasy serves as a retreat from the world of reality and a source of satisfaction. Since it is a solitary pursuit, it increases the sense of loneliness and isolation. But it avoids many of the anxieties of daily experience.

Fantasy as a process should be dealt with before the content of the fantasy. This requires discussing the problems of daily living, and testing the fantasy against the reality. As the person develops some confidence in his ability to deal with the real world, he will need fantasy less and less. Then he may be ready to deal with the content of the fantasy. It is important not to get ahead of the person or he will feel his mind is being read.

Of special interest to the pastoral psychotherapist is the symbolic language of the person. The schizophrenic person sees his conflicts as related to his whole existence, as indeed they are, since they involve the life of the self in relation to the world. The separation of self and world is an artifact of our thinking; actually self and world are two aspects of the life of the organism as a whole. The schizophrenic person withdraws from each and creates a private fantasy world. But feelings from within continue to push into consciousness and the real world brings pressures from without. He feels that his entire life and destiny are at stake, and this involves the cosmic or ultimate dimensions. He finds himself in a struggle between life and death, being or non-being from early infancy. Many of his ideas reflect this profound struggle. His ideas of a religious nature do not mean that religion has made him sick. They rather mean that he senses a religious dimension in his struggles. While it is important to help him work out his problems with everyday reality, it is important also not to repress his concern with a reality beyond his everyday world. Here is where deep issues in the nature of reality are joined in the life of a human being, and these issues need to be understood and respected. They should not be rationalized away, or overly intensified, or repressed, but should rather be dealt with frankly and honestly as are other phases of the person's life. Pastors are more inclined to overemphasize these ideas, while scientifically trained therapists without religious orientation are likely to deny and rationalize them away. They rather need to be respected and understood.

Dealing with intangibles in his experience, the schizophrenic person uses symbolic language.[15] This language, like religious language, points to realities in the person's inner world and in his external world which are felt to have some relationship. His language does not have its traditional meanings. Therefore, it is likely to be called delusional. This is a mistake, since it has profound meaning to the person. But the meaning has to be discovered; sense has to be made out of the nonsense. But this sense has to be in terms of the experience and condition of the person, not the pastor. At times the pastor should share with the person the fact that he does not hold to the same ideas, but he understands something as to why the person holds to them. This should be done with deep acceptance and respect for the person. Again attention should be given to the process and relationship behind these ideas before examining the content. Once process and relationship are understood the content may take care of itself. The pastor may find this difficult, since an abstract ideology has been so emphasized in his training. Any ideology which is held with conviction and purpose is grounded in deep emotional and relational factors, not only in the schizophrenic person, but in all of us.

If the schizophrenic person is listened to attentively and with feelings, it will be found that his ideas reflect much human experience which is common to all persons. Basic human problems such as love and hate, fear and trust, closeness and distance, power and submission, guilt and self-acceptance, hopelessness and hope, faith and anxiety, the meaning of suffering, the nature and purpose of life are all part of his struggles and symbolized in some manner in his ideas. Death and rebirth, the loss of self and the renewal of self, a sense of worthlessness and a sense of mission are also there. In short, he is dealing with the problem of death and is struggling to find life. This gives a definite religious significance to his struggles and to his ideas. This dimension must be respected if there is to be genuine therapy.[16]

It was Freud who pointed out that the ideas of death and of cosmic catastrophe prevalent in the schizophrenic disturbance are reflections of the disintegration of the ego and the loss of self. Boisen[18] indicated that this was in line with his experience. With the emphasis today on the work of the pastor with the terminally ill patient, it is interesting that there is not a comparable emphasis on work with the person who is threatened by a loss of self and inner death. There are many of these in every community. This is a central problem, for example, in youthful drug addicts, and often in their parents. One has to be very comfortable emotionally to work with them.

We have stressed the need for the exploration of the immediate, daily experiences, defense reactions, and relationships of the person in the therapy process. Also needing exploration are the defenses and resistances operating within the therapy hour in relation to the pastor. Attention should be given to repetitive defenses and patterns. An openness and trustworthiness on the part of the pastor are essential here. Whether in the parish or in a professional therapy setting, the pastor should communicate his concern. Interpretations should be kept to a minimum, as the person may have considerable insight but not know what to do about it. He needs help with day-to-day reality. He also needs trustworthy support on a level that he is able to accept.

It is always worthwhile for the pastor to consider the potential psychotherapeutic significance of his general pastoral relationships and of the activities of the church for many persons. This is

of particular importance with the schizophrenic person who may
not be able to utilize formal psychotherapy, but for whom activities and relationships with others within the church may be of
particular importance. Many isolated persons are completely
dependent on the church for contact and communication with
others. In general, any person suffering from a personality
pathology will use the church and its activities for his particular
needs, just as a healthy, mature person might do. The needs,
however, may be different.

THE TRANSIENT SEARCHER

Another category are those we shall call transient searchers.
These people go from pastor to pastor, from church to church,
from psychiatrist or psychologist to pastor and perhaps back
again seeking help. They may fit into various of the diagnostic
groups, but they have one strong factor in common. Their final
defense against any deep search is to become mobile, to move to
another helper. At first they seem to have a good understanding
of their problem. They put together comments from several therapists into a plausible story. But this is also defensive, and they
may repeat, "I understand all of this, but I get no better."
Underneath, the conflict goes on unabated.

These people can be very seductive, bidding for the sympathy
of the pastor. One ploy is to emphasize their need for a
"religious" approach. They are really acting out a negative transference which will occur with successive therapists unless one is
able to break through it. If they are still seeing another therapist,
they should be sent back to him and encouraged to talk about
their negative feelings, their visit to the pastor, and the meaning
of wanting to terminate the present relationship. If that relationship has already been terminated for some time, then inquiry
needs to be made as to why the termination. This should be done
in terms of the relationship with that therapist and the dynamics
of the person. The pastor may be sure that the same factors will
operate again in relationship with him. In short, people should be

discouraged from moving from one therapist to another without full exploration of motivation and transference. They should not be encouraged to avoid their conflicts by acting out in this way.

The pastor should examine his own feelings toward such persons. He may feel quite complimented that he is chosen to do what other therapists have not been able to do, and may rise quickly to the challenge. He should know he is being set up for a fall. On the other hand, he may have negative feelings. He may feel too anxious to confront the person with his pattern of behavior and succumb to the pressure put on him. There is a tradition with many pastors that no one should be turned away, a tradition that needs considerable reinterpretation in its application. If the pastor gets involved with the person against his better judgment or desire, he will have conscious or unconscious anger, and this will seriously interfere with the therapy. Openness, frankness, and honesty are needed with these people, and it may pay off. The person may be looking for someone who can confront him with his acting out.

This has its application to persons who seek a transfer of membership from one parish to another. Sometimes there are legitimate reasons for this. All cases should be carefully examined. If this is done it will be found that some of these persons have made several such moves previously, or that they have projected some of their inner problems on the present parish or its clergy. The desire to move is a way of avoiding facing a problem that needs resolution, and the finding of a new quality of life. In other words, they need to work out their negative transference feelings toward a pastor or others in the parish. On the other hand, some will be frightened by their positive transference feelings toward a pastor, and they need help with these feelings. The frequent interpretation of the church as a family can foster displacement of either positive or negative parental feelings toward the pastor or others in the church. There can be a great deal of sibling rivalry among adults in a parish, or there can also be a great deal of valuable support, encouragement, and experiences that produce growth.

Other groups of persons should receive some special attention of the pastor. One such is those alienated from the church. They may fit into any one of the categories discussed above, but the approach of the pastor should be based on their feelings of separation and hostility. They may also be struggling with guilt problems.

Another group are those who are undergoing severe crises of the sort that leads the community to reject them, or to their withdrawal from the community. This would include families where there has been a divorce. Most communities know how to give support in time of bereavement, but do not know how to meet the loss and bereavement of divorce. Sometimes families in which there has been a crime or delinquency are also isolated or isolates themselves. These situations usually bring a deep sense of shame to the participant families, and a sense of fear to the community. The fear is a projection of insecurity within the community. The shame is strong inner condemnation along with the isolation experienced from the community. The pastor may not be able to do anything on the community level, but we have known pastors who were able to influence community attitudes considerably through sermons. The family in trouble needs to be called on, as usually their sense of shame is too strong for them to reach out for help.

Finally, there are those who are "normal." In a world where human life is a constant process of change, a moving forward and a moving backward, conflict, regression, and growth, the word *normal* suggests a static condition in which one may take pride. Thus the word is used for defense and denial, and has no use in understanding persons. The pastor may need to use it as much as his people. Whoever the person is, or whatever position he occupies in society, there is always the same need for understanding dynamics, motivation, and the inner quality of life behind the "normal" exterior. With the emphasis on this in the Bible, the pastor should be well aware of the problem. If the pastor is to be the first line of defense against mental illness as we believe he is, then he must learn to deal with emotional disturbances in their milder and sometimes chronic forms. The idea of preventing inner problems and conflicts is a false goal in human life. To be alive is to have problems. But to help people to develop the strength that comes from the resolution of conflict, from the development and expression of their own autonomous functions, and from their assumption of responsibility for their own life insofar as humanly possible is the path of prevention of serious disturbances. The pastor has several approaches to this task. This book is about one of them. But "normal" people will not be among those who consult him; or, if they do, it will be about another person (Matt. 9:12).

We have been using categories of diagnosis that grow out of the biomedical model. There is stress today within medicine to consider the sociological and cultural dimensions, particularly family relationships, in searching out the reasons for illness.[19] That emphasis has also been running through this book. Pastors are much more familiar with this than physicians through training in theology, sociology, and cultural anthropology. But pastors have been more interested in the study of theological ideas as such than in the study of persons theologically. With all of the pathological conditions in society, people who can find wholesome person-to-person relationships, particularly in childhood, have a good chance to become mature, loving adults. But many do not find that and need individual attention. It is as though a man contracts a disease through air pollution in his place of work. Correcting the pollution will do him no good after the disease has developed. Now he must have individual treatment, both physical and psychological. Correcting the pollution may prevent others from contracting similar illnesses. The kind of persons discussed in this chapter could benefit from individual attention if it is made available, though some are unable to cooperate in such therapy. For others group therapy, family and marriage therapy, can be very helpful. We have not discussed these modes in this book, but the church and church institutions are suitable locales for them. While it seeks to promote change in unwholesome conditions in society, the church should implement more effectively the concern of the New Testament in the cure of souls, in pastoral psychotherapy. The church has a heavy responsibility here.

We turn now to a further consideration of pastoral therapy as a religious process.

NOTES

1. This chapter is not a thorough discussion of the psychodynamics of various diagnostic groups. It is rather an attempt to outline major transference and countertransference attitudes that may be encountered. There are many books dealing with the dynamics of the various groups. The following are suggested: Roger A. MacKinnon and Robert Michels, *The Psychiatric Interview in Clinical Practice,* Philadelphia: W. B. Saunders, 1971; Harry Guntrip, *Personality Structure and Human Interaction,* New York: International Universities Press, 1964; Theodore Millon, *Modern Psychopathology,* Philadelphia: W. B. Saunders, 1969.

2. Willard Gaylin, *The Meaning of Despair,* New York: Jason Aronson, 1968; Leon Salzman, *The Obsessive Personality,* New York: Jason Aronson, 1973, ch. 5; Sigmund Freud (1915), "Mourning and Melancholia," in *The Standard Edition of the Complete Psychological Works of Sigmund Freud,* vol. 14, trans. James Strachey, London: Hogarth Press, 1957, pp. 243–258.

3. A literary example of this experience is James Agee's *The Morning Watch,* Boston: Houghton-Mifflin, 1950.

4. Paul Tillich, *The Courage To Be,* New Haven: Yale Universities Press, 1952; Paul Tillich, *Dynamics of Faith,* New York: Harper and Row, 1957, pp. 99–127.

5. There are many books that discuss anxiety. The pastor will need to make a distinction between existential anxiety and pathological anxiety. The writings of Rollo May and Paul Tillich will be of help, especially on existential anxiety. Freud has numerous papers on anxiety, which may be found by consulting his complete works. The pastor must learn to reevaluate many of the so-called religious "cures" for anxiety. See also Charles Odier, *Anxiety and Magic Thinking,* New York: International Universities Press, 1956.

6. Paul Tillich, *The Courage to Be; Dynamics of Faith.*

7. See case report in chapter 4.

8. Many parish pastors find hysterical persons interesting, and easy to work with at first. However, this runs into impasses frequently because the pastor does not understand the psychodynamics. One pastoral therapy center receives numerous referrals from pastors who come to feel frustrated with such persons. See also David Moss and Ronald R. Lee, "Homogamous and Heterogamous Marriages," *International Journal of Psychoanalytic Psychotherapy,* vol. 5, 1976, pp. 395–412.

9. Leon Salzman, *The Obsessive Personality.*

10. This occurrence is not frequent, but it does occur in situations where no therapy is being undertaken, as well as in therapy relationships. This is another reason for the pastor to understand psychodynamics thoroughly, to be able to make suitable interventions at times and to know when he is in need of consultation.

11. For a comprehensive study of the so-called "schizophrenic family system" see Theodore Lidz, S. Fleck, and A. R. Cornelison, *Schizophrenia and the Family*; Don Jackson, ed., *The Etiology of Schizophrenia,* New York: Basic Books, 1960. A classic work on psychotherapy with schizophrenic persons is: Frieda Fromm-Reichmann, *Principles of Intensive Psychotherapy,* Chicago: University of Chicago Press, 1950. The pastor would also be helped by the study of Helm Stierlin, *Separating Parents and Adolescents,* New York: Quadrangle/ New York Times, 1974.

12. Erik Erikson, *Identity, Youth and Crisis,* New York: W. W. Norton, 1968, pp. 142–196. On the problem of schizophrenia see Harry Guntrip, *Schizoid Phenomena, Object Relations and the Self,* New York: International Universities Press, 1969; and Sherman C. Feinstein, Peter L. Giovacchini, and Arthur L. Miller, eds., *Adolescent Psychiatry,* vol. I, New York: Basic Books, 1971. An excellent work on psychotherapy with adolescents is John E. Meeks, *The Fragile Alliance,* Baltimore: Williams and Wilkins, 1971.

13. Anton Boisen, *The Exploration of the Inner World,* New York: Harper and Row, 1936.

14. Milton Rokeach, *The Three Christs of Ypsilanti: A Psychological Study,* London: Arthur Barker, Ltd., n.d.

15. Anton Boisen, "The Sense of Isolation in Mental Disorder: Its Religious Significance," *American Journal of Sociology,* vol. 33, no. 4, January, 1928, p. 555; Anton Boisen, "The Problem of Values in the Light of Psychopathology," *American Journal of Sociology,* vol. 38, no. 1, July, 1932, pp. 251–268; Anton Boisen, "Form and Content in Schizophrenic Thinking," *Psychiatry,* vol. 5, no. 1, February, 1942, pp. 23–33; Beulah Parker, *My Language is Me: Psychotherapy with a Disturbed Adolescent,* New York: Basic Books, 1962.

16. The themes of death and resurrection are to be found in several psychological novels: Hannah Green, *I Never Promised You a Rose Garden,* New York: Holt, Rinehart and Winston, 1970; Richard D'Ambrosio, *No Language But a Cry,* New York: Doubleday, 1970. A more concise and poetic expression of the same experience is to be found in Edna St. Vincent Millay's poem, "Renascence," published by Michel Kennerley, 1912.

17. Sigmund Freud (1911), "Psycho-analytic Notes on an Autobiographical Account of a Case of Paranoia (Dementia Paranoides)," *The Standard Edition*

of the Complete Psychological Works of Sigmund Freud, vol. 12, trans. James Strachey, London: Hogarth Press, 1958, pp. 1–82.

18. Anton Boisen, op. cit.

19. George L. Engel, "The Need for a New Medical Model," *Science,* vol. 196, April, 1977, pp. 129–196.

Chapter 9

Pastoral Therapy as a Religious Process

In the previous chapters we have dealt largely with pastoral psychotherapy as a psychological process. In this chapter we shall come back to the main theme of the first chapter, pastoral psychotherapy as a religious process.

Religious experience is a process which involves a relationship with the self, with others, and with God. The goal of the religious process is integration within the self, a sense of belonging with and responsibility to others, and a sense of peace with ultimate or universal meanings, with God. Within such relationships the inner potential of the self for the realization of true individuality may be experienced. It is important to remember that the relationship of a person to self, others, and God partakes of the same quality in all directions. He who seeks to avoid responsibility for self will also seek to avoid responsibility to others and before God.

The pastor often correctly interprets his ministry to others in terms of doing something for them. Out of this comes the emphasis on social change. This has strong Biblical support. However, we have been interpreting pastoral psychotherapy, not as doing something for others but as being something to others, as offering a relationship through which others may do something for themselves. While the emphasis in discussions of pastoral psychotherapy is frequently on the person being helped, the real issue is the response of the pastor to the person. Does it offer freedom,

courage, and understanding, and the opportunity to relive hurt-
ful experiences in a curative manner? This is a question for the
pastor himself.

In the first chapter we interpreted pastoral psychotherapy in
the light of two New Testament concepts "psyche" and "therapeuo." The pastor deals with human beings who have minds and
spirits, or selves, or souls. These are not animistic concepts. They
are rather concepts necessary for anyone who considers the whole
person. The pastor deals with persons in a manner that shares
their burdens while permitting them full freedom to use him for
their own growth and fulfillment, not for neurotic ends. The pastor needs to give much thought as to whether his approach and
relationship brings a helpful or harmful influence to them. The
Bible, however, is concerned with relationships on both the ultimate and human levels. It is not a text on therapeutic techniques,
and he who looks for such will be disappointed. On the other
hand it contains many insights of therapeutic value. The development of pastoral psychotherapy today combines the insights of
religious faith with scientific knowledge of how personality is
formed, how persons become sick, and how they become well.

Religious people have often rejected scientific knowledge
because it seems to rule out direct or miraculous action by God.
Thus, it is felt, the mystery of religion is destroyed. But this is a
fault in human thinking, not in the reality of the situation. For
cause and effect relationships are grounded on just as much
mystery (the mystery of why it should be) as are capricious,
unpredictable events. Real mystery is grounded on the inability of
the finite mind to grasp the infinite, and it leads to humility, not
to pride.

Strong statements of cause and effect relationships are to be
found in the Bible. "In those days they shall no longer say: 'The
fathers have eaten sour grapes, and the children's teeth shall be
set on edge.' . . . Each man who eats sour grapes, his teeth shall
be set on edge" (Jer. 31:29–30). Or again, "For whatever a man
sows, that he will also reap" (Gal. 6:7). The pastor meets many
who use cause and effect to justify their behavior ("My father

made me this way"), but the mature, healthy person uses it as a basis of individual and moral responsibility.

The crucial point, however, is not only what experiences and relationships a person might have met in childhood, but how that person responded to them emotionally and habitually. In previous chapters we have dealt with some of the possibilities of inner response.

Our past cannot be changed. What can be changed, or rather what *we* can change, is the character of our inner responses, our feelings and attitudes and patterns of relationship. There is a danger in using our past experiences to justify present relationships or behavior, or to expect others to change them for us. Religion stresses personal and moral responsibility, and insists that the choices we make, and the nature and depth of our commitments, are determining factors in our becoming. In some, responses have developed into such rigid patterns that it is very difficult or even impossible for them to change.

Pastoral psychotherapy tries to help people discover how to control their own responses and to change their own feelings and attitudes. It is a very popular but falsely satisfying illusion to believe that others, or some external condition, are responsible for our ways of responding. They are not. The mature person is the one who has learned to control his own responses. Our inner life is our own responsibility. The less control over our feelings and responses, the sicker we become.

For example, we may think that something frightens us, when we are really frightened by some of our own impulses, such as sex or anger. Or we may say, "He makes me angry," when we are really angry at something in ourselves, such as our dependence, or because life is not granting some of our wishes, perhaps the wish to control others. It is always comforting to seek the cause of our difficulties in something outside ourselves, and also to demand that the cure come from the outside, rather than through using our own inner resources. This, along with other things, contributes to our having become a nation of pill-poppers. And it is one of the factors in the development of neurotic processes in religion.

A healthy religious process requires honesty with self, others, and God. Some persons dishonestly pile guilt on themselves, while others avoid and deny honest guilt. Only the truth makes us free, not self-deceit or deceit of others, even though it may be covered with pious religiosity. Honesty is often painful. It is a blow to our self-esteem to admit that something is wrong in us. The pain leads us to resist facing the truth, either in therapy or outside of it. The pastor must be able, through his own personal understanding and acceptance of the person, to share this pain and to make it possible for the person to deal with its roots as well as its consequences. Pastoral psychotherapy is neither easy nor magical. It must conform to the nature and laws of human reality, and must distinguish reality from fantasy. Instead of expecting God to remove anxiety in some easy manner, it is a struggle to deal honestly with the total experience of the anxiety. The pastoral psychotherapist needs a strong religious faith to enable him to share painful human experience with understanding, and a knowledge of people that enables him not to interfere with basic healing processes.

RELIGIOUS SYMBOLS AND
THE RELIGIOUS PROCESS

There have been numerous theological interpretations of psychotherapy.[1] These have one thing in common. It is the attempt to generalize and intellectualize the dynamic content of religious experience and the experience of psychotherapy. Such intellectualization moves away from the dynamic content of religious experience toward rational and theoretical considerations. The living person is lost in intellectualized dogma. Such concepts are of little avail in the actual therapy process, just as are psychological formulations and dogma, except as background structure for the pastor. If given by the therapist, such concepts come from outside the person, and he is not likely to see any connection between them and his struggles. If they arise from the person, they come from the surface of the mind. Either way, they fail to get down to the dynamic levels of experience and the symbols are cut off from their non-rational dynamic roots.

Images and symbols hold sway in the deeper, nonrational levels of personal experience. They may express either creative or destructive processes, or conflict between these. Dreams, for example, are not rational creations but segments of living experience in symbolic form. Likewise, living religious symbols embody something of the whole person in depth. They become deeply personal and meaningful, and may or may not be used to communicate experience to others. The intellectual processes are involved in this to comprehend, formulate, retain, and interpret. The more formulations and interpretations move toward rational systems, the more they can lose the vitality of experience. The pastoral psychotherapist, as well as the pastor, is faced with the demand that we theologize, or retheologize, our work. The danger in this is that concepts become a defensive substitute for understanding experience, rather than an aid to understanding.

The most insightful and moving sections of the Bible are those couched in symbols reflecting life experiences rather than in descriptive abstractions. Jesus spoke in parables, and gave as his reason the idea that persons who have eyes to see and ears to hear could discern their meaning (Matt. 13:10-17). In our language this means that persons who open their minds, their feelings, and their wills to these symbolic formulations and to their own inner experiences, will find that they have meaning. This meaning cannot be proven logically. It carries a conviction to which the assent of the total person is asked. In this chapter we shall discuss Biblical symbols as a means to the comprehension of certain aspects of the pastoral psychotherapy process. We shall avoid the tendency to elaborate on their meaning in detail, as this could obscure the living experience. On the other hand, we shall be reminded that symbols never fully comprehend that Personal Presence to whom we are inescapably related and from whom we draw strength. There is always an element of mystery that human pride causes us to forget. We see but through a glass darkly. The finite mind·can only dimly comprehend the Infinite.

Religious faith is grounded on the assumption that underneath the many external appearances and experiences in the physical world, and with other human beings, there are laws, values, and relationships which unify and give meaning and goals for living. To live is not only to enjoy discrete aspects of existence. It is also to experience inner processes that move toward wholeness, integration, and individuation. It is also to experience physical and emotional suffering, frustration, conflict, guilt and anxiety, anger and destructiveness that interfere with the drive toward wholeness. Out of the positive and negative aspects of existence questions arise about the fundamental nature of life. What is the purpose of a life that includes suffering and pain? What is the meaning of a life that is precarious and that may be lost at any time in death? What is the meaning of morality, of responsibility, of the search for what is good and beautiful and true in a world where values seem put at the mercy of destructive forces? If a man dies, shall he live again? What is salvation and how is it achieved? What is my responsibility to others as well as to myself? What is the nature and aim of the forces that have created the universe on which human life is dependent for its existence? Is there a God, and if so what is the nature of God?

These and other such questions point to and formulate deep, intangible issues and insecurities. Since they are not experiences on the external level of life, and since a description of them scientifically or theologically contains no answer, they must be dealt with on the level of insight or interpretative symbolism. Religion throughout the history of mankind has been the means to realized and hoped-for answers. Through symbols that carry insight into the nature and aim of life, religion has sought to express its individual or collective faith. These include verbal symbols such as creeds, object symbols such as altars, and action symbols such as rituals. Sometimes these have been combined. Symbols are the creation of the experiences of gifted individuals combined with historic events and cultural movements. They grow out of dynamic life experiences and express the meaning of those experiences and the relationships to which they point. Symbols are ever meaningful — never capricious.

There is a universal and cosmic aspect to religious symbols and their meaning. This is because the experiences and questions of the individual are not strictly individual but are shared by many. Some are universal and timeless. People share common experiences and meanings within group relationships. The culture becomes a factor in developing religious formulations and their expression in ritual. It adds authority and support to the individual, reinforces his sense of unity and adds cohesiveness to the group. In this way human culture takes on a universal and cosmic significance.

Today there is a marked breakdown and denial of the meaning of traditional Hebrew-Christian language and symbolism. There are many reasons for this. We are concerned with the consequences — the breakdown of inner meaning and values, the loss of a sense of direction, the inability to find motivation for meaningful existence, the reduction or loss of a desirable quality of life and a sense of hope for the future. People ask, How do we live? as though life itself or religion give no clues to this. They must find the answer to this for themselves in meaningful relationships with others. In the past, many human drives and urges were repressed, so people lost their creativity. Today there is more expression of sexuality and destructiveness, but meaningful existence is at a low ebb. People ask whether there is a level of existence beneath the physical and material, one that gives more than momentary answers to the problems of pain, suffering, and frustration.

Repression means shutting out of consciousness, creating dissociation between inner experience and symbolic expression of that experience. If symbols are to remain vital, promote growth, and lead to resolution of conflict and integration on the personal, group, and cosmic levels, the association between the symbol and the reality symbolized must be maintained. For religious symbols, this association is grounded on analogy, not logic. While logic has a place, life is much deeper than logic. Analogy is an emotional association. It is the basis for insight, for the imaginative and emotional relating of events and their meaning. The attempt to intellectualize and systematize symbols destroys the association by analogy. The attempt to accept symbolic systems on authority of others creates a barrier to the integration of the symbols into the dynamic processes of the person. This is another way of describing repression. When there is dissociation between symbol and the reality symbolized, the symbol becomes dead. It has lost its emotional power for effecting resolution of conflict and for integration and wholeness within the individual and the group. It is like the salt that has lost its savor. It now serves the purposes of concealment and avoidance, and creates the basis for a relationship of rebellion or escape — in other words, for neurosis, psychosis, or delinquency. Any of the defense mechanisms outlined by the psychologists can operate in the use of religious symbols. Symbols then lose their creative meaning for the individual and the group. The symbol itself becomes an object of devotion or of rejection, a living communication or an empty form.

The culture participates along with the individual in the processes of growth, breakdown, and re-creation of symbols and their meaning. The culture tends to organize symbols into myths and to propagate these myths. A myth is not a false idea or story. It is a story that carries a profound truth for human life. It reflects the meanings and values of the generations that gave it birth. The Christian myth, for example, began with Jesus of Nazareth, or even before him in prophecy, and has been developed through the generations which followed. In the culture as in the individual, symbols and myths tend to become fixed and hardened through the dissociation of symbol and meaning. The culture then assists in the development of illness and becomes a desert of hopelessness rather than a promised land. We are in that situation today. The church as part of the larger culture participates in it. Many of its once powerful symbols and myths have lost their meaning. The church as a dominant voice in the culture has been greatly diminished. People are left alone with no cohesive forces drawing them together. The dominant symbol-makers of our culture are the movies, television, newspapers, magazines, paperbacks. These have no depth of cohesive power. Since they create isolation, they are participated in only passively. They usually teach a morality grounded in wishes and desires rather than the heroic mastery of life. They fail to create a sense of community.

As an illustration of what we have been saying, consider a symbol of destructiveness that swept the land in the mid-seventies. I refer to "Jaws."[1] Here is a symbol that combines sexuality and destructiveness. Most persons who see the movie are impressed by its techniques for death and destruction. Its impact at the time was intensified by news reports of sharks attacking swimmers. Thus, there is a reality element in the symbol. The sexual aspects of the symbols seem to be held in the unconscious of most viewers, but here at once is the fantasy and desire for male potency and the expression of fear of such mastery. But techniques of destructiveness are uppermost in the consciousness of viewers. The futility of fighting force with force, of allowing anger and revenge to force a power contest in which no one really wins, or wins at great cost is evident. Man must indeed master the forces of nature—and some he has not yet mastered—but through intelligence and understanding he can learn how to cope creatively rather than in a self-destructive manner. This requires that first he learn to deal creatively with destructive forces within himself, rather than project them onto external objects.

Television soon copied the symbol to sell a product. A handsome man, sitting at a table floating on water, is attacked by a shark; the table is destroyed, but the man appears on the remnants. At this moment a beautiful girl arises out of the water (recalling the birth of Venus) with a tray of cocktails in her hand, and a salespitch begins. The sexual aspects control the destructive aspects as the emphasis is placed on oral satisfaction through a substance that both increases desire and decreases performance. (Need I say the latter is not so much as suggested?) In no way is the viewer helped toward creative expression of either sexuality or aggressiveness. In fantasy he experiences a rather blatant expression of these drives, vicariously.

This is not the first time a symbol like "Jaws" was used to convey a message, although it was a much different message. I refer to the story of Jonah in the Old Testament. Jonah received a call from the Lord to go to Nineveh to preach destruction for the sinfulness of the city. Frightened, he decided to flee to Tarshish. He went to Joppa and took passage on a boat to that city. A great storm arose, frightening the sailors, who cast lots to discover who had angered his god. The lot fell on Jonah. The sailors threw Jonah overboard; the storm ceased and a great whale swallowed Jonah. He remained three days in the belly of the whale, and then the Lord heard his prayer for deliverance and caused the whale to vomit Jonah onto dry land. Jonah again received the call of the Lord to go to Nineveh, and this time he went. The people, including the king, listened to his message and repented. The Lord then responded with mercy and forgiveness, and the city was not destroyed. Jonah became angry at the Lord. He felt let down. He went outside the city, made a tent for himself, and waited. The Lord then made a tree grow over Jonah to give him shade. The next morning the Lord appointed a worm to kill the tree, and also appointed a sultry east wind to beat upon the head of Jonah. Jonah pleaded to die. He was angry at the Lord for causing the tree to die. The Lord then pointed out to Jonah that he really felt sorry for the plant and, therefore, he was angry. Should not he, the Lord, then feel sorry for the great city when it repented and not destroy it?

There are many possibilities of interpretation in this mythological figure, but we will emphasize only one. The story points to the creative solution between desire and conscience, between the wish to control God and the need to be obedient to God's call, and in all of this it deals with the problem of evil and destructiveness creatively. Jonah learned that mercy, forgiveness, and new relationships are necessary to the creative solution of human problems.

Jonah and Jaws are symbolic of two worlds, two cultures, two ways in which individuals and groups may deal with conscience, guilt, and destructiveness. Jonah will never have the broad appeal of Jaws because it asks for heroism rather than escape, for courage born out of faith rather than bravado born out of fear, and for love rather than anger. It points to the futility of sedating the inner voices of man, the presence of the Lord. It points to the redemptive experience that comes through mercy and goodness. It is impossible to give Jonah the mass appeal of Jaws. The immature feelings of many persons demand expression followed by punishment. The Mysterium Tremendum of Rudolph Otto[2] appears here only in its negative aspects. The message of the Church must rather be through the seed which is sown and allowed to mature, the light which is set upon a hill, the yeast which leavens the whole lump (Matt. 13:1-8; Matt. 5:14-16; Luke 13:20-21).

Pastoral psychotherapy is a necessity in the present situation. There are many individuals caught up in inner conflicts who are unable to find answers in the present culture. The message of the church is unreal to them, and the processes of the church do not reach their problem, either because of their resistance and defensiveness, or the ineptitude of the church in communicating. They need to experience the ancient religious process of confession in sufficient depth and complexity to meet their problem. This is pastoral psychotherapy. That the modern pastor has learned much from other professional therapists only attests to his willingness to search for truth wherever it may be found for the sake of those to whom he ministers. This means that the attitude of openness needs to be balanced by a critical and evaluative attitude grounded in both experience and understanding. Out of the confusion of tongues in the field of general psychotherapy, the pastor needs to be able to separate the wheat from the chaff, while he maintains his own distinctive religious faith. Furthermore, there are those persons in our culture who view their problem as essentially religious and who want and need a pastoral relationship.

THE INTERPRETATION OF
RELIGIOUS SYMBOLISM

The discussion of Jonah gives data for a consideration of religious symbols and their interpretation. It is an error to make a literal interpretation of religious symbols. Many persons have done this with Jonah, with Genesis, and with other symbolic expressions in the Bible and elsewhere. This is defensive. Religious insight may be clothed in symbols from any aspect of the external world, but their purpose is to convey the meaning of a relationship on both the human and divine levels. These insights and meanings may not be immediately apparent, for the depth of meaning usually requires some reflection. Symbols bring their meaning only as one is open to that meaning and places himself in a mood of emotional and spiritual reflection and receptivity. To take them literally is to block out deeper responses and to destroy their deeper meanings. Jonah, Genesis, and many other portions of the Bible and other religious writings, taken literally, are completely misinterpreted.

Another error is known as reductionism.[3] This is interpreting a symbol in a manner that destroys its higher meanings. This means that a story like Jonah would be interpreted only in terms of archaic, infantile, or pathological meanings. The possibility of such interpretation grows out of the ambiguous nature of religious symbols, as well as a desire on the part of the interpreter to deny religious truth. The ambiguity of religious symbols lies in the fact that they may express truth on various levels of life simultaneously. A person may use religious symbols in a manner which does express infantile or pathological processes, while at the same time expressing truths on much more mature and higher levels. This is part of the power of religious symbols — they pick up energy and goals from deep, instinctive dimensions of being and transform them into higher, creative goals. This is part of the redemptive, healing process of religion. This leads to greater differentiation of the person, fuller development of individuality and a higher level of integration.

Therefore, we cannot deny that religious symbols may carry archaic and pathological meanings. However, to say that a symbol has "only" infantile sexual meanings, or that it is "only" the expression of a father fixation, or that it contains "only" oral aggressiveness or Oedipal guilt, is to deny its creative meaning. We must also look at what symbols say about the way in which such energy is to be expressed. Religious symbols can and do express profound regressive tendencies in human life, but their essential nature is in the manner in which they also express a drive toward growth, integration, and individuation. Many religious persons sense that they are in a struggle with ambivalent processes which threaten them with regression or offer the promise of hope and growth. But only the mature person can go through such a conflict alone and emerge on the positive side. Help is needed. This may come through the fellowship of the church and various functions within the church. It may come through pastoral care or pastoral psychotherapy. It may come through secular therapists who understand the nature of religious experience and who do not seek to destroy the religion of a person.

In addition to expressing psychological meanings, religious symbols may and do reveal the dimensions of height, of breadth, and of depth of life. The dimension of height is found in symbols of the Infinite or Ultimate. God, Christ, the Creator, the Redeemer, are symbols of the Ultimate. Some persons deny that traditional symbols carry meaning for them, but they tend to replace these by other symbols. Life requires some convictions about and faith in an Ultimate Being, else the individual tends to exalt himself to that level. People need a home in the universe.

The breadth dimension of life is found in the attempt to probe the meaning of human relationships. Human need and aggressiveness have brought peoples and nations into severe conflict which is destructive. Furthermore, every human being needs to find an answer to feelings of being alone, of isolation and alienation. The Christian faith traditionally has used such symbols as the Kingdom of God, the Family of God, the fellowship of the saints, to express the need to break down inner barriers and arrive

at a sense of community and communion. It is impossible to estimate the value of the churches in bringing people together in a
sense of community and communion. It is impossible to estimate
the value of the churches in bringing people together in a sense of
fellowship. The fact that conflict may arise within the fellowship,
as within the family, is testimony to the fears that many persons
have of human closeness. They have been hurt in childhood by
persons with whom they were close. To be close to others may
raise sexual issues with which some feel unable to cope. The
Christian faith has used the dimension of breadth to include all
humanity. These symbols express meaning of a universal character. They give people the opportunity to identify with broad
segments of humanity insofar as they are able.

The depth dimension of religious insight concerns the way of
life of the person and the group. This involves moral choices,
decisions, and values. A prominent symbol of this is the
commandments of Moses, commonly called The Ten Commandments (Exod. 20:1-17). Jesus offered two further commandments which combine the three dimensions of which we have been
speaking (Matt. 22:34-40). A fundamental issue in pastoral
psychotherapy is whether moral law is imposed from the outside,
by the pastor, through his authority, of whether it is interpreted in
a relationship of understanding and grace, helping the person to
evaluate his own experience and resolve conflicts in moral choice.
Only as adults have a high degree of autonomy in their own decision making, can they make genuinely moral choices. The pastor
meets some persons who are in severe moral conflict, some others
who have such a rigid sense of right and wrong that their life is in a
straitjacket, and still others whose decisions are under the control
of impulses and whose power of moral control is very weak. All of
these need help on an emotional level. They need also to learn how
to evaluate their own experiences and become aware of the moral
structure in their own life. As persons learn to make genuine moral
choices, they develop deep inner strength.

Today the pastor is in a strategic position to interpret the moral
dimension of religious faith. He is serving in the aftermath of a

period when "law and order" became a dominant symbol in the feelings of many persons. Inwardly the majority of persons know that law and order are the only basis for individual or social living, and the political symbols picked up this inner conviction. But people were disillusioned, and their faith in national leadership was destroyed. Today we are in a period of deep indifference, apathy, and cynicism. Many feel that they "can get away with it too, so why not?" In this situation the pastor is called upon to speak with a love and understanding, an empathy which includes a certainty based on the reality of the situation and his own moral convictions. This will give others the confidence to face their own moral dilemmas courageously.

Symbols and meanings expressing the height, breadth and depth of religious faith are inseparably related or at times are identical. When these symbols are interpreted, all three dimensions must be considered. In addition, the psychological dimension must be considered, especially as it is interwoven with religious meanings. There is no religious experience that does not involve psychological processes. Such interpretation should be more than conceptual and theoretical. The individual needs to experience the feelings involved and to discover how these feelings move him toward relationships and action. The mature and growing aspects of feelings as they are expressed through symbols need attention, as well as the regressive aspects. As we have said, religious symbols partake of deep emotional energy that may be derived from a childish level, but that may also partake of the maturing, growing, integrating energy. Each side needs to be brought out into consciousness. There is no magic formula for doing this. It depends largely on the skill of the pastor and the depth to which he has come to understand his own religious symbols, feelings, and strivings.

This then is a problem for the pastor. Inner, psychological processes may distort the meaning of religious symbols, even as the same symbols embody and seek to express creative energy. For example, if the pastor listens to people, he will find that his sermons often are received with a different meaning from what intended. The communication was distorted or even reversed as it was received. Perhaps it was improved! Perhaps the meaning he intended on the conscious level was not the same as what came from him on the feeling level. He cannot control how others receive his message. He can only examine thoroughly the feelings behind the sermon. Through conversation he may be able to help the other person correct some of his distortions. Sometimes distortion and denial are necessary because the maturing and growing aspects of religion require more strength than a person can give at that time.

This has bearing also on pressures that are being placed today on pastoral psychotherapists to theologize their work. The theologian and philosopher deal with religious symbols in their ontological meaning. The pastoral therapist must work with the experiential meaning. His knowledge of theology can help him understand how ideas and behavior denies or distorts accepted theological truth. The person often sees this, and the issue is how to resolve the conflict. This will not be resolved by rational processes, but only as the inner motivation is changed. This is clear in the New Testament, where commitment often precedes discovery of truth. The pastoral therapist needs to know his way around in the theological disciplines, to have his own theology worked out and continuing to grow, and to be able to relate his theology to his work. In the therapy office he deals with the experience of the individual and his symbols. If he makes religious interpretations, they should be in symbols not in abstractions. They should be in symbols which have meaning within the context of the existing relationship, and should be interpretive of what is being experienced within that relationship.

HUMAN ASPIRATIONS AND
RELIGIOUS SYMBOLS

When religious symbols are used for the purposes of growth and movement toward wholeness, they combine insight and meanings on all four levels simultaneously. This may be illustrated by the Biblical use of religious symbols to express human aspirations. We will be looking at symbols from the point of view of inner processes and meanings rather than the symbolic process itself.

Human beings aspire. It is part of our nature to reach out beyond ourselves, to fervently wish for something we have not yet achieved or experienced, to desire something higher than what we have. Many aspire to move up out of severe or intolerable social and economic conditions. Human beings aspire to knowledge and to achieve. Many deprived peoples aspire today to move up out of unhappy conditions.

Human beings also aspire spiritually. They seek deep, inner satisfactions for themselves and families. They seek to discover life's meanings and how they should live. Religious faith has presented, through its symbols, objects, and goals for human aspiration. To worship God is to aspire to become like him in character. The insight that man was made in the image of God is the highest expression of this aspiration. Religion then gives people an identity, both individually and as a group. It does so not only in terms of insight into the nature of the Ultimate, but also of insight into the nature of man. To know what is in man is to know something about the God who created him.

The profound potentials in human beings also find expression in insights into the relationship of the individual to the group, and to humanity as a whole. "He made of one every nation of men" (Acts 17:26). The same symbols express the urge to moral choices which lead to fulfillment. Human beings cannot escape the necessity of finding a relationship within themselves and between themselves and their world which leads to the fulfillment of their aspirations, the realization of moral values, the improvement of their quality of life and the increase of their love toward God and man. To avoid this is to become less than a complete person. This capacity to aspire toward moving out of where we are is one of the inner resources in individuals which is utilized experientially in pastoral psychotherapy.

Becoming God-like in character does not mean retaining our childish sense of omnipotence. We do not go far along the pathway of the Christian faith before meeting a deep sense of the difference in power between ourselves and our Creator. This is not simply a projection, but a projection that accords with reality. It is attested in the tragedies that occur when men aspire to be God. We also meet up with the necessity of finding ourselves a part of the family of man, a universal brotherhood. Out of our cultural backgrounds we may find ourselves in severe conflict at this point. The sense of moral responsibility to which we are called beckons us to develop the virtue of humility. Humility is honest self-acceptance and the acceptance of others in compassion, not in pride or arrogance.

In psychological terms, one of the powerful contributions of religion has been and still is the offering to human beings of an ego ideal that promises to fulfill human aspirations. An ego ideal is the part of a person that says, "I want to be like another because I trust and love him or her." It cannot be forced by an overriding conscience or external authority. Parents, teachers, and other adults may help a child to develop strong ego ideals through a loving relationship. But human beings are fallible, and sooner or later all of us have found flaws in our ideals. Religious faith offers an ideal in which there are no flaws. Within the Christian faith this ideal is personified in Christ. It is no accident that one of the classics of Christian devotion has been "The Imitation of Christ" by Thomas à Kempis. Today we understand processes deeper than imitation, namely identification and introjection, as a basis for the ideal.

No human being is always true to his ideals or even his accepted moral standards. It is no accident that the story of man's creation in the image of God in Genesis is followed by the story of man's fall. Whether this weakness is constitutional or the result of human upbringing and frustrations, we shall not pause to argue here. The pastor is interested in the motivation of sinful acts, in their consequences and in helping people move toward a higher quality of life. To do this he must distinguish between neurotic guilt, that arising out of unconscious motivation and conflict, and real or healthy guilt which arises as a danger signal indicating that the individual is on the wrong track and needs to turn around. These kinds of guilt may be centered in the same act — the alcoholic, for example, may be driven by unconscious motivation about which he feels guilty in the neurotic sense, but also by real guilt about what he is doing to himself and family. Man aspires, man fails, and here is written the source of much human "grandeur and misery" and the need for a healing ministry.

The healing ministry combines process and quality of relationship in an inextricable manner. The processes are clear. They are repentance, confession and acceptance of forgiveness. The witness to this is the new life which follows.

Repentance, as a process, involves a change of mind or heart, the breaking through of defenses sufficiently to understand that there is underlying pain that needs to be dealt with openly and honestly. Repentance is more than a wish, more than a weak promise that a change will be made, and it is not an attempt to appease another person. It is a profound change of attitude which results in at least becoming a beginner in the discovery of the moral nature of the self and in the moral structure of the universe. It may result in self-exploration or in therapy. Its goal is to change the way of life. It is not an act which is performed once and for all; it is an inner attitude which finds continuing expression and more about the self that needs to be changed. It is the process of looking at one's inner pain and dealing with it as his strength permits.

Repentance leads to confession. This is simply because we live in a universe in which we are closely and deeply related to each other, and whatever pain we are struggling with is greatly lessened as it is shared with a person who is competent to handle it with us. Competency is not a matter of intellectual training. The confessor, pastor, or other person should be one who has come to terms with his own inner pain, and who has worked it through sufficiently that he can speak a healing word to the confessee.

Confession often involves more than an act about which one feels guilty. There is a need for the discovery of the motivation of the act. When feelings of guilt are displaced from the original action to another, then the original action needs again to be related to the guilt. Much guilt is due, not so much to acts as to feelings which have never been expressed in action; for example, a sexual feeling or a wish to hurt someone. Guilt experienced in adult life is often the outgrowth of childhood relationships. Part of the task of the pastor is to help people discover just what it is they need to talk about, to confess, to reveal. Depending on the attitude and strength of the pastor, the confession itself can bring healing. But it must be more than catharsis. In order to be healing it must lead to insight and to change. Confessing to a pastor may also partake of a symbolic experience for the religious person. Confession is the traditional, theological word for what we have been discussing as pastoral psychotherapy.

Everyone wants forgiveness; few want to pay the price. The Christian faith comes with the assurance of God's forgiveness and acceptance of each person. The person must accept that forgiveness in depth, that is in whatever depth he needs it. In order to do this, he or she must forgive others. This is a simultaneous process. As a person gives up his hatred for another, he finds himself able to accept God's forgiveness with a meaning it never had before. The Biblical statement is clear: forgive us as we have forgiven others. We have greatly overemphasized being forgiven; we have greatly underemphasized being forgiving.

The process of the healing ministry requires the underlying qualities of faith, hope, and love. We have discussed these elsewhere in the book, and will not elaborate here. The meaning of these qualities in the inner life of the pastor is central to his entire ministry, but crucial to the healing ministry.

BIBLICAL SYMBOLS AND HUMAN CONFLICT

The early pages of Genesis symbolize the basic human conflict as that of a creature "made in the image of God," but also fallen from grace into sin and tragically needing redemption. Paul expressed the conflict with the symbols "spirit" and "flesh."[4] These words, like others, have a richness of meaning that may become confusing, but again they symbolize living realities in human experience. The Spirit gives life. The flesh is the embodiment of the Spirit and may be transformed by Spirit or self. This illustrates how living symbols carry meaning on several levels simultaneously, but a logical and exact definition tends to destroy the relationship and dynamic connection between symbol and reality. The negative meaning of flesh, like that of sin, is more than sensuality. It means that the whole person is wrongly directed. Spirit, on the other hand, carries meanings such as illumination and guidance, as power, as giving fruits highly desirable, as becoming a basis for a personal response of commitment, as providing freedom from legalism, as searching the deep things of God, among others. It is the Spirit which brings the new birth and leads in the search for the truth which liberates. It is a mistake to interpret the term *spirit* as a hangover from animism. The modern conception of spirit, or self in ego psychology, is a kernel of reality and truth that was present in animistic concepts. Human life cannot be understood religiously or psychologically without some such concept.

We have been discussing in Biblical terms what has been called in psychological terms the ambivalence in human nature. On the one side, there is the physical being, a source of intense pleasure and pain, of fulfillment and frustration, of life and death. It is the ambivalence between the ultimate and the contingent in life, between that which is given as part of our nature and that which is subject to causal relationships, and between the sense of freedom and the large areas where life is determined. Human beings have an image of their high destiny in life, yet they are capable of the most brutal acts and fantasies. Sometimes we seek dependency on forces outside of ourselves, and at other times we are in a state of rebellion and flight. At times we are moved by genuinely altruistic motives, and at other times by a fantasy of ourselves as omnipotent, with a false sense of power. At times we are aware of a deep spiritual hunger, but it is hard for us to discipline our desire for physical gratification. We degrade sex when we use it for purely physical gratification, but to use it for the purpose of expressing genuine love and intimacy often presents internal obstacles such as fear and guilt. Inwardly, we seem to understand that one secret of peace and contentment is to seek to live in accordance with the conditions given by a Creator. At other times we insist that we are the creator, not a creature, and we seek to control through our magical fantasies. At times we know we were made for fellowship; at other times we experience an intolerable sense of alienation. With all of this conflict we are incurably optimistic. We see ourselves as creative, we have achieved marvels in the physical world, we have produced great art and literature, but we have not learned, as individuals or as a society, how to handle our destructiveness and find peace. The issue is how to fulfill the image of God within us rather than succumb to the desire to become God, how to become a whole person rather than a counterfeit god.

Out of this conflict between impulse and conscience, or between opposing wishes, repressed into unconscious processes and complicated by environmental and cultural factors, arise what the psychologist calls symptoms, but what religion interprets as false gods or idolatry. These arise in part because the ego is too weak, with energy absorbed in the conflict, to make a resolution that leads to growth and wholeness. Indeed, the person is unable to keep his attention focused on the realities that are being expressed in his symbols, but rather becomes absorbed with the symbols themselves or some aspect of them. The symbol then becomes the reality. Or if he is unable to become aware of the conflict and to cope with it, he may use one of the numerous defenses against it, and out of this create symptoms. The symptoms then symbolize the conflict, but he is not aware of this. His attention is focused on the symptom or the symbol. It becomes the reality. He is running from part of his self, while over-magnifying another part to which he devotes himself. If he is a person of severe conscience then he will magnify his guilt, and he will reject the forgiving realities in his religion. If a person of weak conscience, then impulses are likely to take control, and he will reject or deny the moral aspects of religion. He may also refuse to accept his responsibility to other persons and to himself. The separation of symbol and reality, and the resulting worship of a symbol means that the Infinite is being replaced by something finite, and there is no healing in this.

IDOLS AS DEAD SYMBOLS

Idolatry expresses aspirations that are misguided and short-circuited. Some idols, such as physical symptoms, are self-destructive. The person not only gets certain satisfactions out of being sick but punishes himself at the same time and prevents himself from becoming whole. Sometimes the destructiveness grows out of the uncontrolled expression of instinctive needs, sex or aggression, with guilt about such expression repressed. False gods, whether the gods of pain or of pleasure, lead to values which do not promote the welfare of the whole person. They repress positive aspects of the person while giving exaggerated expression to negative aspects. There is no long-range growth or lasting satisfaction. Individuals and groups become committed to them in worship and in obedience, as though they were the Ultimate. The finite becomes the Infinite.

We live in a culture lush in the worship of false gods. Some of these arise within the family. A grown-up child worships a parent and maintains a commitment to that parent's ideals and standards in a manner that prevents growth. A parent hangs on to a child in a false kind of love that is crushing, and that leads to the child's fear and hatred of the parent. The object of our anger also becomes the object of our devotion, through dissociation of feeling and symbol. A false god is any object of devotion, any sought-for value, that seems to offer inner satisfaction and fulfillment but in the end only destroys or reduces the quality of personal existence. Activity, such as the making of money or some other achievement, can be a false god, since it promises the satisfaction of inner needs through power. Not many people come to the pastor complaining that they make too much money. They come complaining that their marriage is on the rocks, that their children are in rebellion, or that life has lost its meaning. They do not realize that they have been searching for a high quality of life in a false manner.

A common false god today is the worship of sex and other physical pleasures. The body, or some aspect of it, is the object of devotion and commitment, rather than an instrument through which creative human spirit can give and receive enrichment. The pastor frequently finds himself helping persons find a more satisfying sexual life. He knows that the sexual life is one of the gifts of God to man, part of the creative activity of God in man, not just for procreation, but for the re-creation of persons and for the development of a deep sense of intimacy with and commitment to another person. Many seek to avoid intimacy through commitment to a sexual life that is nothing more than physical activity. Others deny the sexual aspect of their lives. Either attitude is a false god.

Another popular form of idolatry is the erection of altars to the "self." Having discarded the soul, many have discovered that they cannot get away from the spiritual core of their personality. Many have set the self up as the highest value, the great god. Thus we have all sorts of programs for self-development, for discovering our potential, for becoming ourselves.

Some of these programs have values; for many they have become false gods. These have missed an essential aspect of genuine religious faith, which is, however, not opposed to the growth of the self. Jesus is reported to have said that he came to bring people the abundant life, and many have testified to this (John 10:10). A central message of Jesus was that people find their real selves as they commit themselves to the Ultimate Source of life, God. The worship of God in spirit and in truth leads to the amelioration of alienation and a closer, more open and joyful relationship with others (John 4:23–24). Indeed, we find our real selves not by a kind of self-massage and protectiveness, but by losing ourselves in loving service to others. Fulfillment of the self comes as we give of ourselves, but first we must receive. Not to be open to what others have to give us emotionally is to be like an apple that cuts itself off from the tree and lies forlornly on the ground trying to make itself grow. It soon exhausts its strength, since it is not fed from deep roots.

Religion itself can become idolatrous, as the Bible amply testifies. Here again there is dissociation between the symbol and reality on the human and Ultimate dimensions, with a compulsive need to maintain the symbol while denying the inner spirit and truth of the symbol. The Church, religious creeds, religious practices and rituals may become idols. When this occurs, they tend to encourage pathological processes within the individual and in the group. Religious idolatry uses the same symbols as does healthy, living religion, but the manner in which they are used is radically different.

Idolatry is the endeavor to resolve inner conflict and to find satisfaction through devotion and commitment to an aspect of the human, finite existence and its symbols. It is a regressive solution of human conflict. It represents a partial aspect of human personality which has taken over the control of the whole person, and which is dominating human aspirations. The problems of reality testing, of impulse control, of object relationships, and of past, present, and future relationships discussed in a previous chapter have not been resolved.

HUMAN ASPIRATION AND FEAR OF DEATH

One of the profound human conflicts, found both in the Biblical account and in modern life, is that between life and death. Human beings fear death, though they know it is inevitable. This is the fear of the actual death of the body, but also the symbolic or real death of the self or spirit. The loss of mastery over some part of ourselves is often experienced as a kind of death. Many times anxiety about death is really anxiety about life, unfulfilled life. Experiences which deprive us of a special meaning create a kind of living death. Human beings are caught between creative and destructive forces throughout their existence, between conflicting aspirations, or between aspirations and a sense of inadequacy. In pastoral psychotherapy we deal constantly with these forces as they find expression in many human experiences, including the fear of death. Rather than give reassurance, the task of the pastor is to help the person discover whether the fear of death is fear of bodily death, or the fear of the death of the self or the spirit, or a combination of these, and to deal with it accordingly.

The life of Jesus has given some significant symbols which express the realities and conflicts of which we have been speaking. For example, the story of the temptations (Matt. 4:1–11) takes us into the very core of human experience. Here we see the conflict, arising out of human hungers, the demand for immediate, physical satisfaction, and the inner conviction of Jesus of the primacy of the human spirit, that requires that life be lived in terms of higher aspirations. Immediate physical needs are not denied but are carried up into an appropriate relationship to higher needs. The experience can be contrasted with that of Esau, who sold his birthright for a bowl of stew because he was hungry (Gen. 26:29–34). The second temptation symbolizes the need to seek control of the world and of God through magical omnipotence as this conflicts with the nature of both human and Ultimate Reality. In the third we see, through living symbols, the struggle between the impulse to enter in a self-defeating power struggle by the worship of evil (idolatry), and the necessity for single-minded loyalty to the living God.

In each of these temptations the struggle needs to be understood as between motivating elements in Jesus, expressed through symbols that have an external reference but also a profound inner reality. In each the ontological element is strongly present. In each the implications of the experience for humanity as a whole are present. In each the necessity of a clear-cut moral decision, one made through his own freedom, is portrayed. Human aspirations, both healthy and perverted, realistic and unrealistic, are portrayed. In each the possibility of failure with serious consequences is poignantly present. In each there was a movement toward answers which had a creative influence on his life. All of this was expressed in symbols of profound personal significance, which can be understood by those who read the story with openness, imagination, and reflection.

It would be interesting to deal with many of the sayings and parables of Jesus from the point of view of both religious and psychological dynamics as experienced in pastoral therapy. This the reader must do for himself. We move on to another powerful experience, that of Gethsemane (Matt. 26:36–46).

In the Gethsemane story there is the struggle between life and death, between values of the spirit and needs of the flesh, between a quality of love that is redemptive and the need to save one's own life. Here again the usual elements of religious symbols are present. Here the attention of Jesus is focused on the inner realities of the situation, not on the symbols. Here are aspirations, conflict, the possibility of failure, the necessity of moral decision and responsibility, and profound implications for humanity as a whole. Here death is accepted as a means to life. Jesus is reported to have spoken to his disciples about how a seed must drop into the ground and die in order to bring forth new life (John 12:24). Now he faces that issue in his own life. Could he accept a higher purpose than his own continued existence as a human being? This reversal of the usual human values is difficult to understand, though we honor our heroes who lay down their life for others. Our Healer should be like us, and we become frightened and angry when he is not. We insist on the objective truth of our transference reactions.

Because of the nature of the events surrounding it, and the experience which was lived out on it, the Cross of Christ has become a major and inescapable symbol of the crucial conflict between life and death, good and evil. It points to both the human and divine dimensions, to the conflict between the temporal and the eternal, to the human need to hold on and let go of life, to the principle of the renunciation of the infantile, destructive and egocentric in order to become mature, creative, and self-giving. It points to the fact that there is no health or salvation on a purely individual basis, but only as one serves the needs of others and the community in obedience to God. These meanings are inherent in the therapy experience, but are often not brought to the level of consciousness or formulated. The Cross condenses many human experiences and, therefore, it is a potent symbol.

Death, the renunciation of all that conflicts with redemptive love, leads on to the new life of the resurrection, another dominant symbol of the faith. Here is new life. The mystery of the resurrection in the New Testament has a minor parallel in the mystery experienced by some persons at the change within them when they are able to renounce that which blocks growth, and to find release for creative powers from within that they had never before experienced. This is sometimes called the emergence of a new self, or growth to maturity, or personal fulfillment. These words catch only part of the total reality of the religious experience. Genuine new life, the new birth, or the resurrection of the spirit must be experienced in a manner that includes the love and service of others, the giving of oneself as one has been given to, the committing of oneself to a reality that has been felt working within. It is a gift, not an achievement. Though therapy may prepare the way by removing resistances and obstacles to growth, the quality of life to which the Christian faith points involves commitment to the ideals and values of that faith, or to a spiritually mature image of that faith, Christ.

From the resurrection experience, the New Testament moves on to describe the new life in the Spirit, the new Being in Christ, the consequences of the rebirth (Letter to the Galatians). Life in the Spirit is contrasted with life in the flesh. The flesh here is not the body but the hostile, destructive impulses which emerge through the body out of man's omnipotence and distorted narcissism. Life in the Spirit is not a permanent acquisition, but one that needs constantly to be renewed. There is a continual struggle in human life between tendencies to regress and to grow, to experience decay and to experience regeneration. Static morality is a sign of defended regression.

The impulses of the flesh seek their outlet in activities, in works. Performance, not motivation, is the measure of achievement. Right behavior may be performed for the wrong reasons. Not all of the people who follow the impulses of the flesh are to be found on skid row. Some are in the churches where they are struggling to follow the oft disproved doctrine of salvation by works.

The search for salvation by works leads inevitably to the denial of honest motivation, and the depersonalization and mechanization of the person. The question often raised in the therapy process is "How do I do that?" or "How do I achieve that?" or "How do I get over this?" This is the question Nicodemus asked of Jesus (John 3:1-15). Here the pastor is in the presence of defensiveness. The demand for detailed and specific directions is answered in kind by some "healers" who themselves wish to participate in the illusion of omnipotence. It completely ignores the insistence of the New Testament that the way to healing is through the uncovering and transformation of motivations, feelings, and strivings (Matt. 6-8). Rigid intellectual patterns breakdown under the power of honesty in owning one's motivation. This is why in pastoral therapy the giving of advice is usually gratuitous. Advice usually has to do with performance.

In an earlier chapter we spoke of the need for diagnosis. In the fifth chapter of Galatians Paul gives diagnostic material based on the concepts of flesh and Spirit. We notice first that the flesh produces "works" while the Spirit gives "fruits." The list of the works of the flesh sounds like a recitation of symptoms from a modern psychopathology. "The works of the flesh are plain: immorality, impurity, licentiousness, idolatry, sorcery, enmity, strife, jealousy, anger, selfishness, dissension, party spirit, envy, drunkenness, carousing, and the like" (Gal. 5:19-21). These are ways in which men seek salvation through performance, through giving themselves to the service of destructive impulses and the fantasy of omnipotence.

The pastor also sees those on the opposite pole — persons who do not achieve, those afraid to be aggressive, passive persons who depend on others to take care of them and who have many excuses for dealing with neither their problems nor the problems of society. Yet they confess faith. Their goodness is negative; nothing happens except when others make it happen. They are the underachievers, the people who bury their talent (Matt. 25:14-30). Sometimes they withdraw in prayer and contemplation, but this never brings them back into a world of active service as it should. Part of the motivation of these people is the need to suffer.

The faith of a passive person is not grounded in trust. It is grounded in fear and dependency. In the New Testament it is dead and fruitless. "So faith by itself if it has no works is dead" (James 2:17). Genuine faith, grounded in trust and courage to risk is completed and fulfilled by work. The two are inseparable. "For as the body apart from the spirit is dead, so faith apart from works is dead" (James 2:26). Or as Jesus said, "You will know them by their fruits" (Matt. 7:20). Often passive people are experts at telling others what they should do. These people need help on a rather deep level, but often they are too passive to ask for it, or to cooperate in the process. They want it "given" to them.

On the other hand, there is no greater statement of the goals of pastoral therapy, or the results of life in the Spirit than the description of the fruits of the Spirit. "The fruit of the Spirit is love, joy, peace, patience, kindness, goodness, faithfulness, gentleness, self-control; against such there is no law" (Gal. 5:22-23). These are qualities of the human spirit which bring fulfillment. This is life in the Spirit.

THE SEARCH FOR CONSOLATION

There is another experiential use of religious symbols that frequently involves the Cross, as well as other symbols. It is that of consolation or comfort.

To comfort another is a normal, human response when the other is in pain and suffering. To seek comfort in times of crises and pain is also a human response. There are many symbolic expressions of comfort in the Bible, and many of these are used repeatedly in funeral services. They are so familiar that they hardly need to be repeated here.[5]

The word *comfort* has confused meanings, and it is important to understand the meaning we put into symbols of comfort. To some it means a sentimental kind of sympathy which has the result of weakening the resistance of a sufferer. Some persons seem to ask for this, and others want to give it. The real meaning of the word is to give strength and fortitude. The last part of the word is derived from the same root as our word *fort*. To be comforted means to be fortified.

The issue then is how to bring strength and courage to persons in various conditions of suffering. The process of doing this may vary from person to person and with the exact nature of the suffering. A patient suffering from a severe illness needs to be treated differently than a bereaved person.

Some will immediately think of natural evil, such as earthquakes, droughts, fires and pestilences. For these, the victims are not held responsible. It happens to them. The answer seems to be in whatever science can do to prevent them. It has already learned how to prevent many serious diseases, such as polio and typhoid.

Today the horizon surrounding what we believe a person is responsible for is widening. We know today that people have a responsibility for becoming ill. True, a disease germ or a pathological process may be involved, but emotional factors have been shown to play a large part in the production of many illnesses, such as tuberculosis and even cancer.[6] Some emotions, such as grief over the loss of a loved object, if not handled with courage and worked through can make the person a hospitable host to disease process. Other illnesses may have a more direct relationship to personality structure and emotions. Many persons suffering from these illnesses seek the kind of comforting which is weakening and which relieves them from all responsibility. Someone else, or God, must take care of them.

The meaning of the desire for such comfort needs to be looked at from the point of view of psychodynamics. Here it is seen to be regressive, a desire to go back to an early childhood state of being cared for rather than caring for oneself, and a passive and dependent attitude which weakens the moral processes in the person. Therefore, when such needs are gratified through religion or otherwise, the person is weakened. Many seek this kind of comfort through tranquilizers and other drugs, choosing to surrender a part of their personhood for a false kind of strength.

The pastor in the parish and the pastoral therapist meet persons like this frequently. They must be dealt with in terms of their psychodynamics rather than in terms of their symptoms. Their symptoms are indeed idols which they highly value since they seem to justify the kind of childish dependency they seek. If the pastor turns them away, they are hurt. If the pastor gratifies them, he has been drawn into an unhealthy relationship. The pastor must learn how to gradually call these persons to a sense of responsibility for themselves. With some this is a long hard task; with others not so long. Some will respect him, and they will understand what he means if he is firm but kind, stressing more what the person needs rather than what he wants. Sometimes he will be able to effectively interpret some of the consoling passages of the Bible with a mature meaning, but this only if he first offers them a mature relationship.

PASTORAL CARE AND INNER STRENGTHS

If the pastor is able to walk with persons through their pain and suffering, their despair and guilt, their anxiety about life and their fear of death, he may be rewarded by seeing the person emerge with a new sense of strength which he knows is not entirely of human making. We are speaking here of a kind of empathy which communicates that the pastor feels the sufferings of another through the reconciliation of his own human sufferings. Such empathy speaks analogically of a similar but more complete empathy in God through which reconciliation may take place. Out of such a relationship a person may gain strength and become able to accept and become reconciled to their own sufferings. We are speaking here about the sufferings which are residuals of childhood and also with sufferings which originate in the present, such as the fear of death. Only as the pastor has become deeply reconciled with his own death can he feel within himself the fear that another has. Otherwise he will project his own fears on to them.

What are some of the inner resources or strengths which a genuine pastoral relationship may bring out in another? One is certainly the ability to learn how to trust, or to work through mistrust. The ability to increase the sense of autonomy and responsibility for self is another. The ability to love and to experience intimacy, in both the sexual and nonsexual dimensions without fear and guilt is another. The ability to use aggressiveness in a manner that produces human values for self and others rather than destroying them is another. The capacity to continue to clarify one's sense of personal identity within a community of mutually beneficial and responsible relationships, and to give oneself in the nurture of others is another. There are new strengths which may not emerge until age is experienced in the sixties and seventies and beyond, which are grounded in strengths developed in previous stages of the life cycle. From a theological point of view we see these strengths as part of the nature of human personality, a gift of God to man in the process of creation. They may lie dormant or they may be developed. Part of the task of pastoral care and of pastoral therapy, as well as other aspects of the religious life is that of bringing these potentials in human beings to full realization. This in itself becomes an experience of deep reassurance or comfort to a person—to know that one has the strength to meet the crises of life. Such strength does not manifest itself until we are called upon to use it.

Human aspirations, creativity, and strength do not grow apart from an atmosphere of freedom and a deep commitment to the process of growth. This means the willingness to take the next step which is required in the growth process, whatever that is. Such commitment must be without reservation. As with the Prodigal (Luke 15:11–32), there must be a compelling desire to move toward reconciliation and restitution without counting the cost, and to risk the experience of suffering in order to achieve a desirable goal. The demand of Jesus for commitment was uncompromising—there are no halfway measures in the religious search. This is true also in all forms of pastoral care and pastoral therapy. Persons who say, "I will try it to see if it works," or "I want help but I do not want to change," or "I want help but there are some things I won't talk about," or "I want to be cured but at no effort"—these persons must have a change of mind before any help or growth will be experienced. Commitment must counteract resistance.

The chief struggle in either religious or therapeutic processes is the modification of that narcissism or self-centeredness which demands that life and the universe, including others, revolves around us. The task is to learn to use self-concern and self-esteem to make those decisions which enhance rather than destroy the self. When we move out of our self-centeredness, we see that what enhances our own life also enhances the lives of others and that decisions which hurt others also hurt us. Our welfare is inextricably bound to that of others. Life cannot be compared to a circle having a center. Life is rather more like an ellipse with two foci, self and others, held together in all dimensions by a living God. The object of a genuine religious commitment, God, must be large enough to include self and others in a living community of concern and service. The struggle toward this commitment has been symbolized in many ways, but it is deeply one of death and rebirth. It is the death of those feelings, attitudes, and responses which bind us to immature and false values, and to childish narcissism. It is commitment to growth toward those values and relationships where self and others are bound together in mutually enhancing experiences, motivated by love and faith toward God.

The core of the therapy experience, as of Christian experience, may be described by the Biblical statement "For by grace you have been saved through faith; and this is not your own doing, it is the gift of God—not because of works, lest any man should boast" (Eph. 2:8-9). Something of a gracious, beneficent, curative power enters life as the quality of love and trust from another gives a person strength to become open to it in trust. Trust is essentially assent, a saying yes, a receptivity and openness to what is trustworthy in oneself, in others, and in God. Grace is trustworthy. It points to the possibility of acceptance, of affirmation, and of resolution of conflict. Through trust and faith we exercise autonomy as a person; we relax our insistence in our own omnipotence and power; open ourselves up to and accept deep healing and reconciling forces, which then arise within us to resolve our ambivalences. We become aware of those areas of existence where decision is both possible and necessary, and we come to understand those processes which are beyond our control. Destructive aspects of our inner life are neutralized by love; destructive impulses are disciplined by the self.

The healing that takes place in pastoral therapy does not replace the ancient experience of worship. Therapy is essentially the process of discovering the self in relationship to the self, to others and to God. Worship is essentially the discovery of the presence of God, and the self-disclosure, renewal and commitment which takes place through that discovery. Often a person must deal with his own inner attitudes and feelings before he can experience worship. It has been my experience that after pastoral therapy some persons find worship much more meaningful. Neither does worship replace the therapy experience. Either the therapy experience or the worship experience is destroyed if approached in a defensive, demanding manner. Only as we approach these experiences in an open, searching, listening, reflecting manner does the light of the image of God within us become clear.

In this book we have attempted to deal with the understanding and amelioration of human pain and conflict by processes of religion and of pastoral psychotherapy. Psychological understanding of persons and of the various ways of dealing with inner conflict is essential for the pastor. It is also essential that the pastor understand in depth the religious dimensions of persons. This

means that the relation of the individual to whatever he considers
Ultimate, the depth of his identification with humanity as a
whole, as well as with individuals, and the nature of his moral
commitments must be understood as they become involved with
psychological processes. The nature of religious symbols which
carry these meanings, and the processes involved in the use of
symbols for growth and for regression needs to be understood.
This would include the processes by which symbols lose their
power, become dead or become objects of devotion. This understanding must be more than conceptual. The pastor must be able
to enter into the experiences and feelings of a person in an
empathetic manner and respond in a healing manner.

The task of the pastor as a therapist is not to "theologize" with
people. It is in part that of helping a person to discover how he or
she is using religious symbols to support processes of disease and
distress. It is also assisting a person to find the strength through
which those decisions and commitments that lead to change,
growth, and a new quality of life may ne made. If there is theological talk it should grow out of and enhance the immediate context of the conversation, and not be theologizing for its own sake.
Such theologizing will probably mean that the pastor or the person, or both, want to avoid some painful realities in the relationship. The pastor may discover that others do not agree with him
conceptually, either psychologically or theologically, but may
still derive much help from his ministry. His knowledge of processes, along with his own genuine humanity, should help him to
respond in an empathic and healing manner. In the New Testament language we are speaking of the quality of redemptive love,
of a reconciliation which is deeply internal, as well as with others
and with God.

The New Testament concept of human beings is grounded in
an intuitive understanding that sees the person, not just in discrete relationships, but in relationship to both God and man.
The crucial issue in all psychotherapy is: What is a human
being? What does it mean to be human? These questions may be
answered partially by scientific knowledge, but never completely.

Scientific knowledge has expanded greatly during the past decades, and this has resulted in great good. It has also resulted in a Tower of Babel in the psychological and psychotherapy fields as different points of view single out one aspect of man's complex nature to emphasize over other aspects. The same happens in the theological field. Some scientific views attempt a more comprehensive view of human beings, but even these are likely to avoid the person's religion.

The Biblical approach begins with man's wholeness, it becomes concerned with whatever destroys wholeness, and with how wholeness may be restored. It understands wholeness in a three dimensional view, toward God, toward others, and toward self. An essential step to such wholeness often is resolving conflicts within the self, finding a measure of reconciliation within the self so that reconciliation with God and other people may follow. Sometimes it proceeds in the reverse direction (Matt. 5:21-26). Genuine religious experience is primarily a search for a quality of relationship and of selfhood. It is a continual search, never fully achieved. It is not primarily a method of treatment. In the famous words of St. Augustine (almost a cliché), "Thou madest us for thyself, and our heart is restless, until it repose in Thee."

NOTES

1. Peter Benchley, *Jaws,* New York: Doubleday, 1974.

2. Rudolph Otto, *The Idea of the Holy,* New York: Oxford University Press, 1958.

3. The interpretation of the religious questions in a previous chapter comes dangerously close to reductionism. That is being balanced in this chapter.

4. For a concise discussion of the concept of spirit in the Bible see Alan Richardson, *A Theological Word Book of the Bible,* New York: Macmillan, 1951.

5. Perhaps the most commonly used symbols of comfort are to be found in Psalm 23.

6. An excellent discussion of the psychophysiological factors in health and disease is to be found in George L. Engel, *Psychological Development in Health and Disease,* Philadelphia: W. B. Saunders, 1966.

Index